SPEAK BURMESE WITH CONFIDENCE

ESSENTIAL
BURMESE
PHRASEBOOK & DICTIONARY

Hello!
Mingalarbar!

Where are you from?
Ako ga, bar lu myohh lell?

I'm American.
American lu myohh bar.

A Zun Mo

T0160603

Contents

ont	like "ont" in c**ont**inent	တွန့် **tont** shrink
oo	like "oo" in sch**oo**l	အရှူး **ayoo** idiot
oot	like "oot" in sh**oot***	အခု **akhoot** now
out	like "out" in sn**out***	သောက် **thout** drink
'own	like "ow" in **ow**ner	ဖုန် **phown** dust
'ownn/one	like "ow" in **own***	ဖုန်း **phone** phone
ownt	like 'on't' in w**on't***	မုန့် **m'ownt** snack
u	like "u" in s**u**per	ပူ **pu** hot
ut	like "ut" in p**ut***	လွတ် **lut** empty

Basic grammar

Burmese grammar is very easy to learn, although fundamentally different to English. For instance, the subject and object of a Burmese sentence are marked by particles. Many sentences, however can be formed with just a verb and a particle, without using a subject or object. Noun phrases are only added for clarity. This section presents a basic guide to Burmese grammar in terms familiar to English speakers.

1 Word order
The verb always comes at the end of a Burmese sentence. Unlike the word order of English sentences, Burmese word order follows the rule **subject + object + verb.** If place and time are mentioned, they are usually placed at the beginning of the sentence. Adjectives always come before nouns, and adverbs always come before verbs.

Kya naw	myanmar zagarr	ma	pyaww	tat	boo.
I (male speaker)	*Burmese language*	*not*	*speak*	*can*	*not.*

= I can't speak Burmese.

When ending a sentence, add the ending word **dae/tae** (for the past tense and the present tense) or **mae** (for the future tense).

Kya ma	tha yet thee	kyite	tae.
I (female speaker)	*mango*	*like*	*ending particle.*

= I like mangoes.

2 Polite particle

Burmese speakers often use the polite particle **bar/par** after the verb when speaking to older people, teachers, and monks. It is optional and can be left out when speaking to friends.

Kya naw myanmar zagarr ma pyaww tat   bar   boo.
I (male) Burmese language not   speak can polite particle not.
= I don't speak Burmese.

Kya ma   tha yet thee kyite   bar   dae.
I (female) mango   like   polite particle ending particle.
= I like mangoes.

3 Simple sentences

Burmese verbs are never conjugated. You can use the particle **bar** if you want your sentence to sound polite. You leave out **bar** when talking to friends.

Positive statements
Present and past tense: Verb + (**bar**) dae.
  Thwarr (bar) tae.   *I go / I went.*

Future tense: Verb + (**bar**) mae.
  Thwarr mae.   *I will go.*

Present, past or future tense: Noun (+ **bar**).
  Ngarr bar   *It's a fish.*

Negative statements
  Present, past or future tense: **Ma** + verb + (**bar**) boo
  Ma thwarr (bar) boo.   *I didn't go / I don't go / I won't go.*

  Present, past or future tense: Noun + **ma hote** (**bar**) **boo.**
  Ngarr ma hote (bar) boo.   *It's not a fish.*

4 Questions

Yes/No questions:

Verb + **larr** (present and past); verb + **ma larr** (future)

Alote	**thwarr**	**larr?**
Work	*go*	*question particle* = Did / do you go to work?
Alote	**thwarr**	**ma larr?**
Work	*go*	*future question particle* = Will you go to work?

Open questions:

Verb + **lell** (present and past); verb + **ma lell** (future)

Bae	**thwarr**	**lell?**
Where	*go*	*question particle* = Where are you going / did you go?
Bae	**thwarr**	**ma lell?**
Where	*go*	*future question particle* = Where will you go?

5 Plurals

The particle **dway/tway** is added after nouns to make them plural.

Yangon	**mhar**	**karr**	**dway**	**myarr**	**dae.**
Yangon	*in*	*car*	*plural particle*	*a lot*	*(ending particle).*

= There are many cars in Yangon.

6 Commands

It is always better to use the polite particle **bar/par** when you ask someone to do something, although it can be omitted.

Postive: Verb (+ **bar**)

Lar	**(bar).**
Come	*(polite particle).* = Please come.

Negative: Ma + Verb + (**bar**) **naet.**

Ma	**thwarr**	**bar**	**naet.**
Not	*go*	*(polite particle)*	*not.* = Please don't go.

7 Subject marker and object marker

In Burmese, there is no verb for "to be" as there is in English. Instead, the subject marker **ga/ka** is added after the subject, and the object marker **go/ko** is added after the object. However, these are often left out in everyday spoken Burmese and only added for clarity.

Kya ma   ga   american lu myohh bar.
I (female) subject marker American   nationality polite particle.
= I am American.

Kya naw ga   ngarr go   kyite
I (male) subject marker fish   object marker like
bar   dae.
polite particle ending particle.
= I like fish.

8 Prepositions
In/At

The particle **mhar** is added after place or time.

Thu   ga   yangon mhar nay dae.
He/She subject marker Yangon in   live ending particle.
= He/She lives in Yangon.

Kya naw shit nar yi mhar nya sar sarr dae.
I (male) eight o'clock at   dinner eat ending particle.

From

The particle **ga** or **ga nay** is used after nouns to denote place and duration of time.

Alote   ga   lar   dae.
Work   from   came   ending particle.
= I came from work.

Nya nay   chout   nar yi   ga nay   a tann   sa   dae.
Evening   six   o'clock   from   class   start   ending particle.
= The class starts from 6 pm.

To/Until

The particle **go**/**ko** is used after nouns to denote place.

Yangon   go   thwarr   mae.
Yangon   to   go   (ending particle)
= I will go to Yangon.

The particle **ahteet** is used after nouns to express "until."

Nya nay   ngarr nar yi   ahteet   alote   lote   dae.
Evening   five o'clock   until   work   do   ending particle.
= I work until 5 pm.

Mandalay   ga nay   Yangon   ahteet   kohh   nar yi   kyar
Mandalay   from   Yangon   to   nine   hours   take
dae.
(ending particle).
= It takes 9 hours from Mandalay to Yangon.

9 Pronouns

Burmese pronouns vary according to speaker and listener.

I (male speaker)	**kya naw** ကျွန်တော်
I (female speaker)	**kya ma** ကျွန်မ
We (male speaker)	**kya naw doht** ကျွန်တော်တို့
We (female speaker)	**kya ma doht** ကျွန်မတို့
He / she / it	**thu** သူ
They	**thu doht** သူတို့

"You" varies depending on who you are talking to. Burmese speakers often use family terms when addressing people, as follows:

to an elderly man	**oo layy** ဦးလေး (meaning uncle)
to an elderly woman	**adaw** အဒေါ် (meaning aunt)
to an older man	**ako** အစ်ကို (meaning elder brother)
to an older woman	**ama** အစ်မ (meaning elder sister)
to a younger man (male speaker)	**nyi layy** ညီလေး (younger brother)
to a younger man (female speaker)	**maung layy** မောင်လေး (younger brother)
to a younger woman	**nyi ma layy** ညီမလေး (younger sister)
to a boy	**tharr** သား (meaning son)
to a girl	**tha mee** သမီး (meaning daughter).

10 "This" and "That"

This + noun	**di** ဒီ + noun
That + noun	**ho** ဟို + noun
This one	**di har** ဒီဟာ or **dar** ဒါ
That one	**ho har** ဟိုဟာ
These	**di har dway** ဒီဟာတွေ or **dar dway** ဒါတွေ
Those	**ho har dway** ဟိုဟာတွေ

11 Possessives

To indicate possession, simply add the particle **yaet** after the noun or pronoun that indicates the possessor

Kya ma	**yaet**	**sar oat.**
I (female speaker)	*(possessive particle)*	*book*
= My book.		

Nyi ma layy	**yaet**	**phone.**
You (to younger woman)	*(possessive particle)*	*phone*
= Your phone.		

Thoot	**yaet**	**karr.**
He / she	*(possessive particle)*	*car*
= His/her car.		

12 Numbers and counting

In Burmese, there are classifiers that combine with numerals to count objects. These classifiers vary according to the type of object. For numbers up to ten, the sentence structure is noun + number + classifier.

Classifiers	Used for	Examples		
yout	people	**Lu** *person* One person.	**ta** *one*	**yout.** *classifer*
lone	fruit, furniture, electronic devices, round objects	**Kh'own** *chair* Two chairs.	**nha** *two*	**lone.** *classifier*
boo	bottles, cigarette packets	**Yay** *water* Three bottles of water.	**thone** *three*	**boo.** *classifier*
oat	books	**Sar oat** *book*	**layy** *four*	**oat.** *classifier*
chaungg/ jaungg	long object	**Htee** *umbrella* Five umbrellas.	**ngarr** *five*	**jaungg.** *classifier*
kaung	animals	**Khwayy** *dog* Six dogs.	**chout** *six*	**kaung.** *classifier*
see	vehicles	**Karr** *Car* Seven cars.	**khuna** *seven*	**see.** *classifier*
khwet	cup, glass	**Beer** *beer* Eight beers.	**shit** *eight*	**khwet.** *classifier*

To ask how many, use the following sentence structure:

noun + how many + classifier + verb + question particle.

Lu	**bae nha**	**yout**	**sheet**	**lell?**
person	*how many*	*classifier*	*have*	*question particle.*

= How many people are there?

13 Adjectives

Adjectives generally precede the nouns they describe, with the relative pronoun **daet/taet** added in between.

Zayy kyee	**daet**	**phone.**
Expensive	*daet*	*phone* = An expensive phone.

Kyee daet	**zabwell.**
Big daet	*table* = A big table.

Hla	**daet**	**mein kha layy.**
Beautiful	*daet*	*girl* = A beautiful girl.

14 Adverbs

Adverbs are usually placed before the verb or adjective that they describe.

Ngarr	**a yann**	**kyite**	**dae.**
Fish	*very*	*like*	*ending particle.*

= I like fish very much.

Phyayy phyayy	**pyaww**	**bar.**
Slowly	*speak*	*polite particle.*

= Please speak slowly.

Myanmar	**zagarr**	**nell nell**	**pyaww**	**tat**	**dae.**
Myanmar	*language*	*a little*	*speak*	*can*	*ending particle.*

= I can speak Burmese a little.

15 Yes and No

The structure of a response to a yes/no question depends on whether the question focuses on a noun or a verb.

Examples:
1. Answering a noun question.

Dar	**ngarr**	**larr?**
This	*fish*	*question particle.*

= Is this a fish?

Hote (bar) dae.	Yes. (That's true.)
Ma hote (bar) boo.	No. (That's not true.)

2. Answering a verb question. The negative answer repeats the verb.

Alote	**thwarr**	**larr?**	Did you go to work?
work	*go*	*question particle.*	

Hote kaet.	Yes.
Ma thwarr (bar) boo.	No. (I didn't go.)

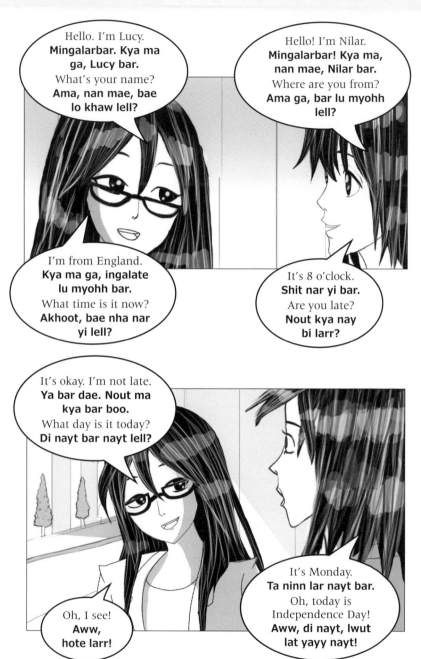

1. The Basics

1.1 Personal details

In Myanmar people do not usually have a family name. Titles come before their given name. For example, Mr. Aung is **U Aung** ဦးအောင် and Mrs. or Ms. Kyi is **Daw Kyi** ဒေါ်ကြည်. However, titles also depend on a person's age. **U** ဦး and **Daw** ဒေါ် are usually used to address people over the age of forty. In some cases, we also use these titles if a person is in a respected position, such as a university lecturer or a manager, even if they are under forty. When we address people who are only slightly older than us or our colleagues, we use the title **Ko** ကို for Mr. and **Ma** မ for Ms./Mrs. For example, Mr. Aung is **Ko Aung** ကိုအောင် and Mrs. or Ms. Kyi is **Ma Kyi**.

name	**nan mae** နာမည်
initials	**nan mae asa salone dway** နာမည်အစစာလုံးတွေ
address	**late sar** လိပ်စာ
street	**lann** လမ်း
unit number	**eain nan bat** အိမ်နံပါတ်

postal code	**sar poht thin gay ta** စာပို့သင်္ကေတ
town	**myoht** မြို့
sex (gender)	**lain** လိင်
male	**kyarr** ကျား
female	**ma** မ
nationality/citizenship	**lu myohh** လူမျိုး
date of birth	**mwayy thet ka rit** မွေးသက္ကရာဇ်
place of birth	**mwayy phwarr theet nay yar** မွေးဖွားသည့်နေရာ
occupation	**alote akai** အလုပ်အကိုင်
marital status	**eain htaung sheet / ma sheet** အိမ်ထောင်ရှိ / မရှိ
married	**eain htaung sheet** အိမ်ထောင်ရှိ
single	**eain htaung ma sheet** အိမ်ထောင်မရှိ
widow	**mote sohh ma** မုဆိုးမ
widower	**mote sohh pho** မုဆိုးဖို
(number of) children	**kha layy oo yay** ကလေးဦးရေ
passport	**passport** ပတ်စ်ပို့
identity card	**mhat p'own tin** မှတ်ပုံတင်
driving license number	**yin maungg lai sin nan bat** ယာဉ်မောင်းလိုင်စင်နံပါတ်
place of issue	**htoat payy theet nay yar** ထုတ်ပေးသည့်နေရာ
date of issue	**htoat payy theet nayt swell** ထုတ်ပေးသည့်နေ့စွဲ
signature	**let mhat** လက်မှတ်

1.2 Today or tomorrow?

What day is it today?	**Di nayt, bar nayt lell?** ဒီနေ့ဘာနေ့လဲ။
Today's Monday.	**Di nayt, ta ninn lar nayt bar.** ဒီနေ့တနင်္လာနေ့ပါ။
Tuesday	**in gar nayt** အင်္ဂါနေ့
Wednesday	**bote da hoo nayt** ဗုဒ္ဓဟူးနေ့
Thursday	**kyar thar ba dayy nayt** ကြာသပတေးနေ့
Friday	**thout kyar nayt** သောကြာနေ့
Saturday	**sa nay nayt** စနေနေ့
Sunday	**ta ninn ga nway nayt** တနင်္ဂနွေနေ့
in January	**january la mhar** ဇန်နဝါရီလမှာ
since February	**february la dell ga** ဖေဖော်ဝါရီလတည်းက
in summer	**nway yar thi mhar** နွေရာသီမှာ
in the rainy season	**mohh yar thi mhar** မိုးရာသီမှာ
in winter	**saungg yar thi mhar** ဆောင်းရာသီမှာ
2019	**nha htaungt saet kohh khoot nhit** နှစ်ထောင့်ဆယ့်ကိုးခုနှစ်
the twentieth century	**nha sae yar soot** နှစ်ဆယ်ရာစု
the twenty-first century	**nha saet tit yar soot** နှစ်ဆယ့်တစ်ရာစု
What's the date today?	**Di nayt, bae nha yet nayt lell?** ဒီနေ့ဘယ်နှစ်ရက်နေ့လဲ။
Today's the 24th.	**Di nayt, nha saet layy yet nayt bar.** ဒီနေ့နှစ်ဆယ့်လေးရက်နေ့ပါ။
Wednesday 3 November	**november la, thone yet nayt, bote da hoo nayt** နိုဝင်ဘာလ ၃ ရက်နေ့၊ ဗုဒ္ဓဟူးနေ့
in the morning	**ma net mhar** မနက်မှာ

in the afternoon	**nayt lae mhar** နေ့လယ်မှာ
in the evening	**nya nay mhar** ညနေမှာ
at night	**nya mhar** ညမှာ
this morning	**di ma net** ဒီမနက်
this afternoon	**di nayt khinn** ဒီနေ့ခင်း
this evening	**di nya nay** ဒီညနေ
tonight	**di nya** ဒီည
yesterday	**ma nayt ga** မနေ့က
last night	**ma nayt nya ga** မနေ့ညက
tomorrow night	**ma net phyan nya** မနက်ဖြန်ည
this week	**di a pat** ဒီအပတ်
last week	**pee khaet daet a pat ga** ပြီးခဲ့တဲ့အပတ်က
next week	**nout a pat** နောက်အပတ်
this month	**di la** ဒီလ
last month	**pee khaet daet la ga** ပြီးခဲ့တဲ့လက
next month	**nout la** နောက်လ
this year	**di nhit** ဒီနှစ်
last year	**ma nhit ga** မနှစ်က
next year	**nout nhit** နောက်နှစ်
in...days	**nout...yet mhar** နောက်...ရက်မှာ
in...weeks	**nout...pat mhar** နောက်...ပတ်မှာ
in…months	**nout...la mhar** နောက်...လမှာ
in...years	**nout...nhit mhar** နောက်...နှစ်မှာ
...weeks ago	**pee khaet daet...pat ga** ပြီးခဲ့တဲ့...ပတ်က

two weeks ago	**pee khaet daet nha pat ga** ပြီးခဲ့တဲ့နှစ်ပတ်က
day off	**pate yet** ပိတ်ရက်

1.3 Months and years

January	**january la** ဇန်နဝါရီလ
February	**february la** ဖေဖော်ဝါရီလ
March	**march la** မတ်လ
April	**april la** ဧပြီလ
May	**may la** မေလ
June	**june la** ဇွန်လ
July	**july la** ဇူလိုင်လ
August	**august la** ဩဂုတ်လ
September	**september la** စက်တင်ဘာလ
October	**october la** အောက်တိုဘာလ
November	**november la** နိုဝင်ဘာလ
December	**december la** ဒီဇင်ဘာလ
year...	**...khoot nhit** ...ခုနှစ်
2019	**Nha htaungt saet kohh khoot nhit** နှစ်ထောင့်ဆယ့်ကိုးခုနှစ်

1.4 One, two, three...

0	**th'own nya** သုည	4	**layy** လေး
1	**tit** တစ်	5	**ngarr** ငါး
2	**nhit** နှစ်	6	**chout** ခြောက်
3	**thone** သုံး	7	**khu nit** ခုနစ်

8	**shit** ရှစ်	20	**nha sae** နှစ်ဆယ်
9	**kohh** ကိုး	21	**nha saet tit** နှစ်ဆယ့်တစ်
10	**ta sae** တစ်ဆယ်	22	**nha saet nhit** နှစ်ဆယ့်နှစ်
11	**saet tit** ဆယ့်တစ်	30	**thone sae** သုံးဆယ်
12	**saet nhit** ဆယ့်နှစ်	31	**thone saet tit** သုံးဆယ့်တစ်
13	**saet thone** ဆယ့်သုံး	40	**layy sae** လေးဆယ်
14	**saet layy** ဆယ့်လေး	50	**ngarr sae** ငါးဆယ်
15	**saet ngarr** ဆယ့်ငါး	60	**chout sae** ခြောက်ဆယ်
16	**saet chout** ဆယ့်ခြောက်	70	**khu na sae** ခုနစ်ဆယ်
17	**saet khu nit** ဆယ့်ခုနစ်	80	**shit sae** ရှစ်ဆယ်
18	**saet shit** ဆယ့်ရှစ်	90	**kohh sae** ကိုးဆယ်
19	**saet kohh** ဆယ့်ကိုး	100	**ta yar** တစ်ရာ

101 **ta ya tit** တစ်ရာ့တစ်

110 **ta ya ta sae** တစ်ရာ့တစ်ဆယ်

111 **ta ya saet tit** တစ်ရာ့ဆယ့်တစ်

200 **nha yar** နှစ်ရာ

300 **thone yar** သုံးရာ

400 **layy yar** လေးရာ

500 **ngarr yar** ငါးရာ

600 **chout yar** ခြောက်ရာ

700 **khu na yar** ခုနစ်ရာ

800 **shit yar** ရှစ်ရာ

900 **kohh yar** ကိုးရာ

1,000 **ta htaung** တစ်ထောင်

2,000	**nha htaung** နှစ်ထောင်	
10,000	**ta thaungg** တစ်သောင်း	
11,000	**ta thaungg ta htaung** တစ်သောင်းတစ်ထောင်	
20,000	**nha thaungg** နှစ်သောင်း	
25,000	**nha thaungg ngarr htaung** နှစ်သောင်းငါးထောင်	
30,000	**thone thaungg** သုံးသောင်း	
45,678	**layy thaungg ngarr htaung chout yar khu na saet shit** လေးသောင်းငါးထောင်ခြောက်ရာခုနှစ်ဆယ့်ရှစ်	
100,000	**ta thein** တစ်သိန်း	
200,000	**nha thein** နှစ်သိန်း	
300,000	**thone thein** သုံးသိန်း	
1,000,000	**sae thein** ဆယ်သိန်း	
10,000,000	**thein ta yar** သိန်းတစ်ရာ	
1st	**pa hta ma** ပထမ	
2nd	**ta ta ya** ဒုတိယ	
3rd	**ta teet ya** တတိယ	
4th	**sa dote hta** စတုတ္ထ	
once	**ta khar** တစ်ခါ	
twice	**nha khar** နှစ်ခါ	
double	**nha sa** နှစ်ဆ	
triple	**thone sa** သုံးဆ	
half	**ta wet** တစ်ဝက်	
a quarter	**ta sate** တစ်စိတ်	
a third	**thone b'own ta b'own** သုံးပုံတစ်ပုံ	
some	**ta choht** တစ်ချို့	

a few	**nell nell** နည်းနည်း

$2 + 4 = 6$ **nhit a paungg layy nyi mhya jinn chout**
နှစ်အပေါင်းလေးညီမျှခြင်းခြောက်

$4 - 2 = 2$ **layy a nhote nhit nyi mhya jinn nhit**
လေးအနုတ်နှစ်ညီမျှခြင်းနှစ်

$2 \times 4 = 8$ **nhit a mhyout layy nyi mhya jinn shit**
နှစ်အမြှောက်လေးညီမျှခြင်းရှစ်

$4 \div 2 = 2$ **layy a sarr nhit nyi mhya jinn nhit**
လေးအစားနှစ်ညီမျှခြင်းနှစ်

even	**s'own** စုံ
odd	**ma** မ
total	**soot soot paungg** စုစုပေါင်း

1.5   What time is it?

What time is it?	**Bae nha nar yi lell?** ဘယ်နှစ်နာရီလဲ။
It's nine o'clock.	**Kohh nar yi bar.** ကိုးနာရီပါ။
10:05	**sae nar yi, ngarr minit** ဆယ်နာရီင်ါးမိနစ်
five past ten	**sae nar yi, htohh pee ngarr minit** ဆယ်နာရီထိုးပြီးင်ါးမိနစ်
11:15	**saet ta nar yi, saet ngarr minit** ဆယ့်တစ်နာရီဆယ့်င်ါးမိနစ်
a quarter past eleven	**saet ta nar yi htohh pee, saet ngarr minit** ဆယ့်တစ်နာရီထိုးပြီးဆယ့်င်ါးမိနစ်
twenty past twelve	**saet nha nar yi htohh pee, nha sae minit** ဆယ့်နှစ်နာရီထိုးပြီးနှစ်ဆယ်မိနစ်
half past one	**ta nar yi khwell** တစ်နာရီခွဲ
twenty-five to three	**thone nar yi htohh poht, nha saet ngarr minit** သုံးနာရီထိုးဖို့နှစ်ဆယ့်င်ါးမိနစ်

a quarter to four	**layy nar yi htohh poht, saet ngarr minit** လေးနာရီထိုးဖို့ဆယ့်ငါးမိနစ်
ten to five	**ngarr nar yi htohh poht, sae minit** ငါးနာရီထိုးဖို့ဆယ်မိနစ်
It's noon.	**Monn taet bi.** မွန်းတည့်ပြီ။
It's 12 p.m.	**Nayt lae, saet nha nar yi par.** နေ့လယ် ၁၂ နာရီပါ။
It's midnight.	**Tha gaung yan bar.** သန်းခေါင်ယံပါ။
half an hour	**nar yi wet** နာရီဝက်
What time?	**Bae achain lell?** ဘယ်အချိန်လဲ။
What time can I come by?	**Bae achain, lar ya ma lell?** ဘယ်အချိန်လာရမလဲ။
at...	**...mhar** ...မှာ
after...	**...pee yin** ...ပြီးရင်
before...	**...ma tai khin** ...မတိုင်ခင်
between 4 and 5 p.m.	**nya nay layy nar yi naet, ngarr nar yi gyarr** ညနေ ၄ နာရီနဲ့ ၅ နာရီကြား
from...to...	**...ga nay...ahteet** ...ကနေ...အထိ
in...minutes	**nout...minit nay yin** နောက်...မိနစ်နေရင်
in an hour	**nout ta nar yi nay yin** နောက်တစ်နာရီနေရင်
in two hours	**nout nha nar yi nay yin** နောက်နှစ်နာရီနေရင်
too early	**saww lite tar** စောလိုက်တာ
too late	**nout kya lite tar** နောက်ကျလိုက်တာ
on time	**achain mi** အချိန်မီ

1.6 The weather

Is the weather good?	**Yar thi oot toot kaungg larr?** ရာသီဥတုကောင်းလား။
Is the weather bad?	**Yar thi oot toot sohh larr?** ရာသီဥတုဆိုးလား။
Is it cold?	**Aye larr?** အေးလား။
Is it hot?	**Pu larr?** ပူလား။
What temperature is it today?	**Di nayt, a pu chain bae lout sheet lell?** ဒီနေ့အပူချိန်ဘယ်လောက်ရှိလဲ။
Is it going to rain today?	**Di nayt, moe ywar ma larr?** ဒီနေ့မိုးရွာမလား။
Is there a storm today?	**Di nayt, m'own daii, sheet larr?** ဒီနေ့မုန်တိုင်းရှိလား။
Is it going to snow today?	**Di nayt, nhinn kya ma larr?** ဒီနေ့နှင်းကျမလား။
Is it going to be foggy today?	**Di nayt, myu saii ma larr?** ဒီနေ့မြူဆိုင်းမလား။
Is there going to be a thunderstorm?	**Di nayt, shat see dway let pee, moe kyee ma larr?** ဒီနေ့လျှပ်စီးတွေလက်ပြီး မိုးကြီးမလား။
The weather's changing.	**Yar thi oot toot, a koo a pyaungg.** ရာသီဥတုအကူးအပြောင်း
It's going to be cold.	**Aye lar dawt mae.** အေးလာတော့မယ်။
What's the weather going to be like today?	**Di nayt, yar thi oot toot bae lo phyit ma lell?** ဒီနေ့ရာသီဥတုဘယ်လိုဖြစ်မလဲ။
What's the weather going to be like tomorrow?	**Ma net phyan, yar thi oot toot, bae lo phyit ma lell?** မနက်ဖြန်ရာသီဥတုဘယ်လိုဖြစ်မလဲ။
rain	**moe** မိုး

heavy rain **moe kyee dae** မိုးကြီးတယ်	cool **aye dae** အေးတယ်	warm **nwayy dae** နွေးတယ်
sunny **nay thar dae** နေသာတယ်	snowing **nhinn kya dae** နှင်းကျတယ်	strong winds **lay byinn tite dae** လေပြင်းတိုက်တယ်
very hot **a yann pu dae** အရမ်းပူတယ်	bleak **aye set dae** အေးစက်တယ်	sunny day **nay thar daet nayt** နေသာတဲ့နေ့
fine **thar yar dae** သာယာတယ်	cloudy **tain htu dae** တိမ်ထူတယ်	overcast **tain phone dae** တိမ်ဖုံးတယ်
ice **yay gell** ရေခဲ	hail **moe thee** မိုးသီး	cold and damp **aye pee so thaii dae** အေးပြီးစိုထိုင်းတယ်
fog **myu** မြူ	heatwave **a pu hlaii** အပူလှိုင်း	clear sky **kaungg kin kyi lin dae** ကောင်းကင်ကြည်လင်တယ်
foggy **myu saii dae** မြူဆိုင်းတယ်	hurricane **hurricane** ဟာရီကိန်း	...degrees (Fahrenheit) **...degree fahrenheit** ...ဒီဂရီဖာရင်ဟိုက်
storm **m'own daii** မုန်တိုင်း	wind **lay** လေ	...degrees (Celsius) **...degree celsius** ...ဒီဂရီဆဲလ်စီးယပ်စ်
humid **so thaii dae** စိုထိုင်းတယ်	windy **lay tite dae** လေတိုက်တယ်	

1.7 Here, there...

See also 5.1 Asking directions

here / over here	**di mhar** ဒီမှာ
there	**ho mhar** ဟိုမှာ
over there	**hohh mhar** ဟိုးမှာ
somewhere	**ta nay yar yar** တစ်နေရာရာ
everywhere	**nay yar daii** နေရာတိုင်း

far away	**a wayy gyee** အဝေးကြီး
near by	**nee nee layy** နီးနီးလေး
(on the) right	**nyar bet mhar** ညာဘက်မှာ
(on the) left	**bae bet mhar** ဘယ်ဘက်မှာ
to the right of	**nyar bet go** ညာဘက်ကို
to the left of	**bae bet go** ဘယ်ဘက်ကို
straight ahead	**taet taet** တည့်တည့်
via	**naet** နဲ့
in	**a htell** အထဲ
to	**go/ko** ကို
on	**a paw** အပေါ်
under	**out** အောက်
against	**sant kyin bet** ဆန့်ကျင်ဘက်
opposite/facing	**myat nha jinn sai** မျက်နှာချင်းဆိုင်
next to	**bayy** ဘေး
beside	**bayy mhar** ဘေးမှာ
near	**narr mhar** နားမှာ
in front of	**a shayt** အရှေ့
in the center	**a lae** အလယ်
forward	**shayt go** ရှေ့ကို
down	**out** အောက်
up	**a paw** အပေါ်
inside	**a htell** အထဲ
outside	**a pyin** အပြင်

English	Burmese romanized	Burmese
at the front	shayt mhar	ရှေ့မှာ
at the back	nout mhar	နောက်မှာ
in the north	myout bet mhar	မြောက်ဘက်မှာ
to the south	taung bet mhar	တောင်ဘက်မှာ
from the west	a nout bet ga nay	အနောက်ဘက်ကနေ
from the east	a shayt bet ga nay	အရှေ့ဘက်ကနေ

What does that sign say?

See also 5.2 Traffic signs

For Hire/Rent
ngharr yan
ငှားရန်

For Sale
yaungg yan
ရောင်းရန်

Sold Out
yaungg pee
ရောင်းပြီး

Post Office
sar dite
စာတိုက်

High Voltage
boht arr pyinn
ဗို့အားပြင်း

Cashier
ngway kai
ငွေကိုင်

Vacant
lit lat nay thi
လစ်လပ်နေသည်

Entrance
win bout
ဝင်ပေါက်

Ticket Office
let mhat yone
လက်မှတ်ရုံး

No Entry
ma win ya
မဝင်ရ

Police Station
yell sa khann
ရဲစခန်း

Traffic Police
yin htein yell
ယာဉ်ထိန်းရဲ

Engaged
ma arr par
မအားပါ

Timetable
achain za yarr
အချိန်ဇယား

Hot Water
yay pu
ရေပူ

Cold Water
yay aye
ရေအေး

Pedestrians
lann thwarr lann lar myarr
လမ်းသွားလမ်းလာများ

Free Entrance
win gyayy a kha maet
ဝင်ကြေးအခမဲ့

Beware of the Dog
khwayy kite tat thi
ခွေးကိုက်တတ်သည်

Wet Paint
sayy thote htarr thi
ဆေးသုတ်ထားသည်

(Emergency) Exit
(a yayy baw) htwet pout
အရေးပေါ်ထွက်ပေါက်

Information
tha dinn a chat a let
သတင်းအချက်အလက်

Water (Not For Drinking)
thout yan yay ma hote
သောက်ရန်ရေမဟုတ်

Hospital
sayy y'own
ဆေးရုံ

Push
tonn bar
တွန်းပါ

Open
phwint bar
ဖွင့်ပါ

Pull
swell bar
ဆွဲပါ

Fire Station
mee that htar na
မီးသတ်ဌာန

Escalator
set hlay garr
စက်လှေကား

Lavatory
thant sin khann
သန့်စင်ခန်း

Full
pyayt nay thi
ပြည့်နေသည်

No Littering
a mhite ma pyit ya
အမှိုက်မပစ်ရ

Out of Order
pyet nay thi
ပျက်နေသည်

Please Do Not Touch
ma kai ya
မကိုင်ရ

No Fishing
ngarr ma mhyarr ya
ငါးမမျှားရ

Fire Hazard
mee bayy an da yae
မီးဘေးအန္တရာယ်

Stop
yat bar
ရပ်ပါ

No Hunting
a mell ma lite ya
အမဲမလိုက်ရ

Emergency Brake
hand brake
ဟန်းဘရိတ်

Money Exchange
ngway lell htar na
ငွေလဲဌာန

Hotel
ho tae
ဟိုတယ်

Not In Use
a thone ma pyoot
အသုံးမပြု

Danger
an da yae sheet thi
အန္တရာယ်ရှိသည်

First Aid
shayy oo thu nar pyoot
ရှေးဦးသူနာပြု

Accident and Emergency (Hospital)
ma taw ta sa mhoot naet a yayy paw htar na
မတော်တဆမှုနှင့်အရေးပေါ်ဌာန

Tourist Information Bureau
nai ngan jarr tharr, kha yee thwarr myarr, s'own zann nai theet htar na
နိုင်ငံခြားသားခရီးသွားများ စုံစမ်းနိုင်သည့် ဌာန

Please Do Not Disturb
ma nhaungt shet bar naet
မနှောင့်ယှက်ပါနဲ့

Danger to Life
a thet an da yae sheet thi
အသက်အန္တရာယ်ရှိသည်

Fire Escape
a yayy paw hlay garr
အရေးပေါ်လှေကား

No Smoking
sa late ma thout ya
ဆေးလိပ်မသောက်ရ

Reserved
reserve lote htarr thi
ရီစာ့ဗ်လုပ်ထားသည်

Legal holidays

Multi-ethnic Myanmar has many festivals to celebrate. The biggest is Thingyan in April, Myanmar New Year. If you are in Myanmar during Thingyan, prepare to get wet! People splash each other with water to wash away the bad luck of the previous year. Below is a list of some of the main public holidays.

January 1 **[january la ta yet nayt]**: International New Year's Day **nai ngan da gar nhit thit koo nayt** နိုင်ငံတကာနှစ်သစ်ကူးနေ့

January 4 **[january la layy yet nayt]**: Independence Day **lwut lat yayy nayt** လွတ်လပ်ရေးနေ့

February 12 **[february la saet nha yet nayt]**: Union Day **pyi htaung zoot nayt** ပြည်ထောင်စုနေ့

March 2 **[march la nha yet nayt]**: Peasants' Day **taung thu lae tha marr nayt** တောင်သူလယ်သမားနေ့

March 27 **[march la nha saet khu na yet nayt]**: Armed Forces Day **tat ma daw nayt** တပ်မတော်နေ့

April 13–16/17 **[april la saet thone yet nayt ga nay saet chout/ saet khu na yet nayt]**: Thingyan Holiday **thingyan pate yet** သင်္ကြန်ပိတ်ရက်

April 18 **[april la saet shit yet nayt]**: Myanmar New Year's Day **myanmar nhit thit koo nayt** မြန်မာနှစ်သစ်ကူးနေ့ (The following day is also a holiday.)

May 1st **[may la ta yet nayt]**: Labor Day **alote tha marr nayt** အလုပ်သမားနေ့

July 19th **[july la saet kohh yet nayt]**: Martyr's Day **ar zar ni nayt** အာဇာနည်နေ့

October: Full Moon Day of Thadingyut **thadingyut la byayt nayt** သီတင်းကျွတ်လပြည့်နေ့

November: Full Moon Day of Tazaungmone **tazaungmone la byayt nayt** တန်ဆောင်မုန်းလပြည့်နေ့

November (tenth day following the Full Moon Day of Tazaungmone): National Day **a myohh tharr nayt** အမျိုးသားနေ့

December 25th **[december la nha saet ngarr yet nayt]**: Christmas Day **christmas nayt** ခရစ္စမတ်နေ့

2. Meet and Greet

2.1 Greetings
2.2 Asking a question
2.3 How to reply
2.4 Thank you
2.5 I'm sorry
2.6 What do you think?

Greetings

It is common for Burmese people to ask "Have you eaten?" or "Where are you going?" as a greeting. There is no standard response, so answer as honestly as you like! Handshaking is not usual among locals unless they work in an international environment or interact with foreigners. Hugging and kissing on the cheek is not common except on occasions involving foreigners.

Hello Mr Williams.	**Mingalarbar Ko Williams.** မင်္ဂလာပါ ကိုဂီလီယမ်စ်။
Good morning, Mr Williams.	**Mingalar nan net khinn bar, Ko Williams.** မင်္ဂလာနံနက်ခင်းပါ ကိုဂီလီယမ်စ်။
Hello Mrs Jones.	**Mingalarbar Ma Jones.** မင်္ဂလာပါ မဂျုံးစ်။
Good morning, Mrs Jones.	**Mingalar nan net khinn bar, Ma Jones.** မင်္ဂလာနံနက်ခင်းပါ မဂျုံးစ်။
Hello, Peter.	**Mingalarbar, Peter.** မင်္ဂလာပါ ပီတာ။
Hi, Helen.	**Mingalarbar, Helen.** မင်္ဂလာပါ ဟယ်လန်။
Good morning (formal).	[male speaker] **Mingalar nan net khinn bar kha myar.** မင်္ဂလာနံနက်ခင်းပါခင်ဗျာ။

	[female speaker] **Mingalar nan net khinn bar shin.** မင်္ဂလာနံနက်ခင်းပါရှင်။
Good afternoon.	**Mingalar nayt lae ginn bar.** မင်္ဂလာနေ့လယ်ခင်းပါ။
Good evening.	**Mingalar nya nay khinn bar.** မင်္ဂလာညနေခင်းပါ။
How are you?	**Nay kaungg larr?** နေကောင်းလား။
Is everything okay?	**A sin pyay larr?** အဆင်ပြေလား။
Fine, thank you, and you?	**Kaungg (bar) dae. Kyayy zoo bar. (Ko/Ma + name) yaww?** ကောင်း (ပါ) တယ်။ ကျေးဇူးပါ။ (ကို / မ + နာမည်) ရော။
Very well, and you?	**A yann kaungg (bar) dae. (Ko/Ma + name) yaww?** အရမ်းကောင်း (ပါ) တယ်။ (ကို / မ + နာမည်) ရော။
in excellent health	**kyann mar yayy, a yann kaung dae** ကျန်းမာရေးအရမ်းကောင်းတယ်
so-so	**di lo bar bell** ဒီလိုပါပဲ
not very well	**thate ma kaungg (bar) boo** သိပ်မကောင်း (ပါ) ဘူး
not bad	**ma sohh (bar) boo** မဆိုး (ပါ) ဘူး
Have you eaten?	**Sarr pee bi larr?** စားပြီးပြီလား။
I have eaten. And you?	**Sarr pee (bar) bi. (Ko/Ma + name) yaww?** စားပြီး (ပါ) ပြီ။ (ကို / မ + နာမည်) ရော။
I haven't eaten yet.	**Ma sarr ya thayy (bar) boo.** မစားရသေး (ပါ) ဘူး။
Where are you going?	**Bae thwarr ma loht lell?** ဘယ်သွားမလို့လဲ။

I'm going to…	**…thwarr ma loht bar.** …သွားမလို့ပါ။
I'm going to leave.	**Thwarr dawt mae naw.** သွားတော့မယ်နော်။
I have to be going. I have to meet someone.	**Thwarr ya dawt mae. Chein htarr dar, sheet thayy dae.** သွားရတော့မယ်။ ချိန်းထားတာရှိသေးတယ်။
Goodbye.	**Ta tar.** တ္တတာ။
See you later.	**Nout mha twayt mae naw.** နောက်မှတွေ့မယ်နော်။
See you in a little while.	**Kha na nay twayt mae naw.** ခဏနေတွေ့မယ်နော်။
Sweet dreams.	**Eain met hla hla met bar zay.** အိပ်မက်လှလှမက်ပါစေ။
Goodnight.	**Kaungg thaww nya bar.** ကောင်းသောညပါ။
All the best. / Good luck.	**Kan kaungg bar zay.** ကံကောင်းပါစေ။
Have fun.	**Kaungg kaungg pyaw gaet naw.** ကောင်းကောင်းပျော်ခဲ့နော်။
Have a nice vacation.	**Pate yet mhar pyaw shwin bar zay.** ပိတ်ရက်မှာပျော်ရွှင်ပါစေ။
Have a good weekend.	**Sa nay, ta ninn ga nway mhar, pyaw shwin bar zay.** စနေ၊ တနင်္ဂနွေမှာ ပျော်ရွှင်ပါစေ။
Bon voyage. / Have a good trip.	**Kha yee mhar kaungg kaungg pyaww gaet par.** ခရီးမှာကောင်းကောင်းပျော်ခဲ့ပါ။
Thank you, the same to you.	**Kyayy zoo tin bar tae. A tutu bell naw.** ကျေးဇူးတင်ပါတယ်။ အတူတူပဲနော်။

Please say hello to...	**...go nhote set dae loht pyaww lite bar ownn naw.** ...ကို နှုတ်ဆက်တယ်လို့ ပြောလိုက်ပါဦးနော်။

2.2 Asking a question

Who?	**Bae thu lell?** ဘယ်သူလဲ။
Who's that?	**Aet dar bae thu lell?** အဲဒါဘယ်သူလဲ။
Who are you?	[to a male] **Ako ga bae thu lell?** အစ်ကိုက ဘယ်သူလဲ။ [to a female] **A ma ga bae thu lell?** အစ်မက ဘယ်သူလဲ။
What?	**Bar lell?** ဘာလဲ။
What's your name?	**Nan mae bae lo khaw lell?** နာမည်ဘယ်လိုခေါ်လဲ။
What time is it?	**Bae nha nar yi (sheet bi) lell?** ဘယ်နှစ်နာရီ (ရှိပြီ) လဲ။
What is there to see?	**Aet mhar, kyeet za yar, bar sheet lell?** အဲမှာကြည့်စရာဘာရှိလဲ။
Where?	**Bae mhar lell?** ဘယ်မှာလဲ။
Where's the bathroom?	**Eain thar, bae mhar lell?** အိမ်သာဘယ်မှာလဲ။
Where are you going?	**Bae thwar ma loht lell?** ဘယ်သွားမလို့လဲ။
Where are you from? (What's your nationality?)	**Bar lu myohh lell?** ဘာလူမျိုးလဲ။
How?	**Bae lo lell?** ဘယ်လိုလဲ။
How far is that?	**Bae lout wayy lell?** ဘယ်လောက်ဝေးလဲ။

How long does that take?	**Bae lout kyar lell?** ဘယ်လောက်ကြာလဲ။
How long is the trip?	**Kha yee ga bae lout kyar lell?** ခရီးကဘယ်လောက်ကြာလဲ။
How much?	**Bae lout lell?** ဘယ်လောက်လဲ။
How much is this?	**Dar, bae lout lell?** ဒါဘယ်လောက်လဲ။
Which one?	**Bae har lell?** ဘယ်ဟာလဲ။
Which ones?	**Bae har dway lell?** ဘယ်ဟာတွေလဲ။
Which glass is mine?	[male speaker] **Bae khwet ga, kya nawt har lell?** ဘယ်ခွက်က ကျွန်တော့်ဟာလဲ။
	[female speaker] **Bae khwet ga, kya ma har lell?** ဘယ်ခွက်က ကျွန်မဟာလဲ။
When was it?	**Bae d'own ga lell?** ဘယ်တုန်းကလဲ။
When will it be?	**Bae dawt lell?** ဘယ်တော့လဲ။
When are you leaving?	**Bae dawt pyan ma lell?** ဘယ်တော့ပြန်မလဲ။
Why?	**Bar phyit loht lell?** ဘာဖြစ်လို့လဲ။
Could you...?	Verb + **payy bar larr?** Verb + ပေးပါလား။
Please...(formal)	**Kyayy zoo pyoot pee...** ကျေးဇူးပြုပြီး...
Are you able to...?	Verb + **nai larr?** Verb + နိုင်လား။
Could you help me, please?	**Ku nyi payy bar larr?** ကူညီပေးပါလား။
Could you show that to me, please?	[male speaker] **Ae dar, kya nawt go, pya bar larr?** အဲဒါကျွန်တော့်ကိုပြပါလား။
	[female speaker] **Ae dar, kya ma go, pya bar larr?** အဲဒါကျွန်မကိုပြပါလား။

Could you come with me, please?	[male speaker] **Kya naw naet lite khaet payy bar larr?** ကျွန်တော်နဲ့လိုက်ခဲ့ပေးပါလား။
	[female speaker] **Kya ma naet lite khaet payy bar larr?** ကျွန်မနဲ့လိုက်ခဲ့ပေးပါလား။
Could you book some tickets for me please?	[male speaker] **Kya nawt go, let mhat booking, lote payy bar larr?** ကျွန်တော့်ကို လက်မှတ်ဘိုကင် လုပ်ပေးပါလား။
	[female speaker] **Kya ma go, let mhat booking, lote payy bar larr?** ကျွန်မကို လက်မှတ်ဘိုကင် လုပ်ပေးပါလား။
Could you recommend another hotel?	**Ta charr hotel nhyon payy bar larr?** တခြားဟိုတယ် ညွှန်ပေးပါလား။
What category of hotel is it? (How many stars?)	**Di hotel ga kyae bae nha pwint a sint sheet daet hotel lell?** ဒီဟိုတယ်က ကြယ်ဘယ်နှစ်ပွင့်အဆင့်ရှိတဲ့ ဟိုတယ်လဲ။
Do you know...?	**...theet larr?** ...သိလား။
Do you have...?	**...sheet larr?** ...ရှိလား။
Do you have any vegetarian dishes, please?	**Thet that lwut hinn bwell dway, sheet larr?** သက်သတ်လွတ်ဟင်းပွဲတွေရှိလား။
I would like a...	**...payy bar.** ...ပေးပါ။
I'd like a kilo of apples, please.	**Pann thee, ta kilo, payy par.** ပန်းသီးတစ်ကီလို ပေးပါ။
May I take this away?	**Dar, yu thwarr loht, ya ma larr?** ဒါယူသွားလို့ရမလား။
Can I smoke here?	**Di mhar, sa late thout loht, ya larr?** ဒီမှာဆေးလိပ်သောက်လို့ရလား။
Could I ask you something?	**Ta khu lout, mayy loht, ya ma larr?** တစ်ခုလောက်မေးလို့ရမလား။

My name is...	[male speaker] **Kya nawt nan mae ga...bar.** ကျွန်တော့်နာမည်က...ပါ။
	[female speaker] **Kya ma nan mae ga...bar.** ကျွန်မနာမည်က...ပါ။
Yes, of course.	**Hote dar bawt.** ဟုတ်တာပွေ့။
No, I'm sorry.	**Ma ya boo. Sorry bar.** မရဘူး။ ဆောရီးပါ။
Yes, what can I do for you?	**Hote kaet, bar ku nyi payy ya ma lell?** ဟုတ်ကဲ့။ ဘာကူညီပေးရမလဲ။
Just a moment, please.	**Kha na layy naw.** ခဏလေးနော်။
No, I don't have time now.	[male speaker] **A khoot, kya nawt mhar, achain ma sheet boo.** အခုကျွန်တော့်မှာ အချိန်မရှိဘူး။
	[female speaker] **A khoot, kya ma mhar, achain ma sheet boo.** အခုကျွန်မမှာ အချိန်မရှိဘူး။
No, that's impossible.	**Aet dar, ma phyit nai bar boo.** အဲဒါမဖြစ်နိုင်ပါဘူး။
No problem.	**Kate sa, ma sheet bar boo.** ကိစ္စမရှိပါဘူး။
I hope so too.	**Aet lo bell, myaw lint bar dae.** အဲလိုပဲမျှော်လင့်ပါတယ်။
No, nothing.	**Bar mha, ma hote bar boo.** ဘာမှမဟုတ်ပါဘူး။
That's right!	**Hote dae.** ဟုတ်တယ်။
Something's wrong.	**Ta khoot khoot, lwell nay dae.** တစ်ခုခုလွဲနေတယ်။

There's a problem.	**Pyat tha nar, sheet dae.** ပြဿနာရှိတယ်။
I agree.	[male speaker] **Kya naw, tha baww tu dae.** ကျွန်တော်သဘောတူတယ်။
	[female speaker] **Kya ma, tha baww tu dae.** ကျွန်မသဘောတူတယ်။
I don't agree.	[male speaker] **Kya naw, tha baww ma tu boo.** ကျွန်တော်သဘောမတူဘူး။
	[female speaker] **Kya ma, tha baww ma tu boo.** ကျွန်မသဘောမတူဘူး။
OK. / It's fine.	**Ya dae.** ရတယ်။
perhaps/maybe	verb + **yin** + verb + **mae** Verb + ရင် + Verb + မယ်
I don't know.	**Ma theet boo.** မသိဘူး။

2.4 Thank you

Thank you.	**Kyayy zoo tin bar dae.** ကျေးဇူးတင်ပါတယ်။
Don't mention it./ No problem.	**Kate sa, ma sheet bar boo.** ကိစ္စမရှိပါဘူး။
Thank you very much.	**Kyayy zoo, a myarr gyee, tin bar dae.** ကျေးဇူးအများကြီးတင်ပါတယ်။
Very kind of you.	**A yann, tha baww kaungg dae naw.** အရမ်းသဘောကောင်းတယ်နော်။
My pleasure. / It's okay.	**Ya bar dae.** ရပါတယ်။
I enjoyed it very much.	**A yann pyaw gaet bar dae.** အရမ်းပျော်ခဲ့ပါတယ်။
Thank you for...	**...a twet kyayy zoo tin bar dae.** ...အတွက် ကျေးဇူးတင်ပါတယ်။

2.5 I'm sorry

Excuse me? (question)	[to male] **A ko yay.** အစ်ကိုရေ [to female] **A ma yay.** အစ်မရေ
Sorry.	**Sorry par. / Taungg pan bar dae.** ဆောရီးပါ။ / တောင်းပန်ပါတယ်။
Excuse me [polite].	**Ta zate lout.** တစ်ဆိတ်လောက်။
Sorry to bother you.	**A nhaungt a shet, payy ya dar, arr nar bar dae.** အနှောင့်အယှက်ပေးရတာ အားနာပါတယ်။
Sorry, I didn't know that...	**Taungg ban bar dae...so dar ma theet loht bar.** တောင်းပန်ပါတယ်။ ...ဆိုတာ မသိလို့ပါ။
I do apologize.	**Ta gae taungg ban bar dae.** တကယ်တောင်းပန်ပါတယ်။
I didn't mean it.	**Ma yee ywae bar boo.** မရည်ရွယ်ပါဘူး။
It was an accident.	**Ma taw ta sa phyit thwarr dar bar.** မတော်တဆဖြစ်သွားတာပါ။
That's all right. / It's okay.	**Ya bar dae.** ရပါတယ်။
Don't worry about it.	**Sate ma pu bar naet.** စိတ်မပူပါနဲ့။
Never mind.	**Kate sa, ma sheet bar boo.** ကိစ္စမရှိပါဘူး။
It could happen to anyone.	**Bae thu ma so, phyit nai bar dae.** ဘယ်သူမဆိုဖြစ်နိုင်ပါတယ်။

Which do you prefer?	**Bae har, po kyite lell?** ဘယ်ဟာပိုကြိုက်လဲ။
Which do you like best?	**Bae har, a kyite sone lell?** ဘယ်ဟာအကြိုက်ဆုံးလဲ။
What do you think?	**Bae lo htin lell?** ဘယ်လိုထင်လဲ။
Don't you like dancing?	**Ka dar, ma kyite boo larr?** ကတာမကြိုက်ဘူးလား။
I don't mind.	[male speaker] **Kya naw ga, kate sa ma sheet boo.** ကျွန်တော်က ကိစ္စမရှိဘူး။
	[female speaker] **Kya ma ga, kate sa ma sheet boo.** ကျွန်မက ကိစ္စမရှိဘူး။
Well done!	**Taw dae!** တော်တယ်။
Not bad!	**Ma soe boo!** မဆိုးဘူး။
Great!/Marvelous!	**Kaungg lite dar!** ကောင်းလိုက်တာ။
I am pleased for you.	**Wann thar bar dae.** ဝမ်းသာပါတယ်။
I'm very happy to...	**...a yann, wann thar bar dae.** ...အရမ်းဝမ်းသာပါတယ်။
It's really nice here!	**Di mhar, a yann kaungg dar bell!** ဒီမှာအရမ်းကောင်းတာပဲ။
How nice!	**Kaungg lite dar!** ကောင်းလိုက်တာ။
I'm very happy with...	**...a yann, pyaw bar dae.** ...အရမ်းပျော်ပါတယ်။
I'm not very happy with...	**...a yann, ma pyaw bar boo.** ...အရမ်းမပျော်ပါဘူး။
I'm glad that...	**...wann thar bar dae.** ...ဝမ်းသာပါတယ်။

I'm having a great time.	**Pyaw nay bar dae.** ပျော်နေပါတယ်။
I'm looking forward to tomorrow.	**Ma net phyan, myan myan, yout chin bi.** မနက်ဖြန်မြန်မြန်ရောက်ချင်ပြီ။
I hope it works out.	**A sin pyay mae loht, myaw lint bar dae.** အဆင်ပြေမယ်လို့ မျှော်လင့်ပါတယ်။
How awful!	**Sate ma chann myayt za yar, kaungg lite dar!** စိတ်မချမ်းမြေ့ စရာ ကောင်းလိုက်တာ။
It's horrible!	**Kyout sa yar, kaungg lite dar!** ကြောက်စရာကောင်းလိုက်တာ။
That's terrible!	**Soe ywarr lite dar!** ဆိုးရွားလိုက်တာ။
What a pity/shame!	**Nha myaww za yar, kaungg lite dar!** နှမြောစရာကောင်းလိုက်တာ။
How disgusting!	**Yon za yar, kaungg lite dar!** ရွံစရာကောင်းလိုက်တာ။
How silly!	**Mite mell lite dar!** မိုက်မဲလိုက်တာ။
That's ridiculous!	**Yee za yar gyee!** ရယ်စရာကြီး။
I don't like it.	**Ma kyite boo.** မကြိုက်ဘူး။
I'm bored to death!	**Pyinn loht, thay dawt mae!** ပျင်းလို့သေတော့မယ်။
I'm fed up!	**Nyee ngwayt nay bi!** ငြီးငွေ့နေပြီ။
This is no good.	**Dar ma kaungg boo.** ဒါမကောင်းဘူး။
This is not what I expected.	[male speaker] **Kya naw myaw lint htarr dar, dar ma hote boo.** ကျွန်တော်မျှော်လင့်ထားတာ ဒါမဟုတ်ဘူး။
	[female speaker] **Kya ma myaw lint htarr dar, dar ma hote boo.** ကျွန်မမျှော်လင့်ထားတာ ဒါမဟုတ်ဘူး။

3. Small Talk

3.1 Introductions

My name's...	[male speaker] **Kya nawt nan mae ga...bar.** ကျွန်တော့်နာမည်က...ပါ။
	[female speaker] **Kya ma nan mae ga...bar.** ကျွန်မနာမည်က...ပါ။
I'm...	[male speaker] **Kya naw ga,...bar.** ကျွန်တော်က...ပါ။
	[female speaker] **Kya ma ga,...bar.** ကျွန်မက...ပါ။
What's your name?	**Nan mae, bae lo khaw lell?** နာမည်ဘယ်လိုခေါ်လဲ။
May I introduce...?	**...naet, mate set payy ya ownn mae?** ...နဲ့ မိတ်ဆက်ပေးရဦးမယ်။
This is my wife.	**Dar, kya nawt, a myohh tha mee bar.** ဒါကျွန်တော့်အမျိုးသမီးပါ။

This is my husband.	**Dar, kya ma, a myohh tharr bar.** ဒါကျွန်မအမျိုးသားပါ။
This is my daughter.	[male speaker] **Dar, kya nawt, tha mee bar.** ဒါကျွန်တော့်သမီးပါ။
	[female speaker] **Dar, kya ma, tha mee bar.** ဒါကျွန်မသမီးပါ။
This is my son.	[male speaker] **Dar, kya nawt, tharr bar.** ဒါကျွန်တော့်သားပါ။
	[female speaker] **Dar, kya ma, tharr bar.** ဒါကျွန်မသားပါ။
This is my mother.	[male speaker] **Dar, kya nawt, a may bar.** ဒါကျွန်တော့်အမေပါ။
	[female speaker] **Dar, kya ma, a may bar.** ဒါကျွန်မအမေပါ။
This is my father.	[male speaker] **Dar, kya nawt, a phay bar.** ဒါကျွန်တော့်အဖေပါ။
	[female speaker] **Dar, kya ma, a phay bar.** ဒါကျွန်မအဖေပါ။
This is my fiancée.	**Dar, kya nawt, tha doht tha mee laungg bar.** ဒါကျွန်တော့်သတို့သမီးလောင်းပါ။
This is my fiancé.	**Dar, kya ma, tha doht tharr laungg bar.** ဒါကျွန်မသတို့သားလောင်းပါ။
This is my girlfriend.	**Dar, kya nawt, chit thu bar.** ဒါကျွန်တော့်ချစ်သူပါ။
This is my boyfriend.	**Dar, kya ma, chit thu bar.** ဒါကျွန်မချစ်သူပါ။
This is my friend.	[male speaker] **Dar, kya nawt, tha ngae jinn bar** ဒါကျွန်တော့်သူငယ်ချင်းပါ။
	[female speaker] **Dar, kya ma, tha ngae jinn bar.** ဒါကျွန်မသူငယ်ချင်းပါ။

Glad to meet you.	**Twayt ya dar, wann thar bar dae.** တွေ့ရတာဂမ်းသာပါတယ်။
Hi, glad to meet you.	**Mingalarbar, twayt ya dar, wann thar bar dae.** မင်္ဂလာပါ။ တွေ့ရတာဂမ်းသာပါတယ်။
It's a pleasure (honor).	**Wann thar bar dae.** ဂမ်းသာပါတယ်။
Which country are you from?	**Bae myoht mhar, nay lell?** ဘယ်မြို့မှာနေလဲ။
What city do you live in?	**Bae nai ngan ga lell?** ဘယ်နိုင်ငံကလဲ။
in…	**…mhar** …မှာ
near...	**…narr mhar** …နားမှာ
How long have you been here?	**Di mhar, bae lout kyar bi lell?** ဒီမှာဘယ်လောက်ကြာပြီလဲ။
A few days.	**Yet nell nell.** ရက်နည်းနည်း။
How long will you be staying here?	**Di mhar, bae lout kyar kyar nay ma lell?** ဒီမှာဘယ်လောက်ကြာကြာနေမလဲ။
We'll be leaving tomorrow.	**Ma net phyan, pyan tawt mae.** မနက်ဖြန်ပြန်တော့မယ်။
We'll be leaving in two weeks.	**Nout nha pat nay yin, pyan dawt mae.** နောက်နှစ်ပတ်နေရင်ပြန်တော့မယ်။
Where are you staying?	**Bae mhar, nay nay lell?** ဘယ်မှာနေနေလဲ။
I'm staying in a hotel.	**Hotel mhar, nay nay dae.** ဟိုတယ်မှာနေနေတယ်။
I'm staying with friends.	**Tha ngae jinn tway naet nay nay dae.** သူငယ်ချင်းတွေနဲ့နေနေတယ်။
I'm staying with relatives.	**A myohh dway naet, nay nay dae.** အမျိုးတွေနဲ့နေနေတယ်။

Are you here by yourself?	**Di mhar, ta yout htell larr?** ဒီမှာတစ်ယောက်တည်းလား။
Are you here with your family?	**Di mhar, meet tharr zoot naet larr?** ဒီမှာမိသားစုနဲ့လား။
I'm on my own.	**Di mhar, ta yout htell bar.** ဒီမှာတစ်ယောက်တည်းပါ။
I came with my wife.	**Kya naw, a myohh tha mee naet, lar dar bar.** ကျွန်တော့်အမျိုးသမီးနဲ့လာတာပါ။
I came with my husband.	**Kya ma, a myohh tharr naet, lar dar bar.** ကျွန်မအမျိုးသားနဲ့လာတာပါ။
I came with my family.	**Meet tharr zoot naet, lar dar bar.** မိသားစုနဲ့လာတာပါ။
I came with my relatives.	**A myohh dway naet, lar dar bar.** အမျိုးတွေနဲ့လာတာပါ။
I came with (a) friend(s).	**Tha ngae jinn (dway) naet, lar dar bar.** သူငယ်ချင်း (တွေ) နဲ့ လာတာပါ။
Are you married?	**Eain daung sheet larr?** အိမ်ထောင်ရှိလား။
Do you have a boyfriend/girlfriend?	**Chit thu sheet larr?** ချစ်သူရှိလား။
I'm married.	**Eain daung sheet dae.** အိမ်ထောင်ရှိတယ်။
I'm single. / I'm not married.	**Eain daung, ma sheet boo.** အိမ်ထောင်မရှိဘူး။
I'm separated.	[male speaker] **Kya naw ga, ta khoot lat bar.** ကျွန်တော်က တစ်ခုလပ်ပါ။
	[female speaker] **Kya ma ga, ta khoot lat bar.** ကျွန်မက တစ်ခုလပ်ပါ။
I'm divorced.	[male speaker] **Kya naw ga, kwar shinn htarr dar bar.** ကျွန်တော်က ကွာရှင်းထားတာပါ။

	[female speaker] **Kya ma ga, ekwar shinn htarr dar bar.** ကျွန်မက ကွာရှင်းထားတာပါ။
I'm a widow.	**Kya ma ga, mote soe ma bar.** ကျွန်မက မုဆိုးမပါ။
I'm a widower.	**Kya naw ga, mote soe bo bar.** ကျွန်တော်က မုဆိုးဖိုပါ။
I live alone.	[male speaker] **Kya naw ga, ta yout htell, nay dar bar.** ကျွန်တော်က တစ်ယောက်တည်းနေတာပါ။
	[female speaker] **Kya ma ga, ta yout htell, nay dar bar.** ကျွန်မက တစ်ယောက်တည်းနေတာပါ။
Do you have children?	**Kha layy sheet larr?** ကလေးရှိလား။
Do you have any grandchildren?	**Myayy sheet larr?** မြေးရှိလား။
How old are you?	**A thet, bae lout sheet bi lell?** အသက်ဘယ်လောက်ရှိပြီလဲ။
How old is she/he?	**Thu ga, a thet bae lout sheet bi lell?** သူက အသက်ဘယ်လောက်ရှိပြီလဲ။
I'm ... years old.	[male speaker] **Kya naw ga, a thet... nhit, sheet bar bi.** ကျွန်တော်က အသက်...နှစ်ရှိပါပြီ။
	[female speaker] **Kya ma ga, a thet... nhit sheet bar bi.** ကျွန်မက အသက်... နှစ်ရှိပါပြီ။
She's/He's ... years old.	**Thu ga, a thet...nhit, sheet bar bi.** သူက အသက်...နှစ်ရှိပါပြီ။
What do you do?	**Bar alote, lote lell?** ဘာအလုပ်လုပ်လဲ။
I work in an office.	**Yone mhar, alote lote bar dae.** ရုံးမှာအလုပ်လုပ်ပါတယ်။

I'm a student.	[male speaker] **Kya naw ga, kyaungg tharr bar.** ကျွန်တော်က ကျောင်းသားပါ။
	[female speaker] **Kya ma ga, kyaungg thu bar.** ကျွန်မက ကျောင်းသူပါ။
I'm unemployed.	**Alote, ma sheet bar boo.** အလုပ်မရှိပါဘူး။
I'm retired.	**Pin sin, yu htarr dar bar.** ပင်စင်ယူထားတာပါ။
I'm on a disability pension.	**Ma than swann pin sin, yu htarr dar bar.** မသန်စွမ်းပင်စင်ယူထားတာပါ။
I'm a housewife.	**Kya ma ga, eain shin ma bar.** ကျွန်မက အိမ်ရှင်မပါ။
Do you like your job?	**A khoot lote nay daet, alote go, kyite larr?** အခုအလုပ်လုပ်နေတဲ့အလုပ်ကို ကြိုက်လား။
Most of the time.	**A myarr arr phyint dawt, kyite bar dae.** အများအားဖြင့်တော့ ကြိုက်ပါတယ်။
Mostly I do, but I prefer vacations.	**A myarr arr phyint dawt, kyite bar dae. Dar bay maet, pate yet tway go, po kyite dar bawt naw.** အများအားဖြင့်တော့ ကြိုက်ပါတယ်။ ဒါပေမဲ့ ပိတ်ရက်တွေကို ပိုကြိုက်တာပေါ့နော်။

3.2 Pardon me, do you speak English?

I don't speak any...	**...zagarr, ma pyaww tat bar boo.** ...စကားမပြောတတ်ပါဘူး။
I speak a little...	**...zagarr, nell nell, pyaww tat bar dae.** ...စကားနည်းနည်းပြောတတ်ပါတယ်။
I'm American.	[male speaker] **Kya naw ga, american lu myohh bar.** ကျွန်တော်က အမေရိကန်လူမျိုးပါ။

[female speaker] **Kya ma ga, american lu myohh bar.** ကျွန်မက အမေရိကန်လူမျိုးပါ။

I'm British.

[male speaker] **Kya naw ga, byeet teet sha lu myohh bar.** ကျွန်တော်က ဗြိတိသျှလူမျိုးပါ။

[female speaker] **Kya ma ga, byeet deet sha lu myohh bar.** ကျွန်မ ဗြိတိသျှလူမျိုးပါ။

I'm Chinese.

[male speaker] **Kya naw ga, ta yote lu myohh bar.** ကျွန်တော်က တရုတ်လူမျိုးပါ။

[female speaker] **Kya ma ga, ta yote lu myohh bar.** ကျွန်မက တရုတ်လူမျိုးပါ။

I'm Singaporean.

[male speaker] **Kya naw ga, singapu lu myohh bar.** ကျွန်တော်က စင်္ကာပူလူမျိုးပါ။

[female spealer] **Kya ma ga, singapu lu myohh bar.** ကျွန်မက စင်္ကာပူလူမျိုးပါ။

I'm Australian.

[male speaker] **Kya naw ga, australia lu myohh bar.** ကျွန်တော်က သြစတြေးလျလူမျိုးပါ။

[female speaker] **Kya ma ga, australia lu myohh bar.** ကျွန်မက သြစတြေးလျလူမျိုးပါ။

I'm French.

[male speaker] **Kya naw ga, pyin thit lu myohh bar.** ကျွန်တော်က ပြင်သစ်လူမျိုးပါ။

[female speaker] **Kya ma ga, pyin thit lu myohh bar.** ကျွန်မက ပြင်သစ်လူမျိုးပါ။

Do you speak English?

Ingalate zagarr, pyaww tat larr? အင်္ဂလိပ်စကားပြောတတ်လား။

Is there anyone who speaks...?	**...zagarr, pyaww tat taet thu, sheet larr?** ...စကားပြောတတ်တဲ့သူရှိလား။
What?	**Bar lell?** ဘာလဲ။
I understand.	**Narr lae bar dae.** နားလည်ပါတယ်။
I don't understand.	**Narr ma lae bar boo.** နားမလည်ပါဘူး။
Do you understand me?	**Narr lae larr?** နားလည်လား။
Could you repeat that?	**Htat pyaww bar ownn?** ထပ်ပြောပါဦး။
Could you speak more slowly, please?	**Phyayy phyayy pyaww bar?** ဖြည်းဖြည်းပြောပါ။
What does this mean?	**Dar, bar a date bae lell?** ဒါဘာအဓိပ္ပါယ်လဲ။
What does that mean?	**Ae dar, bar a date bae lell?** အဲဒါဘာအဓိပ္ပါယ်လဲ။
It's more or less the same as...	**...naet a tu tu lout bell.** ...နဲ့အတူတူလောက်ပဲ။
Could you write that down for me, please?	**Yayy pya bar larr?** ရေးပြပါလား။
Could you spell that for me, please?	**Sa lone paungg pya payy bar larr?** စာလုံးပေါင်းပြပေးပါလား။
Could you point to the phrase in this book?	**Di sar oat htell mhar, pya payy bar larr?** ဒီစာအုပ်ထဲမှာ ပြပေးပါလား။
Just a minute, I'll look it up.	**Kha na layy naw, shar payy mae.** ခဏလေးနော်။ ရှာပေးမယ်။
I can't find the word.	**Sa lone, shar ma twayt boo.** စာလုံးရှာမတွေ့ဘူး။
I can't find the sentence.	**Sar gyaungg, shar ma twayt boo.** စာကြောင်းရှာမတွေ့ဘူး။
How do you say that in...?	**...lo, bae lo pyaww lell?** ...လိုဘယ်လိုပြောလဲ။

| How do you pronounce that word? | **Ae sa lone go, bae lo, a than htwet lell?** အဲစာလုံးကို ဘယ်လိုအသံထွက်လဲ။ |

3.3 Starting and ending a conversation

Could I ask you something?	**Ta khoot lout, mayy loht ya ma larr?** တစ်ခုလောက်မေးလို့ရမလား။
Could you help me?	**Ku nyi payy bar larr?** ကူညီပေးပါလား။
Yes, what's the problem?	**Hote kaet, bar kate sa lell?** ဟုတ်ကဲ့၊ ဘာကိစ္စလဲ။
What can I do for you?	**Bar, ku nyi payy ya ma lell?** ဘာကူညီပေးရမလဲ။
Sorry, I don't have time now.	**Arr nar bar dae. A khoot achain ma sheet loht bar.** အားနာပါတယ်။ အခုအချိန်မရှိလို့ပါ။
Do you have a light?	Mee chit sheet larr? မီးခြစ်ရှိလား။
May I join you?	[male speaker] **Kya naw lell, par loht ya ma larr?** ကျွန်တော်လည်း ပါလို့ရမလား။
	[female speaker] **Kya ma, lell par loht ya ma larr?** ကျွန်မလည်း ပါလို့ရမလား။
Can I take a picture?	**Dat p'own, yite loht ya larr?** ဓာတ်ပုံရိုက်လို့ရလား။
Could you take a picture of me?	[male speaker] **Kya nawt go, dat p'own, yite payy bar larr?** ကျွန်တော့်ကို ဓာတ်ပုံရိုက်ပေးပါလား။
	[female speaker] **Kya ma go, dat p'own, yite payy bar larr?** ကျွန်မကို ဓာတ်ပုံရိုက်ပေးပါလား။
Could you take a picture of us?	[male speaker] **Kya naw doht go, dat p'own, yite payy bar larr?** ကျွန်တော်တို့ကို ဓာတ်ပုံရိုက်ပေးပါလား။

	[female speaker] **Kya ma doht go, dat p'own, yite payy bar larr?** ကျွန်မတို့ကို ဓာတ်ပုံရိုက်ပေးပါလား။
Leave me alone.	[male speaker] **Kya nawt go, ta yout htell, htarr khaet bar.** ကျွန်တော့်ကို တစ်ယောက်တည်းထားခဲ့ပါ။
	[female speaker] **Kya ma go, ta yout htell, htarr khaet bar.** ကျွန်မကို တစ်ယောက်တည်းထားခဲ့ပါ။
Go away!	**Htwet thwarr bar!** ထွက်သွားပါ။
Go away or I'll scream.	**Htwet thwarr bar. Ma hote yin aw lite mhar naw.** ထွက်သွားပါ။ မဟုတ်ရင် အော်လိုက်မှာနော်။

3.4 Chatting about the weather

It's so hot today!	**Di nayt, a yann pu dae!** ဒီနေ့အရမ်းပူတယ်။
It's so cold today!	**Di nayt, a yann aye dae!** ဒီနေ့အရမ်းအေးတယ်။
Isn't it a lovely day?	**Di nayt, yar thi oot toot thar yar dae naw?** ဒီနေ့ရာသီဉတုသာယာတယ်နော်။
It's so windy!	**Lay, a yann tite dae!** လေအရမ်းတိုက်တယ်။
What a storm!	**M'own daii gyee bell!** မုန်တိုင်းကြီးပဲ။
All that rain!	**Moe ywar lite dar!** မိုးရွာလိုက်တာ။
All that snow!	**Nhinn kya lite dar!** နှင်းကျလိုက်တာ။
It's so foggy!	**Myu, a yann saii nay dae!** မြူအရမ်းဆိုင်းနေတယ်။
Has the weather been like this for long?	**Di lo, yar thi oot toot myohh, kyar bi larr?** ဒီလိုရာသီဉတုမျိုးကြာပြီလား။

Is it always this hot here?	**Di mhar, a myell dann, di lo pu larr?** ဒီမှာအမြဲတမ်း ဒီလိုပူလား။
Is it always this cold here?	**Di mhar, a myell dann, di lo aye larr?** ဒီမှာအမြဲတမ်း ဒီလိုအေးလား။
Is it always this dry here?	**Di mhar, a myell dann, di lo chout thwayt nay larr?** ဒီမှာအမြဲတမ်း ဒီလိုခြောက်သွေ့နေလား။
Is it always this humid here?	**Di mhar, a myell dann, di lo so htaii nay larr?** ဒီမှာအမြဲတမ်း ဒီလိုစိုထိုင်းနေလား။

3.5 Hobbies

Do you have any hobbies?	**Bar, war tha nar par lell?** ဘာဝါသနာပါလဲ။
I like reading.	**Sar phat dar, kyite dae.** စာဖတ်တာကြိုက်တယ်။
I like photography.	**Dat p'own pyin nyar go, war tha nar bar dae.** ဓာတ်ပုံပညာကို ဝါသနာပါတယ်။
I enjoy listening to music.	**Tha chinn narr htaung ya dar war tha nar bar dae.** သီချင်းနားထောင်ရတာ ဝါသနာပါတယ်။
I play the guitar.	**Guitar tee ya dar, war tha nar bar dae.** ဂစ်တာတီးရတာ ဝါသနာပါတယ်။
I play the piano.	**Sann da yarr, tee ya dar, war tha nar bar dae.** စန္ဒရားတီးရတာ ဝါသနာပါတယ်။
I like watching movies.	**Yote shin, kyeet ya dar, war tha nar bar dae.** ရုပ်ရှင်ကြည့်ရတာ ဝါသနာပါတယ်။
I like traveling.	**Kha yee, thwarr ya dar, war tha nar bar dae.** ခရီးသွားရတာ ဝါသနာပါတယ်။

3

I like exercising.	**Layt kyint khann, lote ya dar, war tha nar bar dae.** လေ့ကျင့်ခန်းလုပ်ရတာ ဂါသနာပါတယ်။
I like going fishing.	**Ngarr mhyarr htwet ya dar, war tha nar bar dae.** ငါးမျှားထွက်ရတာ ဂါသနာပါတယ်။
I like going for a walk.	**Lann shout htwet ya dar, war tha nar bar dae.** လမ်းလျှောက်ထွက်ရတာ ဂါသနာပါတယ်။

3.6 Invitations

Are you doing anything tonight?	**Di nya, bar lote ma lell?** ဒီညဘာလုပ်မလဲ။
Do you have any plans for today?	**Di nya, bar a si a zin sheet lell?** ဒီနေ့ဘာအစီအစဉ်ရှိလဲ။
Do you have any plans for this afternoon?	**Di nayt lae, bar a si a zin sheet lell?** ဒီနေ့လယ်ဘာအစီအစဉ်ရှိလဲ။
Do you have any plans for tonight?	**Di nya, bar a si a zin sheet lell?** ဒီညဘာအစီအစဉ်ရှိလဲ။
Would you like to go out with me?	[male speaker] **Kya naw doht, a pyin thwarr gya ma larr?** ကျွန်တော်တို့အပြင်သွားကြမလား။
	[female speaker] **Kya ma doht, a pyin thwarr gya ma larr?** ကျွန်မတို့အပြင်သွားကြမလား။
Would you like to go dancing with me?	[male speaker] **Kya naw doht, thwarr ka gya ma larr?** ကျွန်တော်တို့သွားကကြမလား။
	[female speaker] **Kya ma doht, thwarr ka gya ma larr?** ကျွန်မတို့သွားကကြမလား။

Would you like to have lunch with me?	[male speaker] **Kya naw doht, nayt lae zar, sarr gya ma larr?** ကျွန်တော်တို့ နေ့လယ်စာစားကြမလား။
	[female speaker] **Kya ma doht, nayt lae zar, sarr gya ma larr?** ကျွန်မတို့ နေ့လယ်စာစားကြမလား။
Would you like to have dinner with me?	[male speaker] **Kya naw doht, nya zar, sarr gya ma larr?** ကျွန်တော်တို့ ညစာစားကြမလား။
	[female speaker] **Kya ma doht, nya zar, sarr gya ma larr?** ကျွန်မတို့ ညစာစားကြမလား။
Would you like to come to the beach with me?	[male speaker] **Kya naw doht, pin lae kann jay, thwarr gya ma larr?** ကျွန်တော်တို့ ပင်လယ်ကမ်းခြေ သွားကြမလား။
	[female speaker] **Kya ma doht, pin lae kann ,ay, thwarr gya ma larr?** ကျွန်မတို့ ပင်လယ်ကမ်းခြေ သွားကြမလား။
Would you like to come into town with us?	[male speaker] **Kya naw doht naet, atutu, myoht htell go, lite khaet ma larr?** ကျွန်တော်တို့နဲ့အတူတူ မြို့ထဲကို လိုက်ခဲ့မလား။
	[female speaker] **Kya ma doht naet, atutu, myoht htell go, lite khaet ma larr?** ကျွန်မတို့နဲ့အတူတူ မြို့ထဲကို လိုက်ခဲ့မလား။
Shall we dance?	**Ka gya ma larr?** ကကြမလား။
Shall we sit at the bar?	**Barr htai gya ma larr?** ဘားထိုင်ကြမလား။
Shall we get something to drink?	**Ta khoot khoot, thwarr thout gya ma larr?** တစ်ခုခုသွားသောက်ကြမလား။

Shall we go for a walk?	**Lann shout htwet gya ma larr?** လမ်းလျှောက်ထွက်ကြမလား။
Shall we go for a drive?	**Karr shout maungg gya ma larr?** ကားလျှောက်မောင်းကြမလား။
Yes, all right.	**Kaung bar dae.** ကောင်းပါတယ်။
Good idea.	**Thate kaungg daet, a kyan bell.** သိပ်ကောင်းတဲ့အကြံပဲ။
No, thank you.	**Ma lite tawt bar boo, kyayy zoo bar.** မလိုက်တော့ပါဘူး။ ကျေးဇူးပါ။
Maybe later.	**Nout mha bawt.** နောက်မှပေါ့။
I don't feel like it.	**Thwarr jin sate, ma sheet boo, phyit nay dae.** သွားချင်စိတ်မရှိဘူးဖြစ်နေတယ်။
I don't have time.	**Achain ma ya boo.** အချိန်မရဘူး။
I already have a date.	**Chein htarr pee tharr, phyit nay dae.** ချိန်းထားပြီးသားဖြစ်နေတယ်။
I'm not very good at dancing.	**Kaungg kaungg, ma ka tat boo.** ကောင်းကောင်းမကတတ်ဘူး။
I'm not very good at swimming.	**Yay, kaungg kaungg, ma koo tat boo.** ရေကောင်းကောင်းမကူးတတ်ဘူး။

3.7 Paying a compliment

You look great!	[to a male] **Kyeet kaungg nay dae naw!** ကြည့်ကောင်းနေတယ်နော်။
	[to a female] **Hla nay dae naw!** လှနေတယ်နော်။
I like your car!	**Karr ga, kaungg lite dar!** ကားကကောင်းလိုက်တာ။
You are very nice.	**Tha baww kaunng dae naw.** သဘောကောင်းတယ်နော်။

What a good boy/girl!	**Lu kaungg bell!** လူကောင်းပဲ။
You're a good dancer.	**A ka kaungg dae naw.** အကကောင်းတယ်နော်။
You're a very good cook.	**Hinn chet kaungg dae naw.** ဟင်းချက်ကောင်းတယ်နော်။
You're a good soccer player.	**Baw lone kan dar, taw dae naw.** ဘောလုံးကန်တာတော်တယ်နော်။

3.8 Intimate comments and questions

I like being with you.	*(name)* **naet, atutu, sheet nay ya dar go kyite dae.** ...နဲ့ အတူတူရှိနေရတာကိုကြိုက်တယ်။
I've missed you so much.	**A yann, lwann nay dar.** အရမ်းလွမ်းနေတာ။
I dreamt about you.	*(name)* **go, eain met, met khaet dae.** ...ကို အိပ်မက်မက်ခဲ့တယ်။
I think about you all day.	**Ta nayt lone,** *(name)* **a kyaungg twayy nay meet dae.** တစ်နေ့လုံး... အကြောင်းတွေးနေမိတယ်။
I've been thinking about you all day.	**Ta nayt lone,** *(name)* **a kyaungg, twayy nay khaet dar.** တစ်နေ့လုံး... အကြောင်းတွေးနေခဲ့တာ။
You have such a sweet smile.	*(name)* **yaet, a pyone ga, cho lite dar.** ...ရဲ့ အပြုံးက ချိုလိုက်တာ။
You have such beautiful eyes.	*(name)* **yaet, myat wunn layy dway ga hla lite dar.** ...ရဲ့ မျက်ဂန်းလေးတွေက လှလိုက်တာ။
I like (I'm fond of) you.	[male speaker] **Kya naw,** *(name)* **go, tha baww kya dae.** ကျွန်တော်...ကို သဘောကျတယ်။

	[female speaker] **Kya ma,** *(name)* **go, tha baww kya dae.** ကျွန်မ...ကို သဘောကျတယ်။
I'm in love with you.	[male speaker] **Kya naw,** *(name)* **go, chit meet nay bi.** ကျွန်တော်...ကို ချစ်မိနေပြီ။
	[female speaker] **Kya ma,** *(name)* **go, chit meet nay bi.** ကျွန်မ...ကို ချစ်မိနေပြီ။
I'm in love with you too.	[male speaker] **Kya naw lell,** *(name)* **go, chit meet nay bi.** ကျွန်တော်လည်း ...ကို ချစ်မိနေပြီ။
	[female speaker] **Kya ma lell,** *(name)* **go, chit meet nay bi.** ကျွန်မလည်း...ကို ချစ်မိနေပြီ။
I love you.	**Chit dae.** ချစ်တယ်။
I love you too.	[male speaker] **Kya naw lell,** *(name)* **go, chit dae.** ကျွန်တော်လည်း... ကိုချစ်တယ်။
	[female speaker] **Kya ma lell,** *(name)* **go, chit tae.** ကျွန်မလည်း...ကိုချစ်တယ်။
I don't feel as strongly about you.	[male speaker] **Kya naw,** *(name)* **a paw mhar, khan zarr gyet, kyee kyee marr marr, ma sheet bar boo.** ကျွန်တော်...အပေါ်မှာ ခံစားချက်ကြီးကြီးမားမား မရှိပါဘူး။
	[female speaker] **Kya ma,** *(name)* **a paw mhar, khan zarr gyet, kyee kyee marr marr, ma sheet bar boo.** ကျွန်မ...အပေါ်မှာ ခံစားချက်ကြီးကြီးမားမား မရှိပါဘူး။
I already have a girlfriend.	**Kya nawt mhar, chit tu, sheet dae.** ကျွန်တော့်မှာချစ်သူရှိတယ်။

I already have a boyfriend.	**Kya ma mhar, chit thu, sheet dae.** ကျွန်မမှာချစ်သူရှိတယ်။
I'm not ready for that.	[male speaker] **Kya naw, ae dar a twet, a sin thint, ma phyit thayy boo.** ကျွန်တော် အဲဒါအတွက် အဆင်သင့်မဖြစ်သေးဘူး။
	[female speaker] **Kya ma, ae dar a twet, a sin thint, ma phyit thayy boo.** ကျွန်မ အဲဒါအတွက် အဆင်သင့်မဖြစ်သေးဘူး။
I don't want to rush into it.	[male speaker] **Kya naw, ae dar go, a hlyin za lo, ma lote chin thayy boo.** ကျွန်တော် အဲဒါကို အလျင်စလိုမလုပ်ချင်သေးဘူး။
	[female speaker] **Kya ma, ae dar go, a hlyin za lo, ma lote chin thayy boo.** ကျွန်မ အဲဒါကို လျင်စလိုမလုပ်ချင်သေးဘူး။
Take your hands off me.	**Let phae payy bar.** လက်ဖယ်ပေးပါ။
Okay, no problem.	**Kaungg bar bi, kate sa, ma sheet bar boo.** ကောင်းပါပြီ။ ကိစ္စမရှိပါဘူး။
Will you spend the night with me?	**Nya go, atutu k'own sone gya ma larr?** ညကိုအတူတူကုန်ဆုံးကြမလား။
I'd like to sleep with you.	*(name)* **naet, atutu, ate chin dae.** ...နဲ့ အတူတူအိပ်ချင်တယ်။
Only if we use a condom.	**Condom thone mha.** ကွန်ဒုံးသုံးမှ။
We have to be careful about AIDS.	**AIDS go, ga yoot site ya mae.** အေအိုင်ဒီအက်စ်ကို ဂရုစိုက်ရမယ်။
We shouldn't take any risks.	**Bae lo, sont zarr mhoot myohh mha, ma lote dar, kaungg dae.** ဘယ်လိုစွန့်စားမှုမျိုးမ မလုပ်တာကောင်းတယ်။

Do you have a condom?	**Condom sheet larr?** ကွန်ဒုံးရှိလား။
No?	**Ma sheet boo larr?** မရှိဘူးလား။
Then the answer's no.	**Dar so yin dawt, a phyay ga, no bar.** ဒါဆိုရင်တော့အဖြေကနိုးပါ။

3.9 Congratulations and condolences

Happy New Year!	**Nhit thit mhar, pyaw shwin bar zay!** နှစ်သစ်မှာပျော်ရွှင်ပါစေ။
Happy birthday!	**Mwayy nayt mhar, pyaw shwin bar zay!** မွေးနေ့မှာပျော်ရွှင်ပါစေ။
Please accept my condolences.	**A yann bell, wann nell, kyay kwell ya bar dae.** အရမ်းပဲဝမ်းနည်းကြေကွဲရပါတယ်။
My deepest sympathy.	**Sate ma kaungg lite dar.** စိတ်မကောင်းလိုက်တာ။

3.10 Arrangements

When will I see you again?	**Bae dawt, htat twayt gya ma lell?** ဘယ်တော့ထပ်တွေ့ကြမလဲ။
Are you free over the weekend?	**Sa nay, ta ninn ga nway mhar, arr larr?** စနေ၊ တနင်္ဂနွေမှာ အားလား။
What's the plan, then?	**Dar so, bar a si a zin, sheet lell?** ဒါဆိုဘာအစီအစဉ်ရှိလဲ။
Where shall we meet?	**Bae mhar, twayt gya ma lell?** ဘယ်မှာတွေ့ကြမလဲ။
Will you pick me/us up?	[male speaker] **Kya nawt / Kya naw doht go, lar khaw payy ma larr?** ကျွန်တော့ / ကျွန်တော်တို့ကို။ လာခေါ် ပေးမလား။

	[female speaker] **Kya ma doht go, lar khaw payy ma larr?** ကျွန်မ / ကျွန်မတို့ကို လာခေါ် ပေးမလား။
Shall I pick you up?	[male speaker] **Kya naw,** *(name)* **go, lar khaw payy ya ma larr?** ကျွန်တော်…ကို လာခေါ် ပေးရမလား။
	[female speaker] **Kya ma** *(name)* **go, lar khaw payy ya ma larr?** ကျွန်မ…ကို လာခေါ် ပေးရမလား။
I have to be home by…	[male speaker] **Kya naw,** *(time)* **a yout, eain pyan ya mae.** ကျွန်တော်…အရောက် အိမ်ပြန်ရမယ်။
	[female speaker] **Kya ma,** *(time)* **a yout, eain pyan ya mae.** ကျွန်မ…အရောက် အိမ်ပြန်ရမယ်။
I don't want to see you anymore.	[male speaker] **Kya naw,** *(name)* **go, htat, ma twayt chin tawt boo.** ကျွန်တော်…ကို ထပ်မတွေ့ချင်တော့ဘူး။
	[female speaker] **Kya ma,** *(name)* **go, htat, ma twayt chin tawt boo.** ကျွန်မ…ကို ထပ်မတွေ့ချင်တော့ဘူး။

3.11 Being the host(ess)

What would you like to drink?	**Bar thout ma lell?** ဘာသောက်မလဲ။
Something non-alcoholic, please.	**A yet, ma par dar, ta khoot khoot, payy bar.** အရက်မပါတာ တစ်ခုခုပေးပါ။
Would you like a cigarette/cigar?	**Sa late, thout ma larr?** ဆေးလိပ်သောက်မလား။
I don't smoke.	**Sa late, ma thout boo.** ဆေးလိပ်မသောက်ဘူး။

Can I send you home?	[male speaker] **Kya naw, eain lite poht payy loht, ya ma larr?** ကျွန်တော် အိမ်လိုက်ပို့ပေးလို့ရမလား။
	[female speaker] **Kya ma, eain lite poht payy loht, ya ma larr?** ကျွန်မ အိမ်လိုက်ပို့ပေးလို့ရမလား။
Can I email you?	**Email ga nay, set thwae loht, ya ma larr?** အီးမေးလ်ကနေ ဆက်သွယ်လို့ရမလား။
Can I call you?	**Phone set loht, ya ma larr?** ဖုန်းဆက်လို့ရမလား။
Will you text/call me?	[male speaker] **Kya nawt go, [sar poht / phone set] ma larr?** ကျွန်တော့်ကို စာပို့ / ဖုန်းဆက်မလား။
	[female speaker] **Kya ma go, [sar poht / phone set] ma larr?** ကျွန်မကို စာပို့ / ဖုန်းဆက်မလား။
Can I have your mobile number/email address?	[male speaker] **Kya nawt go, [phone nan bat / email late sar] payy htarr bar larr?** ကျွန်တော့်ကို ဖုန်းနံပါတ် / အီးမေးလ်လိပ်စာ ပေးထားပါလား။
	[female speaker] **Kya ma go, [phone nan bat / email late sar] payy htarr bar larr?** ကျွန်မကို ဖုန်းနံပါတ် / အီးမေးလ်လိပ်စာ ပေးထားပါလား။
Thanks for everything.	**A sa sa a yar yar, a twet kyayy zoo tin bar dae.** အစစအရာရာအတွက် ကျေးဇူးတင်ပါတယ်။

It was a lot of fun. Send my regards to...	**A yann pyaw za yar kaungg gaet bar dae.** *(Name)* **go lell, nhote set bar dae loht, pyaww payy bar ownn naw.** အရမ်းပျော်စရာကောင်းခဲ့ပါတယ်။ ...ကိုလည်း နှုတ်ဆက်ပါတယ်လို့ ပြောပေးပါဦးနော်။
All the best!	**Arr lone, a sin pyay bar zay!** အားလုံးအဆင်ပြေပါစေ။
Good luck.	**Kan kaungg bar zay.** ကံကောင်းပါစေ။
When will you be back?	**Bae dawt, pyan lar ma lell?** ဘယ်တော့ပြန်လာမလဲ။
I'll be waiting for you.	**Saungt nay mae naw.** စောင့်နေမယ်နော်။
I'd like to see you again.	**Htat twayt chin thayy bar dae.** ထပ်တွေ့ချင်သေးပါတယ်။
I hope we meet again soon.	**Ma kyar gin mhar, pyan s'own gya boht, mhyaw lint bar dae.** မကြာခင်မှာပြန်ဆုံကြဖို့ မျှော်လင့်ပါတယ်။
Here's my address if you're ever in the United States.	[male speaker] **Dar, kya nawt, late sar bar. American nai ngan go, lar yin, set thwae bar naw.** ဒါကျွန်တော့်လိပ်စာပါ။ အမေရိကန်နိုင်ငံကိုလာရင် ဆက်သွယ်ပါနော်။
	[female speaker] **Dar, kya ma, late sar bar. American nai ngan go, lar yin, set thwae bar naw.** ဒါကျွန်မလိပ်စာပါ။ အမေရိကန်နိုင်ငံကိုလာရင် ဆက်သွယ်ပါနော်။

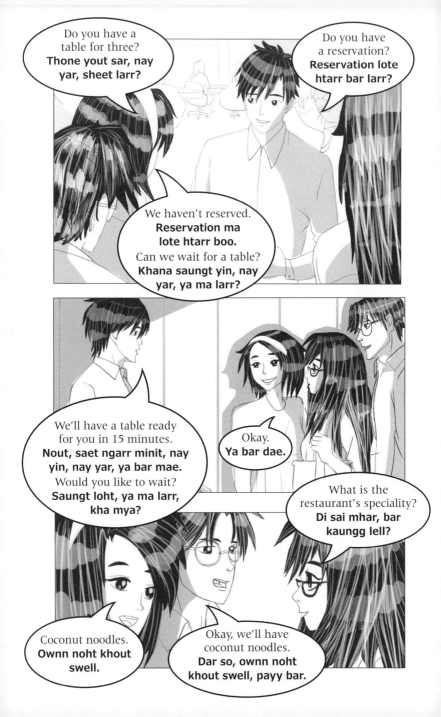

4. Eating Out

Rice is Myanmar's staple food. A typical Burmese meal is rice, meat or vegetable curry, fried vegetables and soup. Mohinga (rice vermicelli in fish soup), coconut noodles and Shan noodles are popular dishes. In Myanmar, the three main meals are:

1. **Ma net sar** မနက်စာ (breakfast), eaten from 6 to 10 a.m. It could consist of noodles, rice, salad or bread, with coffee or tea.

2. **Nayt lae zar** နေ့လယ်စာ (lunch), the main meal of the day, eaten between 11 a.m and 2 p.m. People often take a home-cooked packed lunch to school or work. Lunch usually consists of rice, meat, vegetables, sometimes with soup.

3. **Nya zar** ညစာ (dinner), traditionally eaten at home with the family, from 6 p.m to 9 p.m. If eating at home, lunch and dinner are usually the same.

4.1   At a restaurant

I'd like to reserve a table for seven o'clock, please.	**Khu na na yi a twet, zabwell ta waii, reserve lote chin loht bar.** ခုနစ်နာရီအတွက် စားပွဲတစ်ပိုင်း ရီဇာ့ဗ်လုပ်ချင်လို့ပါ။
A table for two, please.	**Nha yout sar zabwell, lote payy bar.** နှစ်ယောက်စာစားပွဲလုပ်ပေးပါ။

We've reserved.	**Reserve lote htarr pee bi.** ရီဇဗ်လုပ်ထားပြီးပြီ။
We haven't reserved.	**Reserve malote ya thayy boo.** ရီဇဗ်မလုပ်ရသေးဘူး။

ခဏလေးနော်။	A moment, please.
ရီစာပေးရှင်းလုပ်ထားပါလား။	Do you have a reservation?
ဘာနာမည်နဲ့ပါလဲ။	What name please?
ဒီဘက်ကိုကြွပါ။	This way, please.
အားနာပါတယ်။ ဒီစားပွဲက ရီဇဗ်လုပ်ထားလို့ပါ။	Sorry, this table is reserved.
နောက်ဆယ့်ငါးမိနစ်နေရင် နေရာရပါမယ်။	We'll have a table free in fifteen minutes.

Would you mind waiting?	[male speaker] **Saungt loht ya ma larr kha mya.** စောင့်လို့ရမလားခင်ဗျ။
	[female speaker] **Saungt loht ya ma larr shint.** စောင့်လို့ရမလားရှင့်။
Is the restaurant open yet?	**Sai phwint bi larr?** ဆိုင်ဖွင့်ပြီလား။
What time does the restaurant open?	**Sai, bae achain, phwint lell?** ဆိုင်ဘယ်အချိန်ဖွင့်လဲ။
What time does the restaurant close?	**Sai, bae achain, pate lell?** ဆိုင်ဘယ်အချိန်ပိတ်လဲ။
Can we wait for a table?	**Khana saungt yin, nay yar, ya ma larr?** ခဏစောင့်ရင် နေရာရမလား။
Do we have to wait long?	**A kyar gyee, saungt ya ma larr?** အကြာကြီးစောင့်ရမလား။
Is this seat taken?	**Di kh'own arr larr?** ဒီခုံအားလား။

Could we sit here/there? **(Di mhar / Ho mhar) htai loht ya larr?** (ဒီမှာ / ဟိုမှာ) ထိုင်လို့ရလား။

Can we sit by the window? **Bya dinn pout narr mhar, htai loht ya larr?** ပြတင်းပေါက်နားမှာထိုင်လို့ရလား။

Are there any tables outside? **A pyin mhar, zabwell sheet larr?** အပြင်မှာစားပွဲရှိလား။

Do you have another chair for us? **Htai kh'own, sheet thayy larr?** ထိုင်ခုံရှိသေးလား။

Do you have a high chair? **Htai kh'own, a myint, sheet larr?** ထိုင်ခုံအမြင့်ရှိလား။

Could you warm this up (in the microwave)? **Dar layy, nhwayy payy bar larr?** ဒါလေးနွှေးပေးပါလား။

Not too hot, please. **A yann, pu pu gyee, ma hote boo naw.** အရမ်းပူပူကြီးမဟုတ်ဘူးနော်။

Is there somewhere I can change the baby's diaper? **Kha layy diaper lell chin loht, bae mhar lell ya ma lell?** ကလေးဒိုင်ဘာလဲချင်လို့ ဘယ်မှာလဲရမလဲ။

Where are the restrooms? **Eain thar, bae mhar sheet lell?** အိမ်သာဘယ်မှာရှိလဲ။

4.2 Ordering

Waiter/Waitress! [to older-looking person] **Ako! / Ama!** အစ်ကို / အစ်မ။

[male speaker to younger-looking person] **Nyi layy!** ညီလေး။

[female speaker to younger-looking person] **Nyi ma layy!** ညီမလေး။

Madam! **A daw!** အဒေါ်။

Sir! **Oo layy!** ဦးလေး။

We'd like something to eat.	**Ta khoot khoot, sarr jin dae.** တစ်ခုခုစားချင်တယ်။
We'd like something to drink.	**Ta khoot khoot, thout chin dae.** တစ်ခုခုသောက်ချင်တယ်။
Could I have a quick meal?	**Myan daet, a sarr a sar, ya ma larr?** မြန်တဲ့အစားအစာရမလား။
We don't have much time.	**Achain, thate ma sheet boo.** အချိန်သိပ်မရှိဘူး။
We'd like to have a drink first.	**Thout sa yar, a yin lo jin dae.** သောက်စရာအရင်လိုချင်တယ်။
Could we see the menu, please?	**Menu kyeet loht, ya ma larr?** မီနူးကြည့်လို့ရမလား။
Could we see the wine list, please?	**Bar wine dway ya lell, kyeet loht ya ma larr?** ဘာဝိုင်တွေရလဲကြည့်လို့ရမလား။
Do you have an English menu?	**Ingalate lo, yayy htarr daet menu sheet larr?** အင်္ဂလိပ်လိုရေးထားတဲ့မီနူးရှိလား။
Do you have a dish of the day?	**Di nayt a twet, ahtoo hinn pwell sheet larr?** ဒီနေ့အတွက်အထူးဟင်းပွဲရှိလား။
We haven't made a choice yet.	**Ma ywayy ya thayy boo.** မရွေးရသေးဘူး။
What do you recommend?	**Bar sarr yin, kaungg ma lell?** ဘာစားရင်ကောင်းမလဲ။
What are the local specialities?	**Di day tha yaet, a htoo, a sarr a sar dway ga, bar dway lell?** ဒီဒေသရဲ့ အထူးအစားအစာတွေက ဘာတွေလဲ။
What are your specialities?	**Di sai yaet, a htoo a sarr a sar dway ga, bar dway lell?** ဒီဆိုင်ရဲ့ အထူးအစားအစာတွေက ဘာတွေလဲ။

I like chili.	**Nga yote thee, kyite tae.** ငရုတ်သီးကြိုက်တယ်။
I don't like meat.	**A tharr, ma kyite boo.** အသားမကြိုက်ဘူး။
What's this?	**Dar bar lell?** ဒါဘာလဲ။
Does it have...in it?	**Di htell mhar...bar larr?** ဒီထဲမှာ...ပါလား။
What does it taste like?	**Ae dar ga, bae lo a ya thar lell?** အဲဒါက ဘယ်လိုအရသာလဲ။
Is this a hot or cold dish?	**Dar a pu larr, a ayy larr?** ဒါအပူလား၊ အအေးလား။
Is this sweet?	**Dar cho larr?** ဒါချိုလား။
Is this spicy?	**Dar sat larr?** ဒါစပ်လား။
Do you have anything else, by any chance?	**Ta charr har, sheet thayy larr?** တခြားဟာရှိသေးလား။
I'm on a fat-free diet.	**A si, shaung nay dae.** အဆီရှောင်နေတယ်။
I'm on a salt-free diet.	**A ngan, shaung nay dae.** အငန်ရှောင်နေတယ်။
I can't have spicy food.	**A sat, ma sarr nai boo.** အစပ်မစားနိုင်ဘူး။
I can't eat pork.	**Wet tharr, sarr loht ma ya boo.** ဝက်သားစားလို့မရဘူး။
I can't have sugar.	**Tha gyarr, sarr loht ma ya boo.** သကြားစားလို့မရဘူး။
We'll have what those people are having.	**Thu doht, sarr nay daet har, mhar mae.** သူတို့စားနေတဲ့ဟာမှာမယ်။
I'd like...	**...mhar mae.** ...မှာမယ်။

ဘာမှာမလဲ။	What would you like?
ရွေးပြီးပြီလား။	Have you decided?
သောက်စရာအရင်မှာမလား။	Would you like a drink first?
ဘာသောက်မလဲ။	What would you like to drink?
...ကုန်နေတယ်။	We've run out of...
သုံးဆောင်ပါ။	Enjoy your meal.
အဆင်ပြေလား။	Is everything all right?
စားပွဲရှင်းလို့ရမလား။	May I clear the table?

Could I have some
more rice, please?

Hta minn, htat payy bar?
ထမင်းထပ်ပေးပါ။

Could I have a glass of
drinking water, please?

Thout yay, ta khwet, payy bar?
သောက်ရေတစ်ခွက်ပေးပါ။

Another bottle of
drinking water, please.

Thout yay, nout da boo, payy bar.
သောက်ရေနောက်တစ်ဘူးပေးပါ။

Another bottle of wine,
please.

Wine, nout da ba linn, payy bar.
ဝိုင်နောက်တစ်ပုလင်းပေးပါ။

Could I have another
portion of..., please?

...nout da pwell, payy bar?
...နောက်တစ်ပွဲပေးပါ။

Could I have the salt
and pepper, please?

**Sarr naet, nga yote kaungg mhote,
payy bar?** ဆားနဲ့ငရုတ်ကောင်းမှုန့်ပေးပါ။

Could I have a
napkin, please?

Let thote pa war, payy bar?
လက်သုတ်ပဝါပေးပါ။

Could I have a
teaspoon, please?

Laphet yay zonn, payy bar?
လက်ဖက်ရည်ဇွန်းပေးပါ။

Could I have an
ashtray, please?

Salate pyar khwet, payy bar?
ဆေးလိပ်ပြာခွက်ပေးပါ။

Could I have some toothpicks, please?	**Thwarr gyarr htohh dan, payy bar?** သွားကြားထိုးတံပေးပါ။
Cheers!	**Cheers!** ချီးယားစ်။
Could we have a doggy bag, please?	**Parcel, htote payy bar larr?** ပါဆယ်ထုပ်ပေးပါလား။

The bill

How much is this dish?	**Dar ga, bae lout lell?** ဒါကဘယ်လောက်လဲ။
The bill, please.	**Shinn mae.** ရှင်းမယ်။
All together.	**Arr lone paungg.** အားလုံးပေါင်း။
Everyone pays separately.	**That that si, shinn mae.** သပ်သပ်စီရှင်းမယ်။
Let's go Dutch.	**Koht bar thar, shinn gya dar pawt.** ကိုယ့်ဘာသာရှင်းကြတာပေ့ါ။
Could we have the menu again, please?	**Menu, htat payy bar own?** မီနူးထပ်ပေးပါဦး။
The...is not on the bill.	**...ga, bill htell mhar, ma bar boo.** ...က ဘေလ်ထဲမှာမပါဘူး။

Complaints

It's taking a long time.	**A yann, kyar nay bi.** အရမ်းကြာနေပြီ။
This must be a mistake.	**Dar, mharr nay dar, phyit mae.** ဒါမှားနေတာဖြစ်မယ်။
This is not what I ordered.	**Mhar htarr dar, dar ma hote boo.** မှာထားတာ ဒါမဟုတ်ဘူး။
I ordered...	**...mhar htarr dae.** ...မှာထားတယ်။

There's a dish missing.

Hinn bwell, da pwell, lo thayy dae.
ဟင်းပွဲတစ်ပွဲ လိုသေးတယ်။

The plate is broken.

Bagan ga, kwell nay dae.
ပန်းကန်က ကွဲနေတယ်။

The plate is not clean.

Bagan ga, nyit pat nay dae.
ပန်းကန်က ညစ်ပတ်နေတယ်။

The food's cold.

A sarr a thout ga, ayy nay dae.
အစားအသောက်က အေးနေတယ်။

The food's not fresh.

A sarr a thout ga, ma lat sat boo.
အစားအသောက်က မလတ်ဆတ်ဘူး။

The food has gone bad.

A sarr a thout ga, thohh nay bi.
အစားအသောက်က သိုးနေပြီ။

The food's too salty.

A sarr a thout ga, a yann ngan dae.
အစားအသောက်က အရမ်းငန်တယ်။

The food's too sweet.

A sarr a thout ga, a yann cho dae.
အစားအသောက်က အရမ်းချိုတယ်။

The food's too spicy.

A sarr a thout ga, a yann sat tae.
အစားအသောက်က အရမ်းစပ်တယ်။

Could I have something else instead of this?

Dar a sarr, ta charr har, payy bar.
ဒါအစား တခြားဟာပေးပါ။

The bill / this amount is not right.

Di bill ga, mharr nay dae.
ဒီဘေလ်ကမှားနေတယ်။

We didn't have this.

Dar, ma mhar boo. ဒါမှာဘူး။

There's no toilet paper in the restroom.

Eain thar htell mhar, tissue ma sheet boo. အိမ်သာထဲမှာ တစ်ရှူးမရှိဘူး။

Will you call the manager, please?

Manager go, khaw payy bar?
မန်နေဂျာကိုခေါ်ပေးပါ။

4.5 Praising the food

That was a sumptuous meal.	**Shal a sarr a sar bell.** ရှယ်အစားအစာပဲ॥
The food was excellent.	**A sarr a thout ga, taw taw kaungg dae.** အစားအသောက်က တော်တော်ကောင်းတယ်॥
The...in particular was delicious.	**A htoo tha phyint...ga, sarr loht kaungg dae.** အထူးသဖြင့်...က စားလို့ကောင်းတယ်॥

4.6 The menu

Burmese dishes	**myanmar a sarr a sar myarr** မြန်မာအစားအစာများ
rice	**hta minn** ထမင်း
vermicelli in fish soup	**mohinga** မုန့်ဟင်းခါး
coconut noodles	**ownn noht khout swell** အုန်းနို့ခေါက်ဆွဲ
fried rice	**hta minn kyaw** ထမင်းကြော်
fried noodles	**khout swell kyaw** ခေါက်ဆွဲကြော်
fried vermicelli	**kyar zan kyaw** ကြာဆံကြော်
chicken curry	**kyet tharr hinn** ကြက်သားဟင်း
sweet and sour chicken	**kyet cho chin** ကြက်ချိုချဉ်
sour and spicy chicken	**kyet chin sat** ကြက်ချဉ်စပ်
grilled chicken	**kyet kin** ကြက်ကင်
fried chicken	**kyet kyaw** ကြက်ကြော်
pork curry	**wet tharr hinn** ဝက်သားဟင်း
fish curry	**ngarr hinn** ငါးဟင်း

Eating Out

4

fried fish	**ngarr kyaw** ငါးကြော်
steamed fish	**ngarr paungg** ငါးပေါင်း
prawn curry	**bazon hinn** ပုစွန်ဟင်း
prawn salad	**bazon thote** ပုစွန်သုပ်
crab curry	**ga nann hinn** ဂဏန်းဟင်း
beef curry	**a mell tharr hinn** အမဲသားဟင်း
squid salad	**pyi gyee ngarr thote** ပြည်ကြီးငါးသုပ်
duck egg curry	**bell oot hinn** ဘဲဥဟင်း
fried (chicken) egg	**kyet oot kyaw** ကြက်ဥကြော်
omelette	**kyet oot mhway kyaw** ကြက်ဥမွှေကြော်
boiled (chicken) egg	**kyet oot pyote** ကြက်ဥပြုတ်
Shan noodles	**shan khout swell** ရှမ်းခေါက်ဆွဲ
fried watercress	**ga zonn ywet kyaw** ကန်စွန်းရွက်ကြော်
vegetable curry	**thee z'own hinn** သီးစုံဟင်း
tomato salad	**kha yann jin thee thote** ခရမ်းချဉ်သီးသုပ်
tofu salad	**to hoo thote** တိုဟူးသုပ်
tealeaf salad	**laphet thote** လက်ဖက်သုပ်
soup	**hinn jo** ဟင်းချို
fried vegetables	**hinn thee hinn ywet kyaw** ဟင်းသီးဟင်းရွက်ကြော်
International dishes	**nai ngan da gar, a sarr a sar** နိုင်ငံတကာအစားအစာ
biryani	**dan bout** ဒံပေါက်
paratha	**palata** ပလာတာ
bread	**paung mote** ပေါင်မုန့်

cake	**kate mote** ကိတ်မုန့်
ice-cream	**yay khell mote** ရေခဲမုန့်
fried dough stick	**e kyar kwayy** အီကြာကွေး
spring rolls	**kaw pyant late** ကော်ပြန့်လိပ်
fried spring rolls	**kaw pyant kyaw** ကော်ပြန့်ကြော်

4.7 Drinks

drinking water	**thout yay** သောက်ရေ
cold drinks (soft drinks)	**a aye** အအေး
coffee	**kaw fee** ကော်ဖီ
tea (with condensed milk)	**laphet yay** လက်ဖက်ရည်
plain tea	**yay nwayy gyann** ရေနွေးကြမ်း
hot milk	**nwarr noht a pu** နွားနို့အပူ
cold milk	**nwarr noht a aye** နွားနို့အအေး
juice	**phyaw yay** ဖျော်ရည်
mango juice	**tha yet thee phyaw yay** သရက်သီးဖျော်ရည်
beer	**be yar** ဘီယာ
red wine	**wine a ni** ဝိုင်အနီ
white wine	**wine a phyu** ဝိုင်အဖြူ
alcohol	**a yet** အရက်
palm wine	**htann yay** ထန်းရည်

5. Getting Around

5.1 Asking directions

Excuse me, could I ask you something?	[male speaker] **Mingalarbar! Ta khoot lout, mayy loht, ya ma larr kha mya?** မင်္ဂလာပါ။ တစ်ခုလောက်မေးလို့ရမလားခင်ဗျာ။
	[female speaker] **Mingalarbar! Ta khoot lout, mayy loht, ya ma larr shint?** မင်္ဂလာပါ။ တစ်ခုလောက်မေးလို့ရမလားရှင့်။
I've lost my way.	[male speaker **Kya naw, lann pyout nay dae.** ကျွန်တော်လမ်းပျောက်နေတယ်။
	[female speaker] **Kya ma, lann pyout nay dae.** ကျွန်မလမ်းပျောက်နေတယ်။
Is there a...around here?	**Di narr mhar...sheet larr?** ဒီနားမှာ...ရှိလား။
What direction is...?	**...ga, bae bet lell?** ...က ဘယ်ဘက်လဲ။
Excuse me, am I going the right way to get to the bus stop?	**Bus karr mhat tai go, di lann ga, thwarr dar larr?** ဘတ်စ်ကားမှတ်တိုင်ကို ဒီလမ်းကသွားတာလား။
Excuse me, is this the way to the station?	**Dar bu tar go, thwarr daet lann larr?** ဒါဘူတာကိုသွားတဲ့လမ်းလား။

Could you tell me how to get to...?	...go, bae lo, thwarr ya ma lell? ...ကို ဘယ်လိုသွားရမလဲ။
How many miles is it to...?	...go, bae nha mai lout, sheet lell? ...ကို ဘယ်နှစ်မိုင်လောက်ရှိလဲ။
Is it far?	Wayy larr? ဝေးလား။
Can I walk there?	Lann shout thwarr loht, ya larr? လမ်းလျှောက်သွားလို့ရလား။
Is it difficult to find?	Shar ya khet larr? ရှာရခက်လား။

မသိဘူး။ ဒီနားကလမ်းတွေမသိဘူး။	I don't know, I don't know my way around here.
လမ်းမှားနေပြီ။	You're going the wrong way.
နောက်ကိုပြန်သွားရမယ်။	You have to go back.
အဲဒီကနေပြီး လမ်းညွှန်သင်္ကေတတွေအတိုင်း သွားပါ။	From there on just follow the signs.
အဲဒီကိုရောက်ရင် ထပ်မေးလိုက်ပါ။	When you get there, ask again.
တည့်တည့်သွားပါ။	Go straight ahead.
ညာဘက်ချိုးပါ။	Turn right.
ဘက်ဘက်ချိုးပါ။	Turn left.

road/street **lann** လမ်း	overpass **g'ownn kyaw dadarr** ဂုံးကျော်တံတား	the building **a sout a oo** အဆောက်အဦး
river **myit** မြစ်	tunnel **oot min hlai gaungg** ဥမင်လိုဏ်ခေါင်း	at the corner **daungt mhar** ထောင့်မှာ
traffic light **mee point** မီးပွိုင့်	bridge **dadarr** တံတား	arrow sign **mhyarr thin gay ta** မြှားသင်္ကေတ

Intersection/Crossroads
lann s'own
လမ်းဆုံ

Road Assistance (Breakdown service)
yin pyin sin pyoot pyin yayy win saung mhoot
ယာဉ်ပြင်ဆင်ပြုပြင်ရေးဂန်ဆောင်မှု

Stop (Vehicles)
mhat tai
မှတ်တိုင်

Parking for a Limited Period
khit ta karr yat narr yan nay yar
ခေတ္တကားရပ်နားရန်နေရာ

Service Station
wat shawt
ဝပ်ရှော့

Do Not Obstruct
pate ma yat ya
ပိတ်မရပ်ရ။

Broken/Uneven Surface
lann pyet nay thi
လမ်းပျက်နေသည်

Tow-Away Area
yin ma yet ya nay yar
ယာဉ်မရပ်ရနေရာ

No Right/Left Turn
nyar bet/ bae bet, ma kwayt ya
ညာဘက်/ဘယ်ဘက်မကွေ့ရ

Right of Way at End of Road
lann a sone dwin, oo zarr payy lann sheet thi
လမ်းအဆုံးတွင် ဦးစားပေးလမ်းရှိသည်

Roadworks Ahead
shayt dwin lann pyin nay thi
ရှေ့တွင်လမ်းပြင်နေသည်

Curves
a kwayt
အကွေ့

Road Narrows
lann kyinn thi
လမ်းကျဉ်းသည်

Traffic Island / Pedestrian Walk
lu thwarr lann
လူသွားလမ်း

Turn On Headlights (in the Tunnel)
mee gyee phwint bar
မီးကြီးဖွင့်ပါ

Keep Raight/Left
nyar bet thoht / bae bet thoht
ညာဘက်သို့ / ဘယ်ဘက်သို့

Beware of Falling Rocks
Tha deet! Kyout tone myarr pyo kya dat thi.
သတိ။ ကျောက်တုံးများပြိုကျတတ်သည်

Supervised Garage / Parking Lot
karr par kin
ကားပါကင်

Slow Down
phyay phyay maungg bar
ဖြည်းဖြည်းမောင်းပါ

Heavy Trucks
k'own tin yin gyee myarr
ကုန်တင်ယာဉ်ကြီးများ

Maximum Speed
a myint sone a shain nhone
အမြင့်ဆုံးအရှိန်နှုန်း

No Passing
phyat thann ma thwarr ya
ဖြတ်သန်းမသွားရ

Road Blocked
lann pate htarr thi
လမ်းပိတ်ထားသည်။

Traffic Circle (Roundabout)
a waii
အဝိုင်း

Detour **lann hlwell** လမ်းလွှဲ	Beware **tha deet** သတိ	No Hitchhiking **yin ma tarr ya** ယာဉ်မတားရ
Exit **htwet pout** ထွက်ပေါက်	Maximum Height **a myarr sone a myint** အများဆုံးအမြင့်	No Parking **yin ma yet ya** ယာဉ်မရပ်ရ
Emergency Lane **a yayy baw lann** အရေးပေါ်လမ်း	Right of Way **oo zarr payy lann** ဦးစားပေးလမ်း	One Way **ta lann thwarr** တစ်လမ်းသွား
Driveway **phyat lann** ဖြတ်လမ်း	No Entry **ma win ya** မဝင်ရ	Toll Payment **tohh gate** တိုးဂိတ်

5.3 Taking a taxi

Taxis are cheap and plentiful, especially in Yangon, and the easiest way of getting around. Taxis don't have meters, so agree the price with the driver before getting in the car.

I'd like to go to Shwedagon Pagoda. How much is it?	**Shwedagon pha yarr, thwarr jin dae. Bae lout lell?** ရွှေတိဂုံဘုရားသွားချင်တယ်။ ဘယ်လောက်လဲ။
Could you make it lower please?	**Shawt bar ownn.** လျှော့ပါဦး။
Is 2000 okay?	**Nha htaung, ya ma larr?** ၂၀၀၀ ရမလား။
Go straight.	**Taet taet, thwarr bar.** တည့်တည့်သွားပါ။
Turn right.	**Nyar bet, chohh bar.** ညာဘက်ချိုးပါ။
Turn left.	**Bae bet, chohh bar.** ဘယ်ဘက်ချိုးပါ။
Okay, I'll get off here.	**Ya bi. Di mhar, sinn mae.** ရပြီ။ ဒီမှာဆင်းမယ်။
Do you have change?	**Akyway, sheet larr?** အကြွေရှိလား။

5.4 Renting a car

I'd like to rent a car.	**Karr ngharr jin bar dae.** ကားငှားချင်ပါတယ်။
Do I need a (special) license for that?	**Lai sin lo larr?** လိုင်စင်လိုလား။
I'd like to rent it for a day.	**Ta yet, ngharr jin bar dae.** တစ်ရက်ငှားချင်ပါတယ်။
I'd like to rent it for two days.	**Nha yet, ngharr jin bar dae.** နှစ်ရက်ငှားချင်ပါတယ်။
What's the rental cost per day?	**Ta yet, bae lout lell?** တစ်ရက်ဘယ်လောက်လဲ။
What is the rental cost per week?	**Ta bat, bae lout lell?** တစ်ပတ်ဘယ်လောက်လဲ။
How much is the deposit?	**Zabaw ga, bae lout lell?** စပေါ်ကဘယ်လောက်လဲ။
Could I have a receipt for the deposit?	**Zabaw atwet, phyat paii layy payy bar?** စပေါ်အတွက် ဖြတ်ပိုင်းလေးပေးပါ။
Does that include insurance?	**Ar ma gan, par pee tharr larr?** အာမခံပါပြီးသားလား။
What time can I pick the car up?	**Karr go, bae achain, lar yu loht, ya ma lell?** ကားကိုဘယ်အချိန်လာယူလို့ရမလဲ။
When does the car have to be back?	**Karr go, bae dawt, pyan at ya ma lell?** ကားကိုဘယ်တော့ပြန်အပ်ရမလဲ။

5.5 The gas station

How many miles to the next gas station, please?	**Nout si zai ahteet, bae nha mai lout, lo thayy lell?** နောက်ဆီဆိုင်အထိ ဘယ်နှစ်မိုင်လောက်လိုသေးလဲ။
I would like 50 liters of #95.	**Ninety five, ngarr sae liter, htaet mae.** နိုင်တီဖိုက်ငါးဆယ်လီတာထည့်မယ်။

I would like 50 liters of #92.	**Ninety two, ngarr sae liter, htaet mae.** နိုင်တီတူးငါးဆယ်လီတာထည့်မယ်။
I would like 50 liters of diesel.	**Diesel, ngarr sae liter, htaet mae.** ဒီဇယ်ငါးဆယ်လီတာထည့်မယ်။
I would like 10000 kyats worth of #95.	**Ninety five, ta thaungg phohh, htaet mae.** နိုင်တီဖိုက်တစ်သောင်းဖိုးထည့်မယ်။
Fill her up, please.	**A pyayt, htaet mae.** အပြည့်ထည့်မယ်။
Could you check the oil level?	**Si gate, kyeet payy bar larr?** ဆီဂိတ်ကြည့်ပေးပါလား။
Could you check the tire pressure?	**Tar yar lay yawt, ma yawt, sit payy bar larr?** တာယာလေလျော့မလျော့ စစ်ပေးပါလား။
Could you change the (engine) oil, please?	**Engine wai, lell payy bar larr?** အင်ဂျင်ဝိုင်လဲပေးပါလား။
Could you clean the windshield, please?	**Lay gar mhan go, thote payy bar larr?** လေကာမှန်ကိုသုတ်ပေးပါလား။
Could you wash the car, please?	**Karr yay sayy payy bar larr?** ကားရေဆေးပေးပါလား။

5.6 Breakdowns and repairs

My car has broken down, could you give me a hand?	**Karr pyet thwarr loht, ku nyi payy bar ownn?** ကားပျက်သွားလို့ ကူညီပေးပါဦး။
I have run out of gas.	**Si k'own thwarr bi.** ဆီကုန်သွားပြီ။
I've locked the keys in the car.	**Karr htell mhar, thawt kyan gaet dae.** ကားထဲမှာသော့ကျန်ခဲ့တယ်။
The car won't start.	**Karr ga, set nhohh loht, ma ya boo.** ကားကစက်နှိုးလို့မရဘူး။
The motorbike won't start.	**Sai kae ga, set nhohh loht, ma ya boo.** ဆိုင်ကယ်ကစက်နှိုးလို့မရဘူး။

Could you contact the breakdown service for me, please?	**Karr wet shawt go, set thwae payy bar larr?** ကားဂပ်ရှော့ကို ဆက်သွယ်ပေးပါလား။
Could you call a garage for me, please?	**Karr go daung go, phone set payy bar larr?** ကားဂိုဒေါင်ကိုဖုန်းဆက်ပေးပါလား။
Could you give me a lift to the nearest garage?	**A nee sone go, daung ahteet, swell thwarr payy bar larr?** အနီးဆုံးဂိုဒေါင်အထိ ဆွဲသွားပေးပါလား။
Could you give me a lift to the nearest town?	**A nee sone, myoht ahteet, swell thwarr payy bar larr?** အနီးဆုံးမြို့အထိ ဆွဲသွားပေးပါလား။
Can we take my motorcycle?	**Sai kae go, yu thwarr loht, ya ma larr?** ဆိုင်ကယ်ကိုယူသွားလို့ရမလား။
Could you tow me to a garage?	**Go daung go, kyohh naet, swell thwarr payy bar larr?** ဂိုဒေါင်ကိုကြိုးနဲ့ဆွဲသွားပေးပါလား။
There's probably something wrong with...	**...ga, ta khoot khoot, phyit nay dar, phyit mae.** ...က တစ်ခုခုဖြစ်နေတာဖြစ်မယ်။
Can you fix it?	**Pyin dat larr?** ပြင်တတ်လား။
Could you fix my tire?	**Tar yar kyut, phar payy bar?** တာယာကျွတ်ဖာပေးပါ။
Could you change this wheel?	**Di bein, lell payy bar?** ဒီဘီးလဲပေးပါ။
Can you fix it so it'll get me to...?	**...ahteet, thwarr loht ya aung, pyin payy bar larr?** ...အထိသွားလို့ရအောင် ပြင်ပေးပါလား။
When will my car be ready?	**Karr, bae dawt, ya ma lell?** ကားဘယ်တော့ရမလဲ။
When will my bicycle be ready?	**Set bein, bae dawt, ya ma lell?** စက်ဘီးဘယ်တော့ရမလဲ။
Have you already finished?	**Pee thwarr bi larr?** ပြီးသွားပြီလား။

Can I wait for it here?	**Di mhar saungt, loht ya larr?** ဒီမှာစောင့်လို့ရလား။
How much will it cost?	**Bae lout kya ma lell?** ဘယ်လောက်ကျမလဲ။
Could you itemize the bill?	**Baung char htell mhar, a thayy sate, ateet akya, yayy payy bar larr?** ဘောင်ချာထဲမှာ အသေးစိတ်အတိအကျရေးပေးပါလား။
Please give me a receipt for insurance purposes.	**Ar ma gan atwet, phyat paii, phyat payy bar larr.** အာမခံအတွက် ဖြတ်ပိုင်းဖြတ်ပေးပါလား။

ဒီအတွက်ပစ္စည်းမရှိဘူး။	I don't have parts for your vehicle.
တခြားမှာပစ္စည်းသွားဝယ်ရမယ်။	I have to get the parts from somewhere else.
ပစ္စည်းတွေကမှာရမှာ။	I have to order the parts.
နေ့တစ်ဝက်လောက်ကြာမယ်။	That'll take half a day.
တစ်ရက်ကြာမယ်။	That'll take a day.
နှစ်ရက်သုံးရက်လောက်တော့ကြာမယ်။	That'll take a few days (2–3 days).
တစ်ပတ်ကြာမယ်။	That'll take a week.
ကားက တော်တော်ထိထားတာ။	Your car is a write-off.
စက်ဘီးက တော်တော်ထိထားတာ။	Your bicycle is a write-off.
ကားကပြင်လို့မရတော့ဘူး။	Your car can't be repaired.
ဆိုင်ကယ်ကပြင်လို့မရတော့ဘူး။	You motorbike can't be repaired.
စက်ဘီးကပြင်လို့မရတော့ဘူး။	Your bicycle can't be repaired.
...နာရီမှာ ကားရမယ်။	The car will be ready at ...o'clock.
...နာရီမှာ ဆိုင်ကယ်ရမယ်။	The motorbike will be ready at...o'clock.
...နာရီမှာ စက်ဘီးရမယ်။	The bicycle will be ready at... o'clock.

5.7 Motorcycles and bicycles

Motorcycles are prohibited in Yangon, although the use of bicycles and electronic bikes has increased in recent years. People usually take public transport or taxis for daily travel.

The parts of a bicycle

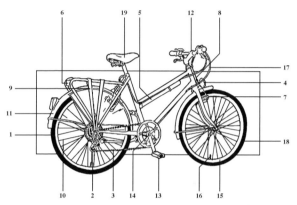

1	rear wheel	**nout bein**	နောက်ဘီး
2	gear change	**gear**	ဂီယာ
3	chain	**chain kyohh**	ချိန်းကြိုး
4	headlight	**shayt mee**	ရှေ့မီး
5	pump	**lay htohh dan**	လေထိုးတံ
6	reflector	**yaung byan**	ရောင်ပြန်
7	brake shoe	**brake shoe**	ဘရိတ်ရှူး
8	brake cable	**brake kyohh**	ဘရိတ်ကြိုး
9	carrier straps	**nout htai kh'own kyohh**	နောက်ထိုင်ခုံကြိုး
10	spoke	**sa mote tan**	စမုတ်တံ
11	mudguard	**thell gar**	သဲကာ
12	handlebars	**let kai tann**	လက်ကိုင်တန်း
13	toe clip	**chay ninn**	ခြေနင်း
14	drum brake	**drum brake**	ဒရမ်ဘရိတ်
15	valve	**gway**	ခွေ
16	valve tube	**kyut**	ကျွတ်
17	gear cable	**gear kyohh**	ဂီယာကြိုး
18	front wheel	**shayt bein**	ရှေ့ဘီး
19	seat	**htai kh'own**	ထိုင်ခုံ

5.8 Getting a lift

It is not common in Myanmar to give someone a lift unless they know you. However, Myanmar is a tourist-friendly country, so in some cases hitchhiking might work, as long as you look decent and can explain in Burmese where you would like to go, either by speaking or with a note written in Burmese. Women are advised to avoid hitching alone. It does not mean that women are not safe in Myanmar, but it is always best to be careful.

Where are you heading?	**Bae thwarr ma loht lell?** ဘယ်သွားမလို့လဲ။
Can you give me a lift?	**Lann ky'own lite loht, ya ma larr?** လမ်းကြုံလိုက်လို့ရမလား။
Can my friend come too?	[male speaker] **Kya nawt, tha ngae jinn yaww, lite loht ya ma larr?** ကျွန်တော့်သူငယ်ချင်းရော လိုက်လို့ရမလား။
	[female speaker] **Kya ma, tha ngae jinn yaww, lite loht ya ma larr?** ကျွန်မသူငယ်ချင်းရော လိုက်လို့ရမလား။
I'd like to go to...	**...go, thwarr jin loht bar.** ...ကို သွားချင်လို့ပါ။
Is that on the way to...?	**Ae dar ga...ko thwarr daet, lann baw mhar larr?** အဲဒါက... ကိုသွားတဲ့လမ်းပေါ်မှာလား။
Could you drop me off at...?	[male speaker]**...mhar, kya nawt go, cha payy bar larr?** ...မှာ ကျွန်တော့်ကို ချပေးပါလား။
	[female speaker]**...mhar, kya ma go, cha payy bar larr?** ...မှာ ကျွန်မကို ချပေးပါလား။
Could you drop me off here?	[male speaker] **Di mhar, kya nawt go, cha payy bar larr?** ဒီမှာ ကျွန်တော့်ကို ချပေးပါလား။

[female speaker] **Di mhar, kya ma go, cha payy bar larr?** ဒီမှာ ကျွန်မကို ချပေးပါလား။

Could you drop me off at the entrance to the highway?

[male speaker] **Highway lann ma baw, awin mhar, kya nawt go, cha payy bar larr?** ဟိုင်းဝေးလမ်းမပေါ် အဝင်မှာ ကျွန်တော့်ကို ချပေးပါလား။

[female speaker] **Highway lann ma baw, awin mhar, kya ma go, cha payy bar larr?** ဟိုင်းဝေးလမ်းမပေါ် အဝင်မှာ ကျွန်မကို ချပေးပါလား။

Could you drop me off at the next intersection highway?

[male speaker] **Highway lann ma baw mhar, nout lann s'own yout yin, kya nawt go, cha payy bar larr?** ဟိုင်းဝေးလမ်းမပေါ်မှာ နောက်လမ်းဆုံရောက်ရင် ကျွန်တော့်ကို ချပေးပါလား။

[female speaker] **Highway lann ma baw mhar, nout lann s'own yout yin, kya ma go, cha payy bar larr?** ဟိုင်းဝေးလမ်းမပေါ်မှာ နောက်လမ်းဆုံရောက်ရင် ကျွန်မကို ချပေးပါလား။

Could you stop here, please?

Di mhar, yat payy bar larr? ဒီမှာရပ်ပေးပါလား။

I'd like to get out here.

Di mhar, sinn lite par mae. ဒီမှာဆင်းလိုက်ပါမယ်။

Thanks for the lift.

Lann ky'own, lite poht payy daet atwet, kyayy zoo tin bar dae. လမ်းကြုံလိုက်ပို့ပေးတဲ့အတွက် ကျေးဇူးတင်ပါတယ်။

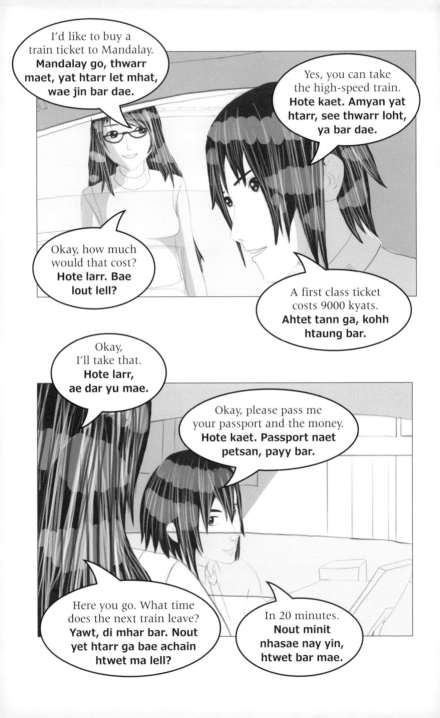

6. Traveling in Myanmar

6.1 Getting around
6.2 Immigration and customs
6.3 Luggage
6.4 Buying a ticket
6.5 Getting travel information

6.1 Getting around

In Myanmar, most people get around by bus (**bus karr** ဘတ်စ်ကား), taxi (**taxi** တက္ကစီ), motorbike (**sai kae** ဆိုင်ကယ်) or train (**yat htarr** ရထား). Motorbikes are prohibited in Yangon, but they are still the most common form of transport elsewhere. You can travel around Yangon by bus, although buses get very crowded during rush hour. Fares are 200 to 300 kyats, which you put in a box (usually next to the driver's seat) when you get on. Make sure you have the correct change before getting on.

Another option is to hail a taxi on the street. Taxis are not metered, and you will need to negotiate a price with the driver before you get in. Alternatively you can use the English-version of the app, Grab, on your smartphone. Grab always has a fixed price, and the cars are air-conditioned, so this could be a good option in hot weather. Grab also accepts credit cards.

If you would like to take a train, tickets can be purchased at the station. Taking express buses or domestic flights is a common way to travel between cities in Myanmar. However, you need to buy the ticket in advance for both options.

6.2 Immigration and customs

Always bring your passport with you when you travel within Myanmar. Anyone staying at the same address for more than a week needs permission from the local ward office. To drive a car or motorbike, you will need an international driving license.

ဆိုက်ရောက်ကတ်ဖြည့်ပေးပါ။	Please fill in the arrival card.
ပတ်စ်ပို့ပြပါ။	Your passport, please.
ဗီဇာပြပါ။	Your visa, please.
ဘယ်မြို့ ကိုသွားမှာလဲ။	Which city are you going to?
ဘယ်လောက်ကြာကြာနေမှာလဲ။	How long are you planning to stay?
ဒီကလဲလုပ်ရမယ့်ပစ္စည်းပါလားား။	Do you have anything to declare?
အိတ်ဖွင့်ပါ။	Open this suitcase, please.

My children are entered on this passport.
Kha layy dway ga, di passport htell mhar, par bar dae. ကလေးတွေက ဒီပတ်စ်ပို့ထဲမှာ ပါပါတယ်။

I'm traveling through.
Kha yee thwarr ma loht bar. ခရီးသွားမလို့ပါ။

I'm going on vacation to...
...go, pate yet kha yee, thwarr ma loht bar. ...ကို ပိတ်ရက်ခရီးသွားမလို့ပါ။

I'm on a business trip.
Alote kate sa naet, lar dar bar. အလုပ်ကိစ္စနဲ့လာတာပါ။

I don't know how long I'll be staying.
Bae lout kyar kyar, nay ma lell, ma theet thayy bar boo. ဘယ်လောက်ကြာကြာနေမလ မသိသေးပါဘူး။

I'll be staying here for just a weekend.
Di mhar, sa nay, ta ninn ga nway bell, nay mhar bar. ဒီမှာ စနေ၊ တနင်္ဂနွေပဲ နေမှာပါ။

I'll be staying here for a few days (2–3 days).
Di mhar, nha yet, thone yet lout bell, nay mhar bar. ဒီမှာ နှစ်ရက်သုံးရက်လောက်ပဲ နေမှာပါ။

I'll be staying here for a week.	**Di mhar, da bet, nay mhar bar.** ဒီမှာ တစ်ပတ်နေမှာပါ။
I'll be staying here for two weeks.	**Di mhar, nha pet ,nay mhar bar.** ဒီမှာ နှစ်ပတ်နေမှာပါ။
I've got nothing to declare.	**Declare lote sayar, bar mha, ma par bar boo.** ဒီကလဲလုပ်စရာ ဘာမှမပါပါဘူး။
I have a carton of cigarettes.	**Cigarette, ta parkin, par bar dae.** စီးကရက်တစ်ပါကင်ပါပါတယ်။
I have a bottle of whisky.	**Whisky, da ba linn, bar dae.** ဂီစကီတစ်ပုလင်းပါတယ်။
I have some souvenirs.	**Amhat ta ya let saung pyit see dway, bar dae.** အမှတ်တရလက်ဆောင်ပစ္စည်းတေ ပါတယ်။
These are personal items.	**Dar dway ga, ko bai pyit see dway bar.** ဒါတွေက ကိုယ်ပိုင်ပစ္စည်းတွေပါ။
These are not new.	**Dar dway ga, a thit, ma hote boo.** ဒါတွေက အသစ်မဟုတ်ဘူး။
Here's the receipt.	**Di mhar, phyat paii bar.** ဒီမှာဖြတ်ပိုင်းပါ။
This is for private use.	**Dar ga, ko dai, thone boht bar.** ဒါကကိုယ်တိုင်သုံးဖို့ပါ။
How much import duty do I have to pay?	**Duty khon, bae lout, saung ya ma lell?** ဂျူတီခွန်ဘယ်လောက်ဆောင်ရမလဲ။
May I go now?	**Thwarr loht, ya bi larr?** သွားလို့ရပြီလား။
Where do I pick up my luggage?	**Luggage, bae mhar, yu ya ma lell?** လက်ဂေ့ဂျ်ဘယ်မှာယူရမလဲ။

6.3 Luggage

Could you take this luggage to...?	**Di luggage go...go, thae thwarr payy bar larr?** ဒီလက်ဂေ့ဂျ်ကို...ကို သယ်သွားပေးပါလား။
How much do I owe you?	**Bae lout, payy ya ma lell?** ဘယ်လောက်ပေးရမလဲ။
Where can I find a trolley?	**Let twonn hlell, bae mhar, shar ya ma lell?** လက်တွန်းလှည်း ဘယ်မှာရှာရမလဲ။
Could you store this luggage for me?	**Di luggage go, thein htarr payy bar larr?** ဒီလက်ဂေ့ဂျ်ကို သိမ်းထားပေးပါလား။
Where are the luggage lockers?	**Luggage locker dway ga bae mhar lell?** လက်ဂေ့ဂျ်လော့ကာတွေက ဘယ်မှာလဲ။
I can't get the locker open.	**Locker phwint loht, ma ya boo.** လော့ကာဖွင့်လို့မရဘူး။
How much is it per item, per day?	**Pyitsee ta khoot go, ta yet, bae lout lell?** ပစ္စည်းတစ်ခုကို တစ်ရက်ဘယ်လောက်လဲ။
This is not my bag/ suitcase.	[male speaker] **Dar, kya nawt ate, ma hote boo.** ဒါကျွန်တော့်အိတ်မဟုတ်ဘူး။
	[female speaker] **Dar, kya ma ate, ma hote boo.** ဒါကျွန်မအိတ်မဟုတ်ဘူး။
My bag/suitcase is damaged.	[male speaker] **Kya nawt ate ga, pyet see nay dae.** ကျွန်တော့်အိတ်က ပျက်စီးနေတယ်။
	[female speaker] **Kya ma ate ga, pyet see nay dae.** ကျွန်မအိတ်က ပျက်စီးနေတယ်။
There's one item missing.	**Pyit see, ta khoot, pyout nay dae.** ပစ္စည်းတစ်ခုပျောက်နေတယ်။
There's one bag/suitcase missing.	**Ate, ta lone, pyout nay dae.** အိတ်တစ်လုံးပျောက်နေတယ်။

My luggage has not arrived.	[male speaker] **Kya nawt ate ga, ma yout thayy boo.**
	ကျွန်တော့်အိတ်က မရောက်သေးဘူး။
	[female speaker] **Kya ma ate ga, ma yout thayy boo.**
	ကျွန်မအိတ်က မရောက်သေးဘူး။
When do you think my luggage will arrive?	[male speaker] **Kya nawt ate, bae dawt lout, yout ma lell?**
	ကျွန်တော့်အိတ် ဘယ်တော့လောက်ရောက်မလဲ။
	[female speaker] **Kya ma ate, bae dawt lout, yout ma lell?** ကျွန်မအိတ် ဘယ်တော့လောက်ရောက်မလဲ။

6.4 Buying a ticket

Where can I buy a ticket?	**Let mhat, bae mhar, wae ya ma lell?**
	လက်မှတ်ဘယ်မှာဝယ်ရမလဲ။
Where can I reserve a seat?	**Bae mhar, htai khown booking, lote ya ma lell?**
	ဘယ်မှာထိုင်ခုံဘွတ်ကင် လုပ်ရမလဲ။
Where can I reserve a flight?	**Bae mhar, lay yin let mhat booking, lote ya ma lell?**
	ဘယ်မှာ လေယာဉ်လက်မှတ် ဘွတ်ကင်လုပ်ရမလဲ။
Could I have a train ticket to Mandalay, please?	**Mandalay go, thwarr maet, yat htarr let mhat, wae jin bar dae?**
	မန္တလေးကိုသွားမယ့်ရထားလက်မှတ ယ်ချင်ပါတယ်။
A one-way ticket to Mandalay please.	**Mandalay athwarr let mhat, payy bar.**
	မန္တလေးအသွားလက်မှတ်ပေးပါ။
A return ticket to Mandalay, please.	**Mandalay apyan let mhat, payy bar.**
	မန္တလေးအပြန်လက်မှတ်ပေးပါ။

I'd like to reserve a berth.	**Ate sin bar daet twell, lo jin bar dae.** အိပ်စင်ပါတဲ့တွဲ လိုချင်ပါတယ်။

6.5 Getting travel information

Where can I find a schedule?	**Achain zayarr, bae mhar, kyeet ya ma lell?** အချိန်ဇယားဘယ်မှာကြည့်ရမလဲ။
Where's the information desk?	**S'own zann daet counter bae mhar lell?** စုံစမ်းတဲ့ကောင်တာဘယ်မှာလဲ။
Do you have a city map with the bus routes on it?	**Bus karr thwarr daet, lann gyaungg dway bar daet, myay b'own sheet larr?** ဘတ်စ်ကားသွားတဲ့လမ်းကြောင်း တွေပါတဲ့ မြေပုံရှိလား။
Do you have a city map with the train routes on it?	**Yat htarr thwarr daet, lann gyaungg dway bar daet, myay b'own sheet larr?** ရထားသွားတဲ့လမ်းကြောင်း တွေပါတဲ့ မြေပုံရှိလား။
Do you have a schedule?	**Achain zayarr, sheet larr?** အချိန်ဇယားရှိလား။
Will I get my deposit back?	**Zabaw ngway ga, pyan ya mhar larr?** စပေါ်ငွေက ပြန်ရမှာလား။
I'd like to confirm my reservation for my trip (by bus) to Taunggyi.	**Taunggyi go thwarr maet, (karr) let mhat, booking lote htarr dar, let mhat phyat chin bar dae.** တောင်ကြီးကိုသွားမယ့်(ကား) လက်မှတ်ဘွတ်ကင်လုပ်ထားတာ လက်မှတ်ဖြတ်ချင်ပါတယ်။
I'd like to cancel my reservation for my trip (by train) to Taunggyi.	**Taunggyi go thwarr maet, (yat htarr) let mhat, booking lote htarr dar, phyet chin bar dae.** တောင်ကြီးကိုသွားမယ့် (ရထား) လက်မှတ်ဘွတ်ကင်လုပ်ထားတာ ဖျက်ချင်ပါတယ်။

I'd like to change my reservation for my trip to Taunggyi.	**Taunggyi go thwarr maet, let mhat, booking lote htarr dar, pyaungg jin loht bar.** တောင်ကြီးကိုသွားမယ့် လက်မှတ်ဘွတ်ကင်လုပ်ထားတာ ပြောင်းချင်လို့ပါ။
I'd like to go to Taunggyi.	**Taunggyi go, thwarr jin bar dae.** တောင်ကြီးကိုသွားချင်ပါတယ်။
What is the quickest way to get there?	**Ae di go, bar naet thwrr dar, amyan sone lell?** အဲဒီကိုဘာနဲ့သွားတာ အမြန်ဆုံးလဲ။
How much is a one-way ticket to Taunggyi?	**Taunggyi go, athwarr let mhat, bae lout lell?** တောင်ကြီးကိုအသွားလက်မှတ် ဘယ်လောက်လဲ။
How much is a return ticket to Taunggyi?	**Taunggyi go, athwarr apyan let mhat, bae lout lell?** တောင်ကြီးကိုအသွားအပြန်လက်မှတ် ဘယ်လောက်လဲ။
Do I have to pay extra?	**Apo gyayy, payy ya mhar larr?** အပိုကြေးပေးရမှာလား။
How much luggage am I allowed?	**Luggage, bae nha lone thae loht ya lell?** လက်ဝေ့ဂျ်ဘယ်နှစ်လုံးသယ်လို့ရလဲ။
Do I have to change buses?	**Karr, pyaungg see ya mhar larr?** ကားပြောင်းစီးရမှာလား။
Do I have to change trains?	**Yat htarr, pyaungg see ya mhar larr?** ရထားပြောင်းစီးရမှာလား။
Do I have to change flights?	**Lay yin, pyaungg see ya mhar larr?** လေယာဉ်ပြောင်းစီးရမှာလား။
Where do I change buses?	**Bae mhar, karr, pyaungg see ya ma lell?** ဘယ်မှာကားပြောင်းစီးရမလဲ။
Where do I change trains?	**Bae mhar, yat htarr, pyaungg see ya ma lell?** ဘယ်မှာရထားပြောင်းစီးရမလဲ။

Where do I change flights?	**Bae mhar, lay yin, pyaungg see ya ma lell?** ဘယ်မှာလေယာဉ်ပြောင်းစီးရမလဲ။
Will there be any stopovers?	**Lann mhar, yat ownn mhar larr?** လမ်းမှာရပ်ဦးမှာလား။
Does the boat stop at any other ports on the way?	**Hlay ga, lann mhar, narr ownn mhar larr?** လှေကလမ်းမှာနားဦးမှာလား။
Does the train stop at...?	**Yat htarr ga...mhar, yat larr?** ရထားက...မှာ ရပ်လား။
Does the bus stop at...?	**Karr ga...mhar, yat larr?** ကားက...မှာ ရပ်လား။
Where do I get off?	**Bae mhar, sinn ya ma lell?** ဘယ်မှာဆင်းရမလဲ။
How long do I have to wait?	**Bae lout kyar kyar, saungt ya ma lell?** ဘယ်လောက်ကြာကြာစောင့်ရမလဲ။
When does the bus leave?	**Karr, bae dawt, htwet ma lell?** ကားဘယ်တော့ထွက်မလဲ။
When does the train leave?	**Yat htarr, dae tawt, htwet ma lell?** ရထားဘယ်တော့ထွက်မလဲ။
When does the boat leave?	**Hlay, bae dawt, htwet ma lell?** လှေဘယ်တော့ထွက်မလဲ။
When does the plane leave?	**Lay yin, bae dawt, htwet ma lell?** လေယာဉ်ဘယ်တော့ထွက်မလဲ။
What time does the first (bus/train/boat) leave?	**Pa hta ma sone (karr/yat htarr/hlay) ga, bae achain, htwet ma lell?** ပထမဆုံး (ကား / ရထား / လှေ)က ဘယ်အချိန်ထွက်မလဲ။
What time does the last (bus/train/plane) leave?	**Nout sone (karr/yat htarr/lay yin) ga, bae achain, htwet ma lell?** နောက်ဆုံး (ကား / ရထား / လေယာဉ်)က ဘယ်အချိန်ထွက်မလဲ။

What time does the next (bus/train/boat/plane) leave?	**Nout (karr/yat htarr/hlay/lay yin) ga bae achain htwet ma lell?** နောက် (ကား / ရထား / လှေ / လေယာဉ်)က ဘယ်အချိန်ထွက်မလဲ။
How long does...take?	**...ga, bae lout kyar lell?** ...က ဘယ်လောက်ကြာလဲ။
What time does... arrive in...?	**...ga...go, bae achain, yout ma lell?** ...က...ကို ဘယ်အချိန်ရောက်မလဲ။
Where does the (bus/train/boat/plane) to... leave from?	**...ko thwarr maet (karr/yat htarr/hlay/lay yin) ga, bae ga nay, htwet ma lell?** ...ကိုသွားမယ့် (ကား / ရထား / လှေ / လေယာဉ်)က ဘယ်ကနေထွက်မလဲ။
Is this the (train/bus) to...?	**Dar...go, thwarr maet, (yat htarr/karr) larr?** ဒါ...ကို သွားမယ့် (ရထား / ကား) လား။

7. Finding a Place to Stay

7.1   **Accommodation in Myanmar**
7.2   **At the hotel**
7.3   **Complaints**
7.4   **Departure**

 7.1 **Accommodation in Myanmar**

In Myanmar, accommodation ranges from basic hostels to five-star hotels with gym, swimming pool, spa, restaurants and bars. Luxury hotels, however, are rarely found outside Yangon and other major tourist destinations.

Do you have any rooms available?	**Akhann sheet larr?** အခန်းရှိလား။
I'm looking for a cheap hotel.	**Zayy thet thar daet hotel, shar nay dar bar.** ဈေးသက်သာတဲ့ဟိုတယ် ရှာနေတာပါ။
I'm looking for a hotel near here.	**Di narr ta wite mhar, hotel shar nay dar bar.** ဒီနားတစ်ပိုက်မှာ ဟိုတယ်ရှာနေတာပါ။
Do you give discounts for students?	**Kyaungg tharr dway atwet, discount sheet larr?** ကျောင်းသားတွေအတွက် ဒစ်စကောင့်ရှိလား။
I'm not sure how long I'm staying.	**Bae lout, tell phyit ma lell, ma thay char thayy boo.** ဘယ်လောက်တည်းဖြစ်မလဲ မသေချာသေးဘူး။
Is there air-conditioning in the room?	**Akhann htell mhar air-con sheet larr?** အခန်းထဲမှာအဲကွန်းရှိလား။
Do you have heating in the room?	**Akhann htell mhar heater sheet larr?** အခန်းထဲမှာ ဟီတာရှိလား။

Do you have hot water all day?	**Ta nayt lone, yay pu, ya larr?** တစ်နေ့လုံးရေပူရလား။
When is the heating turned on?	**Heater, bae achain mhar, phwint payy lell?** ဟီတာဘယ်အချိန်မှာဖွင့်ပေးလဲ။
Do you have room service?	**Room service sheet larr?** ရှန်းဆားဗစ်ရှိလား။
Where's the emergency exit?	**Ayayy baw, htwet pout ga, bae mhar lell?** အရေးပေါ်ထွက်ပေါက်က ဘယ်မှာလဲ။
Where's the fire escape?	**Ayayy baw, hlay garr ga, bae mhar lell?** အရေးပေါ် လှေကားက ဘယ်မှာလဲ။
Can I have two keys, please?	**Thawt, nha chaungg, payy bar.** သော့နှစ်ချောင်းပေးပါ။
The key to room 602, please.	**Akhann, chout ya nhit, thawt payy bar.** အခန်း ၆၀၂ သော့ပေးပါ။
Could you put this in the safe, please?	**Dar go, mee khan thit tar htell mhar, htaet htarr payy bar larr?** ဒါကိုမီးခံသေတ္တာထဲမှာ ထည့်ထားပေးပါလား။
Could you wake me at 7 a.m., tomorrow?	**Ma net phyan, ma net, khuna nar yi mhar, nhohh payy bar larr?** မနက်ဖြန်မနက် ၇ နာရီမှာနှိုးပေးပါလား။
Could I have an extra blanket?	**Saung a po, ta htae, payy bar larr?** စောင်အပိုတစ်ထည်ပေးပါလား။
What time does the gate/door open?	**Bae nha nar yi mhar, dagarr phwint lell?** ဘယ်နှစ်နာရီမှာ တံခါးဖွင့်လဲ။
What time does the gate/door close?	**Bae nha nar yi mhar, dagarr pate lell?** ဘယ်နှစ်နာရီမှာ တံခါးပိတ်လဲ။
Could you get me a taxi, please?	**Taxi ngharr payy bar larr?** တက္ကစီငှားပေးပါလား။

Could you find a babysitter for me?	**Khalay htein, ta yout lout, shar payy bar larr?** ကလေးထိန်းတစ်ယောက်လောက် ရှာပေးပါလား။
Is there any mail for me?	[male speaker] **Kya nawt atwet, sar bar larr?** ကျွန်တော့်အတွက် စာပါလား။
	[female speaker] **Kya ma atwet, sar bar larr?** ကျွန်မအတွက် စာပါလား။

ဒီဖောင်လေးဖြည့်ပေးပါ။	Fill out this form, please.
ပတ်စ်ပို့ပြပါ။	Could I see your passport?
စရံငွေပေးရပါမယ်။	You need to pay a deposit.

 ## 7.2 At the hotel

My name is...	[male speaker] **Kya nawt nan mae ga...bar.** ကျွန်တော့်နာမည်က...ပါ။
	[female speaker] **Kya ma nan mae ga...bar.** ကျွန်မနာမည်က...ပါ။
I've reserved a room.	**Akhann booking, lote htarr dae.** အခန်းဘွတ်ကင်လုပ်ထားတယ်။
I emailed you last month.	**Pee khaet daet la ga, email poht htarr dae.** ပြီးခဲ့တဲ့လက အီးမေးလ်ပို့ထားတယ်။
Here's the confirmation.	**Di mhar, booking lote htarr daet, har bar.** ဒီမှာဘွတ်ကင်လုပ်ထားတဲ့ဟာပါ။
How much is it per night?	**Ta nya, bae lout lell?** တစ်ညဘယ်လောက်လဲ။
How much is it per week?	**Da bat bae lout lell?** တစ်ပတ်ဘယ်လောက်လဲ။

We'll be staying for two nights.	**Nha nya, tell mhar bar.** နှစ်ညတည်းမှာပါ။
We'll be staying for two weeks.	**Nha pat, tell mhar bar.** နှစ်ပတ်တည်းမှာပါ။
I'd like a single room.	**Ta yout khann, payy bar.** တစ်ယောက်ခန်းပေးပါ။
I'd like a double room.	**Nha yout khann payy bar.** နှစ်ယောက်ခန်းပေးပါ။
per person	**ta yout go** တစ်ယောက်ကို
per room	**ta khann go** တစ်ခန်းကို
I'd like a room with twin beds.	**Ta yout ate gadin, nha lone bar daet akann pay bar.** တစ်ယောက်အိပ်ကုတင်နှစ်လုံးပါတ အခန်းပေးပါ။
I'd like a room with a double bed.	**Nha yout ate gadin, bar daet, akhann pay bar.** နှစ်ယောက်အိပ်ကုတင်ပါတဲ့ အခန်းပေးပါ။
I'd like a room with a bathtub.	**Bathtub bar daet, akhann payy bar.** ဘတ်တပ်ပါတဲ့အခန်းပေးပါ။
I'd like a room with a shower.	**Yay bann, bar daet, akhann pay bar.** ရေပန်းပါတဲ့အခန်းပေးပါ။
I'd like a suite.	**Meet tharr zoot, akhann payy bar.** မိသားစုခန်းပေးပါ။
Could we have adjoining rooms?	**Taset htell, akhann dway, payy bar.** တစ်ဆက်တည်းအခန်းတွေပေးပါ။
We'd like a room facing the front.	**Shayt, myat nazar, akhann payy bar.** ရှေ့မျက်နှာစာအခန်းပေးပါ။
We'd like a room at the back.	**Nout phet, akhann payy bar.** နောက်ဘက်အခန်းပေးပါ။

We'd like a room with a view of the street.
Lann go, myin ya daet, akhann payy bar. လမ်းကိုမြင်ရတဲ့အခန်းပေးပါ။

We'd like a room with a view of the river.
Myit go, myin ya daet, akhann payy bar. မြစ်ကိုမြင်ရတဲ့အခန်းပေးပါ။

We'd like a room with a view of the sea.
Pin lae go, myin ya daet, akhann payy bar.
ပင်လယ်ကိုမြင်ရတဲ့အခန်းပေးပါ။

We'd like a non-smoking room.
Salate thout loht, ma ya daet, akhann payy bar.
ဆေးလိပ်သောက်လို့မရတဲ့အခန်းပေးပါ။

Does that include breakfast?
Ma net sar, bar larr? မနက်စာပါလား။

Does that include lunch?
Nayt lae zar bar larr?
နေ့လယ်စာပါလား။

Does that include dinner?
Nya zar, bar larr? ညစာပါလား။

Is there air-conditioning in the room?
Akhann htell mhar, air-con bar larr?
အခန်းထဲမှာ အဲကွန်းပါလား။

Is there heating in the room?
Akhann htell mhar, heater bar larr?
အခန်းထဲမှာ ဟီတာပါလား။

Is there a TV in the room?
Akhann htell mhar, TV bar larr?
အခန်းထဲမှာ တီဗီပါလား။

Is there a refrigerator in the room?
Akhann htell mhar, yay khell thittar bar larr?
အခန်းထဲမှာ ရေခဲသေတ္တာပါလား။

Is there hot water in the room?
Akhann htell mhar, yay pu sheet larr?
အခန်းထဲမှာ ရေပူရှိလား။

Is there an electric kettle in the room?
Akhann htell mhar, yay nwayy ohh sheet larr? အခန်းထဲမှာ
ရေနွေးအိုးရှိလား။

Is there free Wi-Fi in the room?
Akhann htell mhar, wi-fi ya larr?
အခန်းထဲမှာ ဝိုင်ဖိုင်ရလား။

Choosing a hotel

Could I see the room? **Akhann kyeet loht, ya ma larr?**
အခန်းကြည့်လို့ရမလား။

We don't like this one. **Di akhann, ma kyite boo.**
ဒီအခန်းမကြိုက်ဘူး။

Do you have another room? **Ta charr akhann, sheet thayy larr?**
တခြားအခန်းရှိသေးလား။

Do you have a larger room? **Po kyee daet, akhann sheet larr?**
ပိုကြီးတဲ့အခန်းရှိလား။

Do you have a less expensive room? **Zayy po thet thar daet, akhann sheet larr?** ဈေးပိုသက်သာတဲ့အခန်းရှိလား။

We prefer a quiet room. **Tate sate daet, akhann po kyite tae.**
တိတ်ဆိတ်တဲ့အခန်းပိုကြိုက်တယ်။

No, they are all occupied. **Ma sheet boo. Akhann arr lone, pyayt nay bi.** မရှိဘူး။ အခန်းအားလုံးပြည့်နေပြီ။

This room is too hot. **Di akhann ga, a yann, pu lonn dae.**
ဒီအခန်းက အရမ်းပူလွန်းတယ်။

This room is too cold. **Di akhann ga, a yann, aye lonn dae.**
ဒီအခန်းက အရမ်းအေးလွန်းတယ်။

This room is too dark. **Di akhann ga, a yann, mhaung lonn dae.** ဒီအခန်းက အရမ်းမှောင်လွန်းတယ်။

This room is too small. **Di akhann ga, a yann, thayy lonn dae.**
ဒီအခန်းက အရမ်းသေးလွန်းတယ်။

This room is too noisy. **Di akhann ga, a yann, su nyan lonn dae.** ဒီအခန်းက အရမ်းဆူညံလွန်းတယ်။

I'll take this room. **Di akhann, yu mae.** ဒီအခန်းယူမယ်။

Could you put in a cot? **Pakhet, htaet loht ya larr?**
ပုခက်ထည့်လို့ရလား။

What time's breakfast? **Ma net sar ga, bae nha nar yi lell?**
မနက်စာက ဘယ်နှစ်နာရီလဲ။

Where's the dining room? **Hta minn sarr khann ga, bae mhar lell?** ထမင်းစားခန်းက ဘယ်မှာလဲ။

Can I have breakfast in my room? **Akhann htell mhar, ma net sar, sarr loht ya ma larr?** အခန်းထဲမှာ မနက်စာစားလို့ရမလား။

ဒီဘက်ကိုကြွပါ။	This way please.
အခန်းက...လွှာ၊ အခန်းနံပါတ်...ပါ။	Your room is on the... floor, number...
အိမ်သာနဲ့ရေချိုးခန်းက တစ်ထပ်တည်းမှာပါပဲ။	The toilet and shower are on the same floor.
အိမ်သာနဲ့ရေချိုးခန်းက အခန်းထဲမှာပါ။	The toilet and shower are in the room.

How much is the room per night? **Ta nya go, bae lout lell?** တစ်ညကို ဘယ်လောက်လဲ။

Is breakfast included? **Ma net sar, bar larr?** မနက်စာပါလား။

Does this include all three meals? **Hta minn, thone nat lone, bar larr?** ထမင်းသုံးနပ်လုံးပါလား။

Does this include the service charge? **Win saung kha, bar larr?** ဝန်ဆောင်ခပါလား။

7.3 Complaints

We can't sleep because of the noise. [male speaker] **Su nyan nay loht, kya naw doht, ate loht, ma ya boo.** ဆူညံနေလို့ ကျွန်တော်တို့အိပ်လို့မရဘူး။

[female speaker] **Su nyan nay loht, kya ma doht, ate loht, ma ya boo.** ဆူညံနေလို့ ကျွန်မတို့အိပ်လို့မရဘူး။

Could you turn the radio down, please?	**Radio athan tohh payy bar larr?** ရေဒီယိုအသံတိုးပေးပါလား။
We're out of toilet paper.	**Eain thar htell mhar, tissue ma sheet tawt boo.** အိမ်သာထဲမှာ တစ်ရှူးမရှိတော့ဘူး။
There aren't any...	**...ma sheet boo.** ...မရှိဘူး။
There's not enough...	**...a l'own alout ma sheet boo.** ...အလုံအလောက်မရှိဘူး။
The bed linen's dirty.	**Ate yakhinn ga, nyit pat nay dae.** အိပ်ရာခင်းက ညစ်ပတ်နေတယ်။
The room hasn't been cleaned.	**Akhann, thant shinn yayy, ma lote ya thayy boo.** အခန်းသန့်ရှင်းရေး မလုပ်ရသေးဘူး။
The air-conditioning isn't working.	**Air-con ga alote, ma lote boo.** အဲကွန်းက အလုပ်မလုပ်ဘူး။
There's no hot water.	**Yay pu, ma sheet boo.** ရေပူမရှိဘူး။
There's no electricity.	**Mee, ma lar boo.** မီးမလာဘူး။
...doesn't work.	**...ga alote, ma lote boo.** ...က အလုပ်မလုပ်ဘူး။
...is broken.	**...ga pyet nay dae.** ...က ပျက်နေတယ်။
The toilet is blocked.	**Eain thar, a pout, pate nay dae.** အိမ်သာအပေါက် ပိတ်နေတယ်။
The sink is blocked.	**Bay zin, a pout, pate nay dae.** ဘေဇင်အပေါက် ပိတ်နေတယ်။
The tap is dripping.	**Pite gaungg ga, yay kya nay dae.** ပိုက်ခေါင်းကရေကျနေတယ်။
The bulb is burnt out.	**Mee lone, kyonn nay dae.** မီးလုံးကျွမ်းနေတယ်။
The blind is broken.	**Blind ga, kyohh nay dae.** ဘလိုင်းကကျိုးနေတယ်။

Could you have that seen to?	**Lar kyeet payy bar larr?** လာကြည့်ပေးပါလား။
Could I have another room?	**Ta charr, akhann, ya ma larr?** တခြားအခန်းရမလား။
The bed creaks terribly.	**Gadin ga, takyweet kyweet, myi nay dae.** ကုတင်က တကျွီကျွီမြည်နေတယ်။
The bed sags.	**Mwayt yar ga, eet kya nay dae.** မွေ့ယာက အိကျနေတယ်။
It's too noisy.	**Ayann, su nyan lonn dae.** အရမ်းဆူညံလွန်းတယ်။
This place is full of mosquitos.	**Di nay yar ga, chin dway naet, pyayt nay dar bell.** ဒီနေရာက ခြင်တွေနဲ့ပြည့်နေတာပဲ။
This place is full of cockroaches.	**Di nay yar ga, pohh hat tway naet, pyayt nay dar bell.** ဒီနေရာက ပိုးဟပ်တွေနဲ့ပြည့်နေတာပဲ။

 7.4 Departure

I'm leaving (the hotel) tomorrow.	**Manet phyan (hotel ga nay) htwet mae.** မနက်ဖြန် (ဟိုတယ်ကနေ) ထွက်မယ်။
Where can I pay my bill, please?	**Bae mhar, petsan, shinn ya ma lell?** ဘယ်မှာပိုက်ဆံရှင်းရမလဲ။
My room number is 602.	[male speaker] **Kya nawt, akhann nan bat ga, chout ya nhit par.** ကျွန်တော့်အခန်းနံပါတ်က ၆၀၂ ပါ။
	[female speaker] **Kya ma, akhann nan bat ga, chout ya nhit par.** ကျွန်မအခန်းနံပါတ်က ၆၀၂ ပါ။
What time should we check out?	**Bae nhanar yi mhar check-out lote ya ma lell?** ဘယ်နှစ်နာရီမှာ ချက်ကောက်လုပ်ရမလဲ။

I'm leaving early tomorrow.	**Manet phyan, saww saww htwet mae.** မနက်ဖြန်စောစောထွက်မယ်။
Please prepare the bill.	**Petsan shinn poht, bill layy, pyin htarr payy bar.** ပိုက်ဆံရှင်းဖို့ ဘောလ်လေးပြင်ထားပေးပါ။
Could I have my deposit back, please?	**Sa yan payy htarr dar, pyan payy ya ownn mae naw?** စရံပေးထားတာ ပြန်ပေးရဦးမယ်နော်။
I must leave at once.	**Chet chinn, htwet ya mae.** ချက်ချင်းထွက်ရမယ်။
Is this my bill?	[male speaker] **Dar kya nawt bill larr?** ဒါကျွန်တော့်ဘောလ်လား။
	[female speaker] **Dar kya ma bill larr?** ဒါကျွန်မဘောလ်လား။
Is everything included?	**Arr lone, par pee tharr larr?** အားလုံးပါပြီးသားလား။
Do you accept credit cards?	**Credit card naet, payy loht ya larr?** ခရက်ဒစ်ကတ်နဲ့ ပေးလို့ရလား။
I reckon you've made a mistake in the bill.	**Bill htell mhar, mharr nay dae, htin dae naw.** ဘောလ်ထဲမှာ မှားနေတယ်ထင်တယ်နော်။
Could you forward my mail to this address?	[male speaker] **Kya nawt sar go, di late sar go, poht payy bar larr?** ကျွန်တော့်စာကို ဒီလိပ်စာကို ပို့ပေးပါလား။
	[female speaker] **Kya ma sar go, di late sar go, poht payy bar larr?** ကျွန်မစာကို ဒီလိပ်စာကို ပို့ပေးပါလား။
Could I leave my luggage here until leave?	[male speaker] **Kya nawt, luggage go, di mhar, khana, htarr khaet loht, ya I larr?** ကျွန်တော့်လက်ဂေ့ဂျ်ကို ဒီမှာခဏထားခဲ့လို့ရလား။

[female speaker] **Kya ma, luggage go, di mhar, khana, htarr khaet loht, ya larr?** ကျွန်မလက်ဂွေ့ဂျ်က ဒီမှာခဏထားခဲ့လို့ရလား။

Thanks for your hospitality.

Kyayy zoo, a myarr gyee, tin bar dae. ကျေးဇူးအများကြီးတင်ပါတယ်။

We enjoyed it, thank you.

Di mhar, nay ya dar, a sin pyay bar dae. Kyayy zoo bar. ဒီမှာနေရတာ အဆင်ပြေပါတယ်။ ကျေးဇူးပါ။

Hi, where can I change money nearby?
Mingalarbar. Di narr mhar, bae mhar, petsan lell loht, ya lell?

There's a money changer over there.
Ho narr mhar, money changer sheet dae.

Thanks!
Kyayy zoo tin bar dae!

Hello, how can I help you?
Mingalarbar. Bar, ku nyi payy ya ma lell?

I'd like to change USD to kyat. What's the exchange rate?
Dollar ga nay, myanmar kyat, lell jin dae. Bae zayy lell?

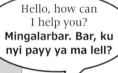

It's 1500 kyat to a dollar.
Da dollar go, htaungt ngarr yar kyat bar.

Okay. Could you give me some small bills with it?
Hote kaet. A ywet thayy layy dway, htaet payy bar naw.

8. Money Matters

In Myanmar, you can exchange foreign currency at the bank or at a money changer. Banks are open Monday to Friday, from 9 a.m to 3 p.m, but local money changers are usually available everyday until 6 p.m. You can also withdraw money from most ATMs using your VISA or Mastercard.

Changing money

Where can I exchange foreign currency?	**Bae mhar, petsan, lell loht ya lell?** ဘယ်မှာပိုက်ဆံလဲလို့ရလဲ။
What's today's exchange rate for US dollars to Myanmar kyat?	**Dollar ga nay, myanmar kyat go, di nayt zayy, bae lout lell?** ဒေါ်လာကနေ မြန်မာကျပ်ကို ဒီနေ့စျေးဘယ်လောက်လဲ။
What's today's exchange rate for Euros to Myanmar kyat?	**Euro ga nay, myanmar kyat go, di nayt zayy, bae lout lell?** ယူရိုကနေ မြန်မာကျပ်ကို ဒီနေ့စျေးဘယ်လောက်လဲ။
What's today's exchange rate for Singapore dollars to Myanmar kyat?	**Singapu dollar ga nay, myanmar kyat go, di nayt zayy, bae lout lell?** စင်ကာပူဒေါ် လာကနေ မြန်မာကျပ်ကို ဒီနေ့စျေးဘယ်လောက်လဲ။
What's today's exchange rate for Thai baht to Myanmar kyat?	**Thai baht ga nay, myanmar kyat ko, di nayt zayy, bae lout lell?** ထိုင်းဘတ်ကနေ မြန်မာကျပ်ကို ဒီနေ့စျေးဘယ်လောက်လဲ။
Can I withdraw money on my credit card here?	**Di mhar, credit card naet, petsan htote loht ya larr?** ဒီမှာ ခရက်ဒစ်ကတ်နဲ့ ပိုက်ဆံထုတ်လို့ရလား။

What's the maximum amount?	**A myarr zone, bae lout, htote loht ya lell?** အများဆုံး ဘယ်လောက်ထုတ်လို့ရလဲ။
What's the minimum amount?	**A nell zone, bae lout, htote loht ya lell?** အနည်းဆုံး ဘယ်လောက်ထုတ်လို့ရလဲ။
I had some money cabled here.	**Di go, petsan hlwell htarr dar, sheet dae.** ဒီကိုပိုက်ဆံလွှဲထားတာရှိတယ်။
These are the details of my bank in the US.	**Dar US ga ban yaet, a chet a let dway bar.** ဒါယူအက်စ်ကဘဏ်ရဲ့ အချက်အလက်တွေပါ။
This is the number of my bank account.	**Dar ban account nan bat par.** ဒါဘဏ်အကောင့်နံပတ်ပါ။
I'd like to change some money.	**Petsan, nell nell, lell jin bar dae.** ပိုက်ဆံနည်းနည်းလဲချင်ပါတယ်။
Could you give me some small change with it?	**A ywet thayy dway payy bar naw.** အရွက်သေးတွေပေးပါနော်။
This is not right.	**Dar ma hote boo.** ဒါမဟုတ်ဘူး။

ဒီမှာလက်မှတ်ထိုးပေးပါ။	Sign here, please.
ဒါဖြည့်ပေးပါ။	Fill this out, please.
ပတ်စ်ပို့ပြပါ။	Could I see your passport, please?
အိုင်ဒီကတ်ပြပါ။	Could I see your identity card, please?
ခရက်ဒစ်ကတ်ပြပါ။	Could I see your credit card, please?

8.2 Settling the bill

Could I have the
bill, please?

Shinn mae. ရှင်းမယ်။

Could you put it on
my bill?

Dar go, bill htell mhar, htaet payy bar?
ဒါကို ဘောလ်ထဲမှာထည့်ပေးပါ။

Is everything included?

Arr lone bar larr? အားလုံးပါလား။

Is the tip included?

Tip yaww bar larr? တစ်(ပ်)ရောပါလား။

Can I pay by credit card?

Credit card naet, payy loht ya larr?
ခရက်ဒစ်ကတ်နဲ့ပေးလို့ရလား။

Can I pay with foreign
currency?

**Nai ngan jarr ngway naet, payy loht
ya larr?** နိုင်ငံခြားငွေနဲ့ပေးလို့ရလား။

You've given me too
much change.

Pyan ann ngway ga, po nay dae.
ပြန်အမ်းငွေကပိုနေတယ်။

You haven't given me
enough change.

Pyan ann ngway ga, lo thayy dae.
ပြန်အမ်းငွေကလိုသေးတယ်။

Could you check this
again, please?

Dar go, pyan sit payy bar larr?
ဒါကိုပြန်စစ်ပေးပါလား။

Could I have a receipt,
please?

Baung char layy, payy bar?
ဘောင်ချာလေးပေးပါ။

Keep the change.

Pyan ann ngway go, yu htarr lite par.
ပြန်အမ်းငွေကိုယူထားလိုက်ပါ။

ဆောရီးပါ။ ခရက်ဒစ်ကတ်နဲ့ ပေးလို့မရပါဘူး။

Sorry, we don't accept
credit cards.

နိုင်ငံခြားငွေနဲ့ပေးလို့မရပါဘူး။

We don't accept foreign
currency.

Money Matters

8

117

9. Mail, Phone and Internet

9.1   Mail
9.2   Phones
9.3   Internet access

 9.1   Mail

Myanmar Post is open Monday to Friday, 9:30 a.m. to 4:30 p.m. It is open weekend mornings for sending express mail only.

stamp **dazate gaungg** တံဆိပ်ခေါင်း	money order **ngway hlwell** ငွေလွှဲ	postcard **postcard** ပို့စ်ကတ်
parcel **parcel** ပါဆယ်	registered mail **register** ရက်ဂျစ်စတာ	express mail **a myan chaww poht** အမြန်ချောပို့

Where is the nearest post office?
: **A nee sone, sar tite ga, bae mhar sheet lell?** အနီးဆုံးစာတိုက်က ဘယ်မှာရှိလဲ။

Where is the nearest mail box?
: **A nee sone, sar tite bone ga, bae mhar sheet lell?** အနီးဆုံးစာတိုက်ပုံးက ဘယ်မှာရှိလဲ။

Which counter should I go to to wire a money order?
: **Ngway hlwell boht, bae counter go, thwarr ya ma lell?** ငွေလွှဲဖို့ ဘယ်ကောင်တာကိုသွားရမလဲ။

Which counter should I go to for general delivery?
: **Pyit see htote boht, bae counter go, thwarr ya ma lell?** ပစ္စည်းထုတ်ဖို့ ဘယ်ကောင်တာကိုသွားရမလဲ။

Is there any mail for me?
: [male speaker] **Kya nawt sar bar larr?** ကျွန်တော့်စာပါလား။

	[female speaker] **Kya ma sar bar larr?** ကျွန်မစာပါလား။
What's the postage for a letter to America?	**American go, sar poht kha, bae lout lell?** အမေရိကန်ကိုစာပို့ခဘယ်လောက်လဲ။
What's the postage for a postcard to America?	**American go, postcard poht kha, bae lout lell?** အမေရိကန်ကိုစာပို့ခ ဘယ်လောက်လဲ။
I'd like two 10 kyat stamps.	**Sae kyat tan, dazate gaungg, nha khoot, payy bar.** ဆယ်ကျပ်တန်တံဆိပ်ခေါင်းနှစ်ခုပေးပါ။
I'd like to send this letter by express mail.	**Di sar go, amyan chaww poht naet, poht jin bar dae.** ဒီစာကို အမြန်ချောပို့နဲ့ပို့ချင်ပါတယ်။
I'd like to send this letter by air mail.	**Di sar go, lay yin naet, poht jin bar dae.** ဒီစာကို လေယာဉ်နဲ့ပို့ချင်ပါတယ်။
I'd like to send this letter by registered mail.	**Di sar go, register ga nay, poht jin bar dae.** ဒီစာကို ရက်ဂျစ်စတာကနေပို့ချင်ပါတယ်။
I'd like to send this letter by surface mail.	**Di sar go, thinn baww naet, poht jin bar dae.** ဒီစာကို သင်္ဘောနဲ့ပို့ချင်ပါတယ်။
I'd like to send a courier package.	**Pyit see poht jin bar dae.** ပစ္စည်းပို့ချင်ပါတယ်။
Which counter should I go to to send a courier package?	**Pyit see poht boht, bae counter go, thwarr ya ma lell?** ပစ္စည်းပို့ဖို့ ဘယ်ကောင်တာကိုသွားရမလဲ။
Can you help me send this package by courier?	**Di pyit see poht jin loht, ku nyi payy bar larr?** ဒီပစ္စည်းပို့ချင်လို့ ကူညီပေးပါလား။
What is the cost?	**Bae lout kya lell?** ဘယ်လောက်ကျလဲ။

9.2 Phones

To use your phone in Myanmar, you need a local SIM card and a prepaid card. Buy them at the airport or a convenience store.

Where can I get a SIM card?	**Bae mhar SIM kat, wae loht ya lell?** ဘယ်မှာဆင်းမ်ကတ်ဂယ်လို့ရလဲ။
Where can I get a prepaid card?	**Bae mhar phone ngway phyayt kat, wae loht, ya lell?** ဘယ်မှာဖုန်းငွေဖြည့်ကတ်ဂယ်လို့ရလဲ။
Could you connect me to room number 602?	**Akhann nan bat, chout ya nhit ko, set thwae payy bar larr?** အခန်းနံပါတ် ၆၀၂ ကို ဆက်သွယ်ပေးပါလား။
Could you give me the country code for the UK?	**UK go, khaw daet, kote nan bat payy bar larr?** ယူကေကိုခေါ်တဲ့ ကုဒ်နံပါတ်ပေးပါလား။
Could you give me Yangon's area code?	**Yangon kote nan bat, payy bar larr?** ရန်ကုန်ကုဒ်နံပါတ် ပေးပါလား။
Can I dial international (long distance) direct?	**Nai ngan jarr go, dite yite khaw loht ya larr?** နိုင်ငံခြားကို တိုက်ရိုက်ခေါ် လို့ရလား။
Could you dial this number for me, please?	**Di nan bat layy, nhate payy bar larr?** ဒီနံပါတ်လေး နှိပ်ပေးပါလား။
I'd like to place a long-distance collect call.	**Nae wayy phone khaw jin bar dae.** နယ်ဝေးဖုန်းခေါ် ချင်ပါတယ်။
Hello, this is...	**Hello, ...bar.** ဟဲလို၊...ပါ။
Who is this, please?	**Akhoot pyaww nay dar, bae thu bar lell?** အခုပြောနေတာ ဘယ်သူပါလဲ။
Is this...?	**...larr?** ...လား။
I'm sorry, I've dialed the wrong number.	**Sorry bar. Phone mharr nhate meet dar bar.** ဆောရီးပါ။ ဖုန်းမှားနှိပ်မိတာပါ။

I can't hear you.	**Ma kyarr ya boo.** မကြားရဘူး။
I'd like to speak to...	**...naet, pyaww jin loht bar.** ...နဲ့ ပြောချင်လို့ပါ။
Do you speak English?	**Ingalate lo, pyaww loht ya larr?** အင်္ဂလိပ်လိုပြောလို့ရလား။
Extension..., please.	**Extension nan bat...go, hlwell payy bar.** အိပ်စ်တန်းရှင်းနံပါတ်...ကို လွဲပေးပါ။
Could you ask him/her to call me back?	**Thoot go, pyan khaw boht, pyaww payy bar larr.** သူ့ကိုပြန်ခေါ် ဖို့ ပြောပေးပါလား။
My name's...	[male speaker] **Kya nawt nan mae ga, ...par.** ကျွန်တော့်နာမည်က...ပါ။
	[female speaker] **Kya ma nan mae ga, ...par.** ကျွန်မနာမည်က...ပါ။
My number's...	[male speaker] **Kya nawt, phone nan bat ga...par.** ကျွန်တော့်ဖုန်းနံပါတ်က...ပါ။
	[female speaker] **Kya ma, phone nan bat ga...par.** ကျွန်မဖုန်းနံပါတ်က...ပါ။
Could you tell him/her I called?	[male speaker] **Kya naw, phone set tae loht, pyaww payy bar larr?** ကျွန်တော်ဖုန်းဆက်တယ်လို့ ပြော ဟပေးပါလား။
	[female speaker] **Kya ma, phone set tae loht, pyaww payy bar larr?** ကျွန်မဖုန်းဆက်တယ်လို့ ပြောပေးပါလား။
I'll call him/her back tomorrow.	[male speaker] **Ma net phyan, kya naw, phone pyan khaw mae.** မနက်ဖြန်ကျွန်တော်ဖုန်းပြန်ခေါ် မယ်။
	[female speaker] **Ma net phyan, kya ma, phone pyan khaw mae.** မနက်ဖြန်ကျွန်မဖုန်းပြန်ခေါ် မယ်။

ဖုန်းလာတယ်။	There's a phone call for you.
သူ့ညကိုအရင်နှိပ်ပါ။	You have to dial "0" first.
ခဏလေးနော်။	One moment, please.
ဖုန်းမကိုင်ဘူး။	There's no answer.
ဖုန်းမအားဘူး။	The line's busy.
ကိုင်ထားမလား။	Do you want to hold?
ဖုန်းမှားနေတယ်။	You've got a wrong number.
သူအခုဒီမှာမရှိဘူး။ ...မှာပြန်ရောက်မယ်။	He's/She's not here right now. He'll/She'll be back at...

9.3 Internet access

Myanmar's commercial capital Yangon ranks high in East Asia for download and upload speeds. Free Wi-Fi is available in most cafés, hotels and bars.

Internet café	portable power	blog	Wi-Fi router
internet café	**power bank**	**blog**	**wi-fi set**
အင်တာနက်ကဖေး	ပါဝါဘဏ်	ဘလော့	ဝိုင်ဖိုင်စက်
social media	email	app	
lu mhoot khon yet	**email**	**app**	
လူမှုကွန်ယက်	အီးမေးလ်	အက်ပ်	

Is there free Wi-Fi here?	**Di mhar, wi-fi alagarr ya larr?** ဒီမှာ ဝိုင်ဖိုင်အလကားရလား။
What is your email address?	**Email late sar layy, payy bar?** အီးမေးလ်လိပ်စာလေးပေးပါ။
My email address is...	[male speaker] **Kya nawt email late sar ga...** ကျွန်တော့်အီးမေးလ်လိပ်စာက...

	[female speaker] **Kya ma email late sar ga...** ကျွန်မအီးမေးလ်လိပ်စာက...
Could you send me an email?	[male speaker] **Kya nawt go, email poht lite bar larr?** ကျွန်တော့်ကို အီးမေးလ်ပို့လိုက်ပါလား။
	[female speaker] **Kya ma go, email poht lite bar larr?** ကျွန်မကို အီးမေးလ်ပို့လိုက်ပါလား။
I will get back to you via email.	**Email naet, pyan pyaww bar mae.** အီးမေးလ်နဲ့ ပြန်ပြောပါမယ်။
The Internet connection is unstable.	**Laii ma kaungg boo.** လိုင်းမကောင်းဘူး။
The Internet connection is slow.	**Laii kya dae.** လိုင်းကျတယ်။
Can I borrow a Wi-Fi router?	**Wi-fi set, ngharr bar larr?** ဝိုင်ဖိုင်စက် ငှားပါလား။
Can I borrow a portable charger?	**Power bank, ngharr bar larr?** ပါဝါဘဏ့် ငှားပါလား။
Let's take a selfie.	**Selfie swell ya aung.** ဆယ်ဖီဆွဲရအောင်။
Add me on Facebook.	**Facebook mhar, add payy bar.** ဖေ့စ်ဘွတ်မှာ အက်ဒ်ပေးပါ။
I will send you the picture via Facebook.	**Facebook ga nay, p'own poht lite mae.** ဖေ့စ်ဘွတ်ကနေ ပုံပို့လိုက်မယ်။
I have uploaded our photos on Facebook.	**Facebook mhar, p'own dway, tin lite bi.** ဖေ့စ်ဘွတ်မှာ ပုံတွေတင်လိုက်ပြီ။
Do you have a Facebook account?	**Facebook account sheet larr?** ဖေ့စ်ဘွတ်အကောင့်ရှိလား။
Can I add you on Facebook?	**Facebook mhar, add lite ya ma larr?** ဖေ့စ်ဘွတ်မှာ အပ်လိုက်ရမလား။

What is your mobile phone number?	**Phone nan bat, bae lout lell?** ဖုန်းနံပါတ်ဘယ်လောက်လဲ။
Do you have this translation app?	**Di, barthar pyan application, sheet larr?** ဒီဘာသာပြန်အက်ပလီကေးရှင်းရှိလား။
Do you have this train ticket booking app?	**Di, yet htarr let mhat, booking lote taet application, sheet larr?** ဒီ ရထားလက်မှတ် ဘွတ်ကင်လုပ်တဲ့အက်ပလီကေးရှင်း ရှိလား။
Do you have this hotel booking app?	**Di, hotel booking lote daet application, sheet larr?** ဒီ ဟိုတယ်ဘွတ်ကင်လုပ်တဲ့အက်ပလီကေး ရှင်း ရှိလား။
Do you have a printer here?	**Di mhar, printer sheet larr?** ဒီမှာ ပရင်တာရှိလား။
How much would it cost to print one sheet of paper in black and white?	**Aphyu amell naet, print htote tar, ta ywet, bae lout lell?** အဖြူအမည်းနဲ့ ပရင့်ထုတ်တာ တစ်ရွက်ဘယ်လောက်လဲ။
It's my ticket confirmation.	**Dar, let mhat, booking lote htarr daet har bar.** ဒါ လက်မှတ်ဘွတ်ကင်လုပ်ထားတဲ့ဟာပါ။
It's my hotel reservation.	**Dar, hotel booking lote htarr daet har bar.** ဒါ ဟိုတယ်ဘွတ်ကင်လုပ်ထားတဲ့ဟာပါ။
It's my boarding pass.	**Dar, boarding pass par.** ဒါ ဘောဒင်းပွ့ါစ်ပါ။

10. Shopping

Department stores, supermarkets and most shops in Myanmar are open daily, from 9 a.m. until 9 or 10 p.m. Convenience stores are open 24 hours. Morning and evening street markets, where it's acceptable to bargain, are common.

supermarket
supermarket
စူပါးမားကတ်

department store
k'own dite
ကုန်တိုက်

fruit shop
athee sai
အသီးဆိုင်

vegetable shop
hinn thee hinn ywet sai
ဟင်းသီးဟင်းရွက်ဆိုင်

grocery
k'own z'own sai
ကုန်စုံဆိုင်

florist
pann sai
ပန်းဆိုင်

market
zayy
ဈေး

fishmonger
ngarr sai
ငါးဆိုင်

household goods
eain thone pyit see, a yaungg sai
အိမ်သုံးပစ္စည်းအရောင်း ဆိုင်

household appliances
eain thone hlyat sit pyit see a yaungg sai
အိမ်သုံးလျှပ်စစ်ပစ္စည်း အရောင်းဆိုင်

household linen shop
eain thone pate sa, a yaungg sai
အိမ်သုံးပိတ်စအရောင်း ဆိုင်

watches and clocks
nar yi sai
နာရီဆိုင်

optician
myet mhan sai
မျက်မှန်ဆိုင်

clothing shop
ahtae sai
အထည်ဆိုင်

ice-cream stand
yay khell mote sai
ရေခဲမုန့်ဆိုင်

music shop
(CDs, DVDs, etc)
akhway sai
အခွေဆိုင်

barber
amyohh tharr zabin nhyat sai
အမျိုးသားဆံပင်ညှပ်ဆိုင်

hairdresser
amyohh thamee zabin nhyat sai
အမျိုးသမီးဆံပင်ညှပ်ဆိုင်

perfumery
yay mhwayy sai
ရေမွှေးဆိုင်

leather goods
tha yay pyit see, a yaungg sai
သားရေပစ္စည်း အရောင်းဆိုင်

Burmese medicine shop
myanmar sayy sai
မြန်မာဆေးဆိုင်

goldsmith
badain
ပန်းထိမ်

toy shop
a yote sai
အရုပ်ဆိုင်

jeweler
kyout myet yadanar sai
ကျောက်မျက်ရတနာဆိုင်

beauty salon
ahla pyin sai
အလှပြင်ဆိုင်

laundry
a wit shaw sai
အဝတ်လျှော်ဆိုင်

bakery
paung mote sai
ပေါင်မုန့်ဆိုင်

cobbler
phanat chote sai
ဖိနပ်ချုပ်ဆိုင်

camera shop
camera sai
ကင်မရာဆိုင်

stationery shop
sar yayy kariyar sai
စာရေးကိရိယာဆိုင်

sporting goods
arr gazarr pyit see sai
အားကစားပစ္စည်းဆိုင်

bookshop
sar oat sai
စာအုပ်ဆိုင်

cake shop
mote sai
မုန့်ဆိုင်

motorbike/bicycle repairs
sai kae / set bein pyin sai
ဆိုင်ကယ် / စက်ဘီးပြင်ဆိုင်

pharmacy
sayy zai
ဆေးဆိုင်

newsstand
jar nae sai
ဂျာနယ်ဆိုင်

delicatessen
nai ngan jarr, asarr asar sai
နိုင်ငံခြား အစားအစာဆိုင်

10.1 At a store

Where can I get...?

...bae mhar ya lell? ...ဘယ်မှာရလဲ။

When is this shop open?

Bae nha nar yi, sai phwint lell?
ဘယ်နှစ်နာရီဆိုင်ဖွင့်လဲ။

Could you tell me where the ... department is?

...ga, bae mhar lell, theet larr?
...က ဘယ်မှာလဲသိလား။

Could you help me, please?

Ku nyi payy bar larr. ကူညီပေးပါလား။

I'm looking for...

...shar nay dar bar. ...ရှာနေတာပါ။

Do you sell English language newspapers?

Ingalate thadinn zar, yaungg larr?
အင်္ဂလိပ်သတင်းစာရောင်းလား။

No, I'd like...
Ma hote boo, ...payy bar.
မဟုတ်ဘူး။ ...ပေးပါ။

I'm just looking, if that's all right?
Di taii, shout kyeet nay dar bar. Ya larr? ဒီတိုင်းလျှောက်ကြည့်နေတာပါ။ ရလား။

မှာထားတာလား။ — Are you being served?

ဘာယူဦးမလဲ။ — Anything else?

Yes, I'd also like...
Hote kaet, ...payy bar. ဟုတ်ကဲ့၊ ...ပေးပါ။

No, thank you. That's all.
Ma yu dawt boo. Kyayy zoo bar.
မယူတော့ဘူး။ ကျေးဇူးပါ။

Could you show me...?
...pya payy bar larr? ...ပြပေးပါလား။

I'd prefer...
...po kyite dae. ...ပိုကြိုက်တယ်။

This is not what I'm looking for.
[male speaker] **Kya naw shar nay dar, dar ma hote boo.**
ကျွန်တော်ရှာနေတာ ဒါမဟုတ်ဘူး။

[female speaker] **Kya ma shar nay dar, dar ma hote boo.**
ကျွန်မရှာနေတာ ဒါမဟုတ်ဘူး။

Thank you, I'll keep looking.
Kyayy zoo tin bar dae. Set shar kyeet lite ownn mae. ကျေးဇူးတင်ပါတယ်။ ဆက်ရှာကြည့်လိုက်ဦးမယ်။

Do you have something less expensive?
Zayy po thet thar dar, sheet larr?
ဈေးပိုသက်သာတာ ရှိလား။

Do you have something smaller?
Po thayy dar, sheet larr?
ပိုသေးတာရှိလား။

Do you have something larger?
Po kyee dar, sheet larr?
ပိုကြီးတာရှိလား။

I'll take this one.	**Dar yu mae.** ဒါယူမယ်။
Does it come with instructions?	**A nhyonn, bar larr?** အညွှန်းပါလား။
It's too expensive.	**A yann, zayy kyee lonn dae.** အရမ်းဈေးကြီးလွန်းတယ်။
I'll give you...	**...payy mae.** ...ပေးမယ်။
Could you keep this for me?	**Dar layy, thein htarr payy bar larr?** ဒါလေး သိမ်းထားပေးပါလား။
I'll come back for it later.	**Nout mha, pyan lar khaet mae.** နောက်မှ ပြန်လာခဲ့မယ်။
Do you have a bag for me, please?	**Ate layy, payy bar larr?** အိတ်လေး ပေးပါလား။
Could you gift-wrap it, please?	**Parkin set ku naet, htote payy bar larr?** ပါကင်စက္ကူနဲ့ ထုပ်ပေးပါလား။

ဆောရီးပါ။ ဒါမရှိပါဘူး။	I'm sorry, we don't have this.
ဆောရီးပါ။ ကုန်သွားပြီ။	I'm sorry, we're sold out.
ဆောရီးပါ။ ...မှ ရောက်ပါမယ်။	I'm sorry, it won't come in until...
ကက်ရှာမှာ ပေးပေးပါ။	Please pay at the cash register
ခရက်ဒစ်ကတ်နဲ့ ပေးလို့မရပါဘူး။	We don't accept credit cards.

10.2 At a food market

Traditional Burmese units of measure for weight are the viss and the tical. 1 viss is about 3½ pounds (1.5 kilos) and 1 tical is about ½ an ounce (15 grams).

I'd like 50 ticals of beef.	**Amell tharr, ngarr zae tharr, payy bar.** အမဲသား ၅၀ သား ပေးပါ။

I'd like a viss of chicken.	**Kyet tharr, da bate thar, payy bar.** ကြက်သားတစ်ပိဿာပေးပါ။
Could you cut it up for me, please?	**Hlee payy bar larr?** လှီးပေးပါလား။
Can I order it?	**Mhar loht ya larr?** မှာလို့ရလား။
I'll pick it up tomorrow at...	**Ma net phyan...mhar, lar yu mae.** မနက်ဖြန်...မှာ လာယူမယ်။
Is it okay to eat this?	**Dar, sarr loht ya larr?** ဒါစားလို့ရလား။
Is it okay to drink this?	**Dar, thout loht ya larr?** ဒါသောက်လို့ရလား။
What's in it?	**Di htell mhar, bar par lell?** ဒီထဲမှာ ဘာပါလဲ။

10.3 Clothing and shoes

I'd like something to go with this.	**Dar naet wit boht, lo jin dae.** ဒါနဲ့ဝတ်ဖို့ လိုချင်တယ်။
Do you have shoes to match this?	**Dar naet lite daet, phanat sheet larr?** ဒါနဲ့လိုက်တဲ့ ဖိနပ်ရှိလား။
I'm a size...in the U.S.	**U.S. site...bar.** ယူအက်စ်ဆိုဒ်...ပါ။
Can I try this on?	**Wit kyeet loht ya larr?** ဝတ်ကြည့်လို့ရလား။
Where's the fitting room?	**A wit lell khann ga, bae mhar lell?** အဝတ်လဲခန်း ကဘယ်မှာလဲ။
It doesn't suit me.	**Ma taw boo.** မတော်ဘူး။
This is the right size.	**A taw bell.** အတော်ပဲ။
Do you have these in white?	**Dar, aphyu yaung, sheet larr?** ဒါ အဖြူရောင်ရှိလား။
Do you have these in black?	**Dar, amell yaung, sheet larr?** ဒါ အမည်းရောင်ရှိလား။

Do you have these in green?	**Dar, asein yaung, sheet larr?** ဒါ အစိမ်းရောင်ရှိလား။
Do you have these in red?	**Dar, ani yaung, sheet larr?** ဒါ အနီရောင်ရှိလား။
Do you have these in blue?	**Dar, apyar yaung, sheet larr?** ဒါ အပြာရောင်ရှိလား။
The heel's too high.	**Dout ga, ayann, myint lonn dae.** ဒေါက်က အရမ်းမြင့်လွန်းတယ်။
The heel's too low.	**Dout ga, ayann, naint lonn dae.** ဒေါက်က အရမ်းနိမ့်လွန်းတယ်။
Is this real leather?	**Dar, tha yay, a sit larr?** ဒါ သားရေအစစ်လား။
I'm looking for a dress for a four-year-old child.	**Lay nhit kha layy atwet, gar win, shar nay dar bar.** လေးနှစ်ကလေးအတွက် ဂါဝန်ရှာနေတာပါ။
I'd like a silk blouse.	**Pohh ein gyi, payy bar.** ပိုးအကျီ ပေးပါ။
I'd like a cotton shirt.	**Chi shat ein gyi, payy bar.** ချည်ရှပ်အကျီ ပေးပါ။
I'd like a woolen jacket.	**Thohh mwayy jarkin ein gyi, payy bar.** သိုးမွေးဂျာကင်အကျီ ပေးပါ။
I'd like a pair of linen pants.	**Linin baungg bi tahtae, payy bar.** လီနင်ဘောင်းဘီတစ်ထည် ပေးပါ။
Will it shrink in the wash?	**Shaw pee yin, ky'ownt thwarr ma larr?** လျှော်ပြီးရင် ကျုံ့သွားမလား။
Could you mend these shoes?	**Di phanat, chote payy bar larr?** ဒီဖိနပ်ချုပ်ပေးပါလား။
Could you resole these shoes?	**Di phanat sole, pyan htaet payy bar larr?** ဒီဖိနပ်ဆိုးလဲပြန်ထည့်ပေးပါလား။
When will they be ready?	**Bae dawt, ya ma lell?** ဘယ်တော့ရမလဲ။

| I'd like a can of shoe polish, please. | **Phanat ayaung tin si, taboo payy bar.** ဖိနပ်အရောင်တင်ဆီတစ်ဘူးပေးပါ။ |
| I'd like a pair of shoe laces, please. | **Shoo phanat kyohh, da z'own payy bar.** ရှူးဖိနပ်ကြိုးတစ်စုံပေးပါ။ |

10.4 At the hairdresser

Do I have to make an appointment?	**Appointment kyo yu ya ma larr?** အပွိုင့်မန့်ကြိုယူရမလား။
Can I come in right now?	**Akhoot, win lar loht ya bi larr?** အခုဝင်လာလို့ရပြီလား။
How long will I have to wait?	**Bae lout, saungt ya ownn ma lell?** ဘယ်လောက်စောင့်ရဦးမလဲ။
I'd like a shampoo.	**Gaungg shaw mae.** ခေါင်းလျှော်မယ်။
I'd like a haircut.	**Zabin nhyat mae.** ဆံပင်ညှပ်မယ်။
I'd like a shampoo for oily hair, please.	**Si myarr daet, zabin atwet, htote htarr daet, shampoo naet, shaw payy bar.** ဆီများတဲ့ဆံပင်အတွက်ထုတ်ထားတဲ့ ရှန်ပူနဲ့လျှော်ပေးပါ။
I'd like a shampoo for dry hair, please.	**Chout daet, zabin atwet, htote htarr daet, shampoo naet, shaw payy bar.** ခြောက်တဲ့ဆံပင်အတွက်ထုတ်ထားတဲ့ ရှန်ပူနဲ့လျှော်ပေးပါ။
I'd like an anti-dandruff shampoo.	**Bout pyout shampoo naet, shaw payy bar.** ဘောက်ပျောက်ရှန်ပူနဲ့ လျှော်ပေးပါ။
I'd like a color-rinse shampoo, please.	**Ayaung kyut daet, shampoo naet, shaw payy bar.** အရောင်ကျွတ်တဲ့ရှန်ပူနဲ့ လျှော်ပေးပါ။
I'd like a shampoo with conditioner, please.	**Pyawt zayy bar daet, shampoo naet, shaw payy bar.** ပျော့ဆေးပါတဲ့ရှန်ပူနဲ့ လျှော်ပေးပါ။

I'd like highlights, please.	**Highlight phout payy bar.** ဟိုင်းလိုက်ဖောက်ပေးပါ။
Do you have a color chart, please?	**Zabin a yaung dway, kyeet boht, sar oat sheet larr?** ဆံပင်အရောင်တွေကြည့်ဖို့စာအုပ်ရှိလား။
I'd like to keep the same color.	**Di a yaung bell, htarr mae.** ဒီအရောင်ပဲထားမယ်။
I'd like it darker.	**A yaung, po yint payy bar.** အရောင်ပိုရင့်ပေးပါ။
I'd like it lighter.	**A yaung, po phyawt payy bar.** အရောင်ပိုဖျော့ပေးပါ။
I'd like my hair dyed.	**Zabin sayy sohh mae.** ဆံပင်ဆေးဆိုးမယ်။
I don't want my hair-dyed.	**Zabin sayy ma sohh boo.** ဆံပင်ဆေးမဆိုးဘူး။
I'd like gel.	**Gel lein mae.** ဂျယ်လိမ်းမယ်။
I don't want lotion.	**Lotion ma lein boo.** လိုးရှင်းမလိမ်းဘူး။
I'd like short bangs.	**Shayt zabin toh toh, nhyat payy bar.** ရှေ့ဆံပင်တိုတို ညှပ်ပေးပါ။
Not too short at the back.	**Anout ko, a yann, ma toh boo.** အနောက်ကို အရမ်းမတိုဘူး။
Not too long.	**A yann, ma shay boo.** အရမ်းမရှည်ဘူး။
I'd like it curly.	**Kout mae.** ကောက်မယ်။
I don't like it too curly.	**A yann, ma kout boo.** အရမ်းမကောက်ဘူး။
It needs a little taken off.	**Nell nell, nhyat payy bar.** နည်းနည်းညှပ်ပေးပါ။
It needs a lot taken off.	**Myarr myarr, nhyat payy bar.** များများညှပ်ပေးပါ။

I'd like a completely different style.	**Zabin p'own, lone wa, pyaungg jin dae.** ဆံပင်ပုံ လုံးဝပြောင်းချင်တယ်။
I'd like it the same as in this photo.	**Di p'own htell ga, a taii, lote payy bar.** ဒီပုံထဲကအတိုင်း လုပ်ပေးပါ။
I'd like it the same as that woman's.	**Ae deet, amyohh thamee lo, lote payy bar.** အဲဒီအမျိုးသမီးလို လုပ်ပေးပါ။
Could you turn the drier up a bit?	**Drier go, nell nell mhyint payy bar larr.** ဒရိုင်ယာကိုနည်းနည်းမြှင့်ပေးပါလား။
Could you turn the drier down a bit?	**Drier go, nell nell nhaint payy bar larr.** ဒရိုင်ယာကို နည်းနည်းနှိမ့်ပေးပါလား။
I'd like a facial.	**Myet nhar sayy mae.** မျက်နှာဆေးမယ်။
I'd like a manicure.	**Let thell lote mae.** လက်သည်းလုပ်မယ်။
Could you trim my bangs please?	**Shayt zabin teet payy bar larr?** ရှေ့ဆံပင် တိပေးပါလား။
Could you trim my beard please?	**Mote sate mhwayy teet payy bar larr?** မုတ်ဆိတ်မွေးတိပေးပါလား။
Could you trim my moustache please?	**Nhakhann mhwayy teet payy bar larr?** နှုတ်ခမ်းမွေးတိပေးပါလား။
I'd like a shave, please.	**Mote sate yate mae.** မုတ်ဆိတ်ရိတ်မယ်။

ညှပ်ချင်တဲ့ပုံ ရှိလား။	What style did you have in mind?
ဘာအရောင်ဆိုးချင်လဲ။	What color did you want it?
အပူချိန်က အဆင်ပြေလား။	Is the temperature all right for you?
တစ်ခုခု ဖတ်မလား။	Would you like something to read?
တစ်ခုခု သောက်မလား။	Would you like a drink?

How do we get to Shwedagon Pagoda?
Shwedagon pha yarr go, bae lo, thwarr ya ma lell?

Take bus line 8.
Bus karr, nan bat shit, see thwarr bar.

You can also take a cab. It is easier.
Taxi see thwarr loht lell, ya dae. Po lwae dar bawt.

Okay, thanks.
Hote kaet, kyayy zoo bar.

11. Tourist Activities

11.1 Places of interest
11.2 Going out
11.3 Booking tickets

Local magazines such as Myanmore (myanmore.com) and
Frontier Myanmar (frontiermyanmar.net) have information
about events and places to visit. Have your hotel concierge write
down (in Burmese characters) the places you want to go to, so
you can show them to the cab driver, bus driver or train staff.

11.1 Places of interest

Where's the Tourist Information, please?	**Tourist information counter ga, bae mhar lell?** တိုးရစ်အင်ဖော်မေးရှင်းကောင်တာက ဘယ်မှာလဲ။
Do you have a city map?	**Myoht pya myay b'own, sheet larr?** မြို့ပြမြေပုံ ရှိလား။
Where is the museum?	**Pya dite ga, bae mhar lell?** ပြတိုက်က ဘယ်မှာလဲ။
Where can I find a church?	**Kharit yan, pha yarr kyaungg, bae mhar sheet lell?** ခရစ်ယာန်ဘုရားကျောင်း ဘယ်မှာရှိလဲ။
Could you give me some information about...?	**...akyaungg, nell nell, pyaww pya bar larr?** ...အကြောင်း နည်းနည်းပြောပြပါလား။
How much is this?	**Dar, bae lout lell?** ဒါဘယ်လောက်လဲ။
What are the main places of interest?	**Bae nay yar dway ga, sate win zarr boht akaungg zone lell?** ဘယ်နေရာတွေက စိတ်ဝင်စားဖို့အကောင်းဆုံးလဲ။

Could you point them out on the map?	**Myay b'own baw mhar, htout pya bar larr?** မြေပုံပေါ်မှာ ထောက်ပြပါလား။
What do you recommend?	**Bar akyan payy ma lell?** ဘာအကြံပေးမလဲ။
We'll be here for a few hours (3–4 hours).	**Di mhar, thone layy nar yi lout, nay mae.** ဒီမှာ ၃-၄ နာရီလောက်နေမယ်။
We'll be here for a week.	**Di mhar, da bat nay mae.** ဒီမှာ တစ်ပတ်နေမယ်။
We're interested in…	**…go, sate win zarr dae.** …ကို စိတ်ဝင်စားတယ်။
How long does it take?	**Bae lout kyar lell?** ဘယ်လောက်ကြာလဲ။
Where does it start?	**Bae ga sa lell?** ဘယ်ကစလဲ။
Where does it end?	**Bae mhar, sone lell?** ဘယ်မှာဆုံးလဲ။
Are there any boat trips?	**Hlay kha yee zin, sheet larr?** လှေခရီးစဉ်ရှိလား။
Where can we board?	**Bae ga, tet ya ma lell?** ဘယ်ကတက်ရမလဲ။
Are there any bus tours?	**Bus karr naet thwarr daet, kha yee zin, sheet larr?** ဘတ်စ်ကားနဲ့ သွားတဲ့ခရီးစဉ် ရှိလား။
Where do we get on?	**Bae ga, tet ya ma lell?** ဘယ်ကတက်ရမလဲ။
Is there a guide who speaks English?	**Ingalate zagarr pyaw tat daet, guide sheet larr?** အင်္ဂလိပ်စကားပြောတတ်တဲ့ ဂိုက်ရှိလား။
What trips can we take around the area?	**Di narr ta wite mhar, bae dway, thwarr loht ya lell?** ဒီနားတစ်ဝိုက်မှာ ဘယ်တွေသွားလို့ရလဲ။
Are there any excursions?	**Layt lar yayy, kha yee, sheet larr?** လေ့လာရေးခရီးရှိလား။

Where do they go?	**Thu doht, bae thwarr dar lell?** သူတို့ဘယ်သွားတာလဲ။
How long is the excursion?	**Layt lar yayy, kha yee ga, bae lout kyar lell?** လေ့လာရေးခရီးက ဘယ်လောက်ကြာလဲ။
We'd like to go to Shwedagon Pagoda.	**Shwedagon pha yarr, thwarr jin dae.** ရွှေတိဂုံဘုရား သွားချင်တယ်။
We'd like to go to Karaweik Palace.	**Karaweik nann daw, thwarr jin dae.** ကရဝိက်နန်းတော် သွားချင်တယ်။
How much does it cost to…?	**...go, bae lout lell?** ...ကို ဘယ်လောက်လဲ။
How much is the admission ticket?	**Win jayy, bae lout lell?** ဝင်ကြေးဘယ်လောက်လဲ။
How long do we stay in…?	**...mhar, bae lout kyar kyar, nay ma lell?** ...မှာ ဘယ်လောက်ကြာကြာနေမလဲ။
Are there any guided tours?	**Guide bar daet, kha yee zin dway, sheet larr?** ဂိုက်ပါတဲ့ ခရီးစဉ်တွေရှိလား။
Do you have an English tour?	**Ingalate lo pyaww daet, kha yee zin, sheet larr?** အင်္ဂလိပ်လိုပြောတဲ့ ခရီးစဉ်ရှိလား။
How much free time will we have there?	**Ae deet mhar, achain, bae lout ya ma lell?** အဲဒီမှာ အချိန်ဘယ်လောက်ရမလဲ။
We want to have a walk around.	**Lann shout kyeet jin dae.** လမ်းလျှောက်ကြည့်ချင်တယ်။
Can we hire a guide?	**Guide ngharr loht ya larr?** ဂိုက်ငှားလို့ရလား။
What time does…open?	**...ga, bae nha nar yi, phwint lell?** ...က ဘယ်နှစ်နာရီဖွင့်လဲ။
What time does…close?	**...ga, bae nha nar yi, pate lell?** ...က ဘယ်နှစ်နာရီပိတ်လဲ။

What days are…open?	**…ga, bae yet dway, phwint lell?** …က ဘယ်ရက်တွေဖွင့်လဲ။
What days are…closed?	**…ga, bae yet dway, pate lell?** …က ဘယ်ရက်တွေပိတ်လဲ။
What's the admission price?	**Win jayy, bae lout lell?** ဝင်ကြေးဘယ်လောက်လဲ။
Is there a child discount?	**Kha layy atwet, discount sheet larr?** ကလေးအတွက် ဒစ်စကောင့်ရှိလား။
Is there a student discount?	**Kyaungg tharr dway atwet, discount sheet larr?** ကျောင်းသားတွေအတွက် ဒစ်စကောင့်ရှိလား။
Is there a discount for senior citizens?	**Thet kyee ywae o dway atwet, discount sheet larr?** သက်ကြီးရွယ်အိုတွေအတွက် ဒစ်စကောင့်ရှိလား။
Can I film here?	**Video yite loht ya larr?** ဗီဒီယိုရိုက်လို့ရလား။
Do you have an English catalog?	**Ingalate lo, yayy htarr daet catalog, sheet larr?** အင်္ဂလိပ်လိုရေးထားတဲ့ကတ်တလော့ ရှိလား။
Do you have an English travel brochure?	**Ingalate lo, kha yee zin dway, yayy htarr daet, let kann sar zaung, sheet larr?** အင်္ဂလိပ်လိုခရီးစဉ်တွေရေးထားတဲ့ လက်ကမ်းစာစောင်ရှိလား။

 Going out

Myanmar has an increasing number of bars, night clubs and late-night coffee shops. Try to see the cultural performance at Karaweik Palace one evening, which has a Burmese buffet.

| What's on tonight? | **Di nya, bar sheet lell?** ဒီညဘာရှိလဲ။ |

Do you have this week's entertainment guide?	**Di apat atwet, phyaw phyay yayy, a si a zin, lann nhyon, sheet larr?** ဒီအပတ်အတွက် ဖျော်ဖြေရေးအစီအစဉ်လမ်းညွှန် ရှိလား။
We want to go to…	**…go, thwarr jin dae.** …ကို သွားချင်တယ်။
What's playing at the cinema?	**Yote shin y'own mhar, bar karr, pya nay lell?** ရုပ်ရှင်ရုံမှာဘာကားပြနေလဲ။
This film has subtitles.	**Di yote shin ga, sar dann htohh dae.** ဒီရုပ်ရှင်က စာတန်းထိုးတယ်။
This film is dubbed in English.	**Di yote shin ga, ingalate than naet bar.** ဒီရုပ်ရှင်က အင်္ဂလိပ်သံနဲ့ပါ။
What's on at the theater?	**Pya zat y'own mhar, bar pya nay lell?** ပြဇာတ်ရုံမှာ ဘာပြနေလဲ။
Where can I find a good nightclub?	**Di narr mhar, bae nightclub kaungg lell?** ဒီနားမှာ ဘယ်နိုက်ကလပ်ကောင်းလဲ။
Should I/we dress up?	**Pwell tet wit s'own, wit ya mhar larr?** ပွဲတက်ဝတ်စုံ ဝတ်ရမှာလား။
What time does the show start?	**Pya pwell ga, bae achain, sa ma lell?** ပြပွဲက ဘယ်အချိန်စမလဲ။
Could you reserve some tickets for us?	[male speaker] **Kya naw doht atwet, booking lote htarr payy bar larr?** ကျွန်တော်တို့အတွက် ဘွတ်ကင်လုပ်ထားပေးပါလား။ [female speaker] **Kya ma doht atwet, booking lote htarr payy bar larr?** ကျွန်မတို့အတွက် ဘွတ်ကင်လုပ်ထားပေးပါလား။
We'd like to book three seats.	**Thone yout sar, booking lote chin bar dae.** သုံးယောက်စာ ဘွတ်ကင်လုပ်ချင်ပါတယ်။

We'd like to book a table for three.	**Thone yout sar zabwell, booking lote chin bar dae.** သုံးယောက်စားပွဲ ဘွတ်ကင်လုပ်ချင်ပါတယ်။

11.3 Booking tickets

Could I reserve three seats for the eight o'clock performance?	**Shit nar yi pwell atwet, thone yout sar, booking lote chin bar dae?** ရှစ်နာရီပွဲအတွက် သုံးယောက်စာဘွတ်ကင် လုပ်ချင်ပါတယ်။
Could I reserve front row seats?	**Shayt dann, booking lote loht, ya ma larr?** ရှေ့တန်း ဘွတ်ကင်လုပ်လို့ရမလား။
Could I reserve a table for eight people at the front?	**Shayt dann mhar, shit yout sar, booking lote chin bar dae?** ရှေ့တန်းမှာ ရှစ်ယောက်စာဘွတ်ကင် လုပ်ချင်ပါတယ်။
Could I reserve seats in the middle?	**Alae mhar, booking lote loht, ya ma larr?** အလယ်မှာ ဘွတ်ကင်လုပ်လို့ရမလား။
Could I reserve a table in the middle?	**Alae mhar, zabwell ta lone lout, booking lote loht, ya ma larr?** အလယ်မှာ စားပွဲတစ်လုံးလောက် ဘွတ်ကင်လုပ်လို့ရမလား။
Are there any seats left for tonight?	**Di nya atwet, kh'own kyan thayy larr?** ဒီညအတွက် ခုံကျန်သေးလား။
How much is a ticket?	**Let mhat, dazaung, bae lout lell?** လက်မှတ်တစ်စောင် ဘယ်လောက်လဲ။
When can I pick up the tickets?	**Bae achain, let mhat, lar yu ya ma lell?** ဘယ်အချိန်လက်မှတ်လာယူရမလဲ။
I've got a reservation. My name's…	**…nan mae naet, booking lote htarr dae.** …နာမည်နဲ့ ဘွတ်ကင်လုပ်ထားတယ်။

ဘယ်ပွဲအတွက် ဘွတ်ကင်လုပ်မှာလဲ။	Which performance would you like to reserve tickets for?
ဘယ်မှာထိုင်ချင်လဲ။	Where would you like to sit?
အားလုံးကုန်သွားပြီ။	Everything's sold out.
မတ်တပ်ရပ်ကြည့်ရမှာပါ။	It's standing room only.
ရှေ့ တန်းအတွက်ပဲ လက်မှတ်ကျန်တော့တယ်။	We've only got tickets for the front row.
နောက်တန်းအတွက်ပဲ လက်မှတ်ကျန်တော့တယ်။	We've only got tickets for the back row.
လက်မှတ်ဘယ်နှစ်စောင်ယူမလဲ။	How many tickets would you like?
နာရီမထိုးခင် လက်မှတ်လာယူရပါမယ်။	You'll have to pick up the tickets before ...o'clock.
လက်မှတ်ပြပါ။	Tickets, please.
ခုံကဒီမှာပါ။	This is your seat.
ဆောရီးပါ။ ခုံမှားနေပါတယ်။	Sorry, you are in the wrong seat.

12. Sports & Activities

12.1 Sports

cycling **set bein see** စက်ဘီးစီး	fishing **ngarr mhyarr** ငါးမျှား	tennis **tennis** တင်းနစ်
mountain climbing **taung tet** တောင်တက်	soccer **baw lone** ဘောလုံး	table tennis **zabwell tin tennis** စားပွဲတင်တင်းနစ်
martial arts **ko khan pyin nyar** ကိုယ်ခံပညာ	badminton **kyet taung yite** ကြက်တောင်ရိုက်	golf **gout yite** ဂေါက်ရိုက်
swimming **yay koo** ရေကူး	volleyball **baw li baww** ဘော်လီဘော	caneball **jinn lone** ခြင်းလုံး
hiking **taung tet** တောင်တက်	basketball **basketball** ဘက်စကတ်ဘော	

Where's the stadium? — **Arr gazarr gwinn ga, bae mhar lell?** အားကစားကွင်း ကဘယ်မှာလဲ။

Where's the gym? — **Gym ga, bae mhar lell?** ဂျင်က ဘယ်မှာလဲ။

Can we see a soccer match? — **Baw lone pwell, kyeet loht ya larr?** ဘောလုံးပွဲ ကြည့်လို့ရလား။

Can we see a basketball game? — **Basketball pwell, kyeet loht ya larr?** ဘက်စကတ်ဘောပွဲ ကြည့်လို့ရလား။

Can we see a badminton game? — **Kyat taung yite pwell, kyeet loht ya larr?** ကြက်တောင်ရိုက်ပွဲ ကြည့်လို့ရလား။

When does the game begin?	**Bae achain, pwell sa ma lell?** ဘယ်အချိန်ပွဲစမလဲ။
What's the score?	**Bae nhamhat ya lell?** ဘယ်နှစ်မှတ်ရလဲ။
I've won.	**Nai dae.** နိုင်တယ်။
I've lost.	**Sh'own dae.** ရှုံးတယ်။
We're even.	**Tha yay bell.** သရေပဲ။

12.2 At the beach

Is it far (to walk) to the sea?	**Pin lae go, lann shout thwarr yin, wayy larr?** ပင်လယ်ကို လမ်းလျှောက်သွားရင် ဝေးလား။
Is there a swimming pool around here?	**Di narr mhar, yay koo kan, sheet larr?** ဒီနားမှာ ရေကူးကန်ရှိလား။
Is there a beach around here?	**Di narr mhar, kann jay, sheet larr?** ဒီနားမှာ ကမ်းခြေရှိလား။
Are there any rocks here?	**Di mhar, kyout saung dway, sheet larr?** ဒီမှာကျောက်ဆောင်တွေရှိလား။
When's high tide?	**Bae achain, yay tet lell?** ဘယ်အချိန် ရေတက်လဲ။
When's low tide?	**Bae achain, yay kya lell?** ဘယ်အချိန် ရေကျလဲ။
What's the water temperature?	**Yay apu jain, bae lout sheet lell?** ရေအပူချိန် ဘယ်လောက်ရှိလဲ။
Is it deep here?	**Di mhar, yay net larr?** ဒီမှာရေနက်လား။
Is it safe for children to swim here?	**Di mhar, kha layy dway, yay koo loht, ya larr?** ဒီမှာကလေးတွေ ရေကူးလို့ရလား။

Are there any currents?	**Hlaii sheet larr?** လှိုင်းရှိလား။
Are there any sharks?	**Nga mann sheet larr?** ငါးမန်းရှိလား။
Are there any jellyfish?	**Jelly ngarr sheet larr?** ဂျယ်လီငါးရှိလား။
What does that flag mean?	**Aet alan ga, bar adate bae lell?** အဲ့အလံက ဘာအဓိပ္ပါယ်လဲ။
What does that buoy mean?	**Ae deet, yay baw mhar, paw nay dar ga, bar lell?** အဲဒီ ရေပေါ်မှာပေါ်နေတာက ဘာလဲ။
Is there a lifeguard on duty?	**Kae sae yayy thamarr dway, sheet larr?** ကယ်ဆယ်ရေးသမားတွေရှိလား။
Where can I get a chair?	**Kh'own, bae mhar ya nai ma lell?** ခုံ ဘယ်မှာရနိုင်မလဲ။
Where can I get a beach umbrella?	**Htee, bae mhar ya nai ma lell?** ထီး ဘယ်မှာရနိုင်မလဲ။
Where can I get a towel?	**Thabet, bae mhar ya nai ma lell?** သဘက် ဘယ်မှာရနိုင်မလဲ။
Where can I get sunglasses?	**Nay gar myet mhan, bae mhar ya nai ma lell?** နေကာမျက်မှန် ဘယ်မှာရနိုင်မလဲ။
Where can I get sunscreen?	**Nay laung dan khan daet lotion, bae mhar ya nai ma lell?** နေလောင်ဒဏ်ခံတဲ့လိုးရှင်း ဘယ်မှာရနိုင်မလဲ။
Where can I have a shower?	**Bae mhar, yay chohh loht ya lell?** ဘယ်မှာရေချိုးလို့ရလဲ။

Danger **an da yae, sheet thi** အန္တရာယ်ရှိသည်	No Swimming/Fishing Here **yay ma koo ya / ngarr ma mhyarr ya** ရေမကူးရ / ငါးမမျှားရ

12.3 Trekking

| How long is the walk? | **Lann shout thwarr yin, bae lout kyar ma lell?** လမ်းလျှောက်သွားရင် ဘယ်လောက်ကြာမလဲ။ |

How long does it take from here?

Di ga nay, bae lout kyar ma lell? ဒီကနေ ဘယ်လောက်ကြာမလဲ။

Are the paths in [good/bad] condition?

Lann [kaungg/sohh] larr? လမ်း [ကောင်း / ဆိုး] လား။

Is the walk difficult?

Lann shout thwarr ya dar, khet larr? လမ်းလျှောက်သွားရတာ ခက်လား။

Where can we find a guide?

Guide, bae mhar, shar loht ya ma lell? ဂိုက်ဘယ်မှာရှာလို့ရမလဲ။

What should I bring?

Bar dway, yu thwarr boht lo lell? ဘာတွေယူသွားဖို့လိုလဲ။

Can we get food and water along the way?

Lann mhar, a sarr a thout, ya nai ma larr? လမ်းမှာအစားအသောက်ရနိုင်မလား။

Where can we stay?

Bae mhar, tell loht ya ma lell? ဘယ်မှာတည်းလို့ရမလဲ။

What is the accommodation like?

Tell ya maet nay yar ga, bae lo myohh lell? တည်းရမယ့်နေရာက ဘယ်လိုမျိုးလဲ။

Is it okay to walk this way?

Di lann ga, thwarr loht ya larr? ဒီလမ်းကသွားလို့ရလား။

Do we walk back the way we came?

Alar lann ataii, pyan shout ya mhar larr? အလာလမ်းအတိုင်း ပြန်လျှောက်ရမှာလား။

Are there any dangerous animals around here?

Di narr mhar, an da yae sheet daet, tarate san dway, sheet larr? ဒီနားမှာ အန္တရာယ်ရှိတဲ့တိရစ္ဆာန်တွေရှိလား။

Is this area safe?

Di nay yar ga, an da yae kinn larr? ဒီနေရာက အန္တရာယ်ကင်းလား။

Are there any...?	**...sheet larr?** ...ရှိလား။
Can we stay here tonight please?	[male speaker] **Kya naw doht, di nya, di mhar, tell loht ya ma larr?** ကျွန်တော်တို့ဒီည ဒီမှာတည်းလို့ရမလား။
	[female speaker] **Kya ma doht, di nya, di mhar, tell loht ya ma larr?** ကျွန်မတို့ဒီည ဒီမှာတည်းလို့ရမလား။
Can I stay here tonight please?	[male speaker] **Kya naw, di nya, di mhar, tell loht ya ma larr?** ကျွန်တော်ဒီည ဒီမှာတည်းလို့ရမလား။
	[female speaker] **Kya ma, di nya, di mhar, tell loht ya ma larr?** ကျွန်မဒီည ဒီမှာတည်းလို့ရမလား။
It's too dark to keep walking.	**Lann set shout poht, a yann, mhaung nay bi.** လမ်းဆက်လျှောက်ဖို့ အရမ်းမှောင်နေပြီ။
We are afraid we will get lost.	[male speaker] **Kya naw doht, lann pyout thwarr mhar, kyout dae.** ကျွန်တော်တို့ လမ်းပျောက်သွားမှာကြောက်တယ်။
	[female speaker] **Kya ma doht, lann pyout thwarr mhar, kyout dae.** ကျွန်မတို့ လမ်းပျောက်သွားမှာကြောက်တယ်။
Thank you for your kindness.	**Kyin nar, ga yoot site payy daet atwet, kyayy zoo tin bar dae.** ကြင်နာရှုစိုက်ပေးတဲ့အတွက် ကျေးဇူးတင်ပါတယ်။

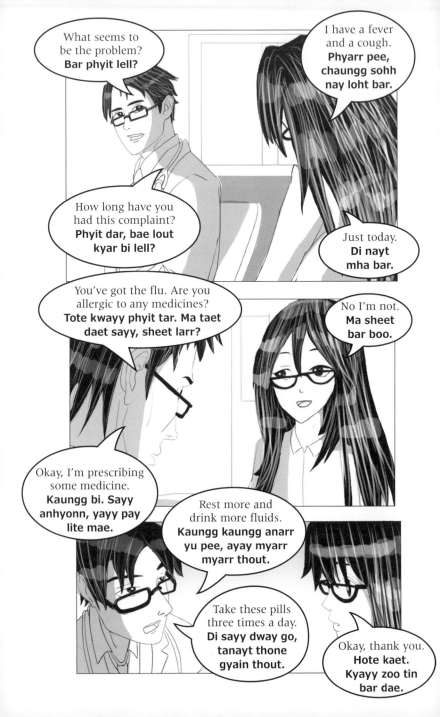

13. Health Matters

If you become ill in Myanmar, there are special departments in many large hospitals with better facilities for foreigners, although they are more expensive. Otherwise, go to the nearest clinic. You should register first, see the doctor and have your illness treated, and then settle the bill.

13.1 Calling a doctor

Could you call (get) a doctor quickly, please?	**Sayar win, myan myan, khaw payy bar larr?** ဆရာဝန်မြန်မြန်ခေါ်ပေးပါလား။
When are the doctor's working hours?	**Sayar win, bae achain, htai lell?** ဆရာဝန်ဘယ်အချိန်ထိုင်လဲ။
When can the doctor come?	**Sayar win, bae achain, lar nai ma lell?** ဆရာဝန်ဘယ်အချိန်လာနိုင်မလဲ။
Could I make an appointment to see the doctor?	**Sayar win pya boht, booking lote loht, ya ma larr?** ဆရာဝန်ပြဖို့ ဘွတ်ကင်လုပ်လို့ရမလား။
I've got an appointment to see the doctor at four o'clock.	**Layy nar yi mhar, sayar win pya boht, booking lote htarr dae.** လေးနာရီမှာ ဆရာဝန်ပြဖို့ ဘွတ်ကင်လုပ်ထားတယ်။
Which pharmacy is on night duty?	**Bae sayy zai ga, nya bet, phwint lell?** ဘယ်ဆေးဆိုင်က ညဘက်ဖွင့်လဲ။

| Which pharmacy is on weekend duty? | **Bae sayy zai ga, sa nay ta ninn ga nway, phwint lell?** ဘယ်ဆေးဆိုင်က စနေ၊ တနင်္ဂနွေဖွင့်လဲ။ |

13.2 What's wrong?

I don't feel well.	**Nay loht, ma kaungg boo.** နေလို့မကောင်းဘူး။
I'm ill.	**Phyarr nay dae.** ဖျားနေတယ်။
I'm dizzy.	**Gaungg muu nay dae.** ခေါင်းမူးနေတယ်။
I feel sick (nauseous).	**An jin nay dae.** အန်ချင်နေတယ်။
I've got a cold.	**A aye, meet htarr dae.** အအေးမိထားတယ်။
I've got a cough.	**Chaungg sohh nay dae.** ချောင်းဆိုးနေတယ်။
I've got diarrhea.	**Wann thwarr nay dae.** ဝမ်းသွားနေတယ်။
I have trouble breathing.	**Athet shu kyet nay dae.** အသက်ရှူကြပ်နေတယ်။
I feel tired all over.	**Tago lone nyaungg nay dae.** တစ်ကိုယ်လုံးညောင်းနေတယ်။
It hurts here.	**Di mhar, nar nay dae.** ဒီမှာနာနေတယ်။
I've been sick (vomited).	**An nay dae.** အန်နေတယ်။
I'm running a temperature of…degrees	**Aphyarr…degree, sheet dae.** အဖျား…ဒီဂရီရှိတယ်။
I've been stung by an insect.	**Insect a kite, khan ya dae.** အင်းဆက်အကိုက်ခံရတယ်။
I've been stung by a jellyfish.	**Jelly ngarr a kite, khan ya dae.** ဂျယ်လီငါးအကိုက်ခံရတယ်။
I've been bitten by a dog.	**Khwayy kite khan ya dae.** ခွေးကိုက်ခံရတယ်။

I've been bitten by a snake.

Mway kite khan ya dae.
မြွေကိုက်ခံရတယ်။

I've cut myself (with a knife).

Darr sha htarr dae. ဓားရှထားတယ်။

I've burned myself.

Apu laung htarr dae.
အပူလောင်ထားတယ်။

I've grazed myself.

Pwonn htarr dae. ပွန်းထားတယ်။

I've had a fall.

Chaw lell htarr dae. ချော်လဲထားတယ်။

13.3 The consultation

I've sprained my ankle.

Chay dout, khout thwarr dae.
ခြေထောက်ခေါက်သွားတယ်။

Could I have a female doctor, please?

A myohh tha mee, sayar win naet, pya jin dae?
အမျိုးသမီးဆရာဝန်နဲ့ပြချင်တယ်။

I'd like the morning-after pill.

Tarr zayy payy bar.
တားဆေးပေးပါ။

I'm a diabetic.

See jo, sheet dae. ဆီးချိုရှိတယ်။

I'm asthmatic.

Pann nar yin kyat, sheet dae.
ပန်းနာရင်ကြပ်ရှိတယ်။

I'm allergic to penicillin.

Pennicillin naet, ma taet boo.
ပင်နီဆလင်နဲ့မတည့်ဘူး။

I'm allergic to amoxicillin.

Amoxicillin naet, ma taet boo.
အမောက်ဆလင်နဲ့မတည့်ဘူး။

I have a heart condition.

Nha lone yaww gar, sheet dae.
နှလုံးရောဂါရှိတယ်။

I'm five months pregnant.

Ko win, ngarr la, sheet bi.
ကိုယ်ဝန်ငါးလရှိပြီ။

I'm on a diet.	**Wate shawt nay dae.** ဂိတ်လျှော့နေတယ်။
I'm on medication.	**Sayy thout nay dae.** ဆေးသောက်နေတယ်။
I'm on the pill.	**Tarr zayy, thout nay dae.** တားဆေးသောက်နေတယ်။
I've had a heart attack once before.	**Takhar ga, heart attack, phyit phoo dae.** တစ်ခါက ဟတ်အတက်ဖြစ်ဖူးတယ်။
I've had a(n)…operation.	**…khwell sate htarr dae.** …ခွဲစိတ်ထားတယ်။
I've been ill recently.	**Di yet paii, phyarr nay dae.** ဒီရက်ပိုင်းဖျားနေတယ်။

မတည့်တာရှိလား။	Do you have any allergies?
လက်ရှိသောက်နေတဲ့ဆေးရှိလား။	Are you on any medication?
ဂိတ်လျှော့နေလား။	Are you on a diet?
ကိုယ်ဝန်ရှိလား။	Are you pregnant?
မေးခိုင်ကာကွယ်ဆေးထိုးထားလား။	Have you had a tetanus injection?
ဖြစ်တာ ဘယ်လောက်ကြာပြီလဲ။	How long have you had these complaints?
အရင်က ဖြစ်ဖူးလား။	Have you had this trouble before?
အကျီ်ကြယ်သီး ဖြုတ်လိုက်ပါ။	Open your shirt, please.
ခါးအထိ ချွတ်လိုက်ပါ။	Strip to the waist, please.
အကျီ်ဘယ်ဘက်လက် တင်လိုက်ပါ။	Roll up your left sleeve, please.
အကျီ်ညာဘက်လက် တင်လိုက်ပါ။	Roll up your right sleeve, please.

13.4 The diagnosis

စိုးရိမ်စရာမရှိပါဘူး။	It's nothing serious.
...ကျိုးသွားတာ။	Your...is broken.
...ခေါက်သွားတာ။	You've got a sprained...
...ပြဲသွားတာ။	You've got a torn...
ပိုးဝင်သွားတာ။	You've got an infection.
နည်းနည်းယောင်နေတယ်။	You've got some inflammation.
အူအတက်ယောင်နေတာ။	You've got appendicitis.
လေပြွန်ယောင်နေတာ။	You've got bronchitis.
ကာလသားရောဂါဖြစ်နေတာ။	You've got a venereal disease.
တုပ်ကွေးမိနေတာ။	You've got the flu.
ဟတ်အတက်ဖြစ်သွားတာ။	You've had a heart attack.
အဆုတ်ရောင်နေတာ။	You've got pneumonia.
အစာအိမ်ယောင်နေတာ။	You've got gastritis.
ပြည်တည်နေတာ။	You've got an ulcer.
အရွတ်ပြဲသွားတာ။	You've pulled a muscle.
မိန်းမကိုယ်ပိုးဝင်သွားတာ။	You've got a vaginal infection.
အစာအဆိပ်ဖြစ်တာ။	You've got food poisoning.
အပူရှပ်တာ။	You've got sunstroke.
...နဲ့မတည့်ဘူး။	You're allergic to...
ကိုယ်ဝန်ရှိနေတယ်။	You're pregnant.
သွေးစစ်ကြည့်ချင်တယ်။	I'd like to have your blood tested.
ဆီးစစ်ကြည့်ချင်တယ်။	I'd like to have your urine tested.
ဂမ်းစစ်ကြည့်ချင်တယ်။	I'd like to have your stool tested.
ချုပ်ရမယ်။	It needs stitches.
အထူးကုဥ္ဏန်ပေးလိုက်မယ်။	I'm referring you to specialist.
ဆေးရုံလွှတ်လိုက်မယ်။	I'm sending you to the hospital.
ဓာတ်မှန်ရိုက်ရမယ်။	You'll need some x-rays taken.
ခွဲစိတ်ရမယ်။	You'll need an operation.

I need something for diarrhea.	**Wann thwarr nay loht, sayy lo jin dae.** ဝမ်းသွားနေလို့ ဆေးလိုချင်တယ်။
I need something for a cold.	**A aye meet nay loht, sayy lo jin dae.** အအေးမိနေလို့ ဆေးလိုချင်တယ်။
I've got a stomach ulcer.	**A sar eain mhar, pyi tae nay dae.** အစာအိမ်မှာ ပြည်တည်နေတယ်။
I've got my period.	**Yar thi lar nay dae.** ရာသီလာနေတယ်။
Is it contagious?	**Kuu larr?** ကူးလား။
How long do I have to stay in bed?	**Ate yar htell mhar, bae lout nay ya ma lell?** အိပ်ရာထဲမှာ ဘယ်လောက်နေရမလဲ။
How long do I have to stay in the hospital?	**Sayy y'own mhar, bae lout nay ya ma lell?** ဆေးရုံမှာဘယ်လောက်နေရမလဲ။
Do I have to go on a special diet?	**A sarr, shaung ya ma larr?** အစားရှောင်ရမလား။
Am I allowed to travel?	**Kha yee, thwarr loht ya larr?** ခရီးသွားလို့ရလား။
Can I make another appointment?	**Ta charr appointment, lote loht ya larr?** တခြားအပွိုင့်မန့်လုပ်လို့ရလား။
How do I take this medicine?	**Di sayy go, bae lo thout ya mhar lell?** ဒီဆေးကို ဘယ်လိုသောက်ရမှာလဲ။

13.5 Medications and prescriptions

ပဋိဇီဝဆေးပေးလိုက်မယ်။	I'm prescribing antibiotics.
ချောင်းဆိုးပျောက်ဆေးပေးလိုက်မယ်။	I'm prescribing a cough mixture.
စိတ်ငြိမ်ဆေးပေးလိုက်မယ်။	I'm prescribing a tranquilizer.
အကိုက်အခဲပျောက်ဆေးပေးလိုက်မယ်။	I'm prescribing painkillers.

များများအနားယူ။	Have lots of rest.
အိမ်ထဲမှာပဲနေ။	Stay indoors.
အိပ်ရာထဲမှာပဲနေ။	Stay in bed.
မနက်ဖြန်ပြန်လာခဲ့။	Come back tomorrow.
သုံးရက်ပြည့်ရင်ပြန်လာခဲ့။	Come back in three days' time.

How many pills
  each time?

Ta khar thout, bae nha lone lell?
တစ်ခါသောက် ဘယ်နှစ်လုံးလဲ။

How many drops
  each time?

Ta khar thout, bae nha set lell?
တစ်ခါသောက် ဘယ်နှစ်စက်လဲ။

How many spoonfuls
  each time?

Ta khar thout, bae nha zonn lell?
တစ်ခါသောက် ဘယ်နှစ်ဇွန်းလဲ။

How many tablets
  each time?

Ta khar thout, bae nha pyarr lell?
တစ်ခါသောက် ဘယ်နှစ်ပြားလဲ။

How many injections
  each time?

Ta khar htohh, bae nha lone lell?
တစ်ခါထိုး ဘယ်နှစ်လုံးလဲ။

How many times a day?

Ta nayt, bae nha jain lell?
တစ်နေ့ဘယ်နှစ်ကြိမ်လဲ။

I've forgotten my
  medication.

**Thout nay daet sayy dway,
mayt nay dae.** သောက်နေတဲ့ဆေးတွေ
မေ့နေတယ်။

At home I take…

Eain mhar,...thout tae.
အိမ်မှာ...သောက်တယ်။

Could you write a
  prescription for me,
  please?

Sayy anhyonn, yayy payy bar larr?
ဆေးအညွှန်းရေးပေးပါလား။

rub on
pwut lein bar
ပွတ်လိမ်းပါ

before meals
a sar ma sarr mi
အစာမစားမီ

after meals
a sar sarr pee
အစာစားပြီး

for…days
…yet sar
…ရက်စာ

injections
htohh sayy
ထိုးဆေး

ointment
lein sayy
လိမ်းဆေး

spoonful
zonn
ဇွန်း

teaspoonful
laphet yay zonn
လက်ဖက်ရည်ဇွန်း

finish the prescription
sayy anhyonn a taii,
k'own aung thout
ဆေးအညွှန်းအတိုင်း
ကုန်အောင်သောက်

every…hours
…nar yi charr
…နာရီခြား

swallow
myo cha bar
မျိုချပါ

…times a day
ta nayt…jain
တစ်နေ့…ကြိမ်

take (drink)
thout par
သောက်ပါ

13.6 At the dentist

Do you know a good
dentist?

Thwarr sayar win, kaungg kaungg,
theet larr?
သွားဆရာပန်ကောင်းကောင်းသိလား။

Could you make a
dentist's appointment
for me?

Thwarr sayar win naet, yet chein,
yu payy bar larr?
သွားဆရာပန်နဲ့ ရက်ချိန်းယူပေးပါလား။

It's urgent.

A yayy kyee nay dae.
အရေးကြီးနေတယ်။

Can I come in today,
please?

Di nayt, lar loht ya ma larr?
ဒီနေ့လာလို့ရမလား။

I have a (terrible)
toothache.

Thwarr (a yann) kite nay dae.
သွားအရမ်းကိုက်နေတယ်။

Could you prescribe/give
me a painkiller?

Thwarr kite pyout sayy, payy bar larr?
သွားကိုက်ပျောက်ဆေး ပေးပါလား။

I've got a broken tooth.	**Thwarr kyohh thwarr bi.** သွားကျိုးသွားပြီ။
I've got a broken crown.	**Swut htarr daet thwarr, paet thwarr bi.** စွပ်ထားတဲ့သွားပဲ့သွားပြီ။
I've got a broken denture.	**An gat, kyohh thwarr bi.** အံကပ်ကျိုးသွားပြီ။
My filling's come out.	**Phar htarr dar, kyut thwarr bi.** ဖာထားတာကျွတ်သွားပြီ။
I'd like a local anesthetic.	**Ht'own zayy, htohh mae.** ထုံဆေးထိုးမယ်။
I don't want a local anesthetic.	**Ht'own zayy, ma htohh jin boo.** ထုံဆေးမထိုးချင်ဘူး။

ထုံဆေးထိုးမယ်။	I'm giving you a local anaesthetic.

Could you do a temporary repair?	**Yar yi, lote payy loht ya larr?** ယာယီလုပ်ပေးလို့ရလား။
I don't want this tooth pulled.	**Di thwarr, ma nhote chin boo.** ဒီသွားမနုတ်ချင်ဘူး။

14. Emergencies

14.1 Asking for help

Help!	**Ku nyi bar!** ကူညီပါ။
Get help, quickly!	**Myan myan, a ku a nyi, taungg bar!** မြန်မြန်အကူအညီတောင်းပါ။
Fire!	**Mee!** မီး။
Police!	**Yell!** ရဲ။
Get a doctor!	**Sayar win, khaw payy bar!** ဆရာဝန်ခေါ်ပေးပါ။
Quick!/Hurry!	**Myan myan!** မြန်မြန်။
Watch out!/Be careful!	**Tha deet htarr!** သတိထား။
Danger!	**An da yae sheet dae!** အန္တရာယ်ရှိတယ်။
Stop!	**Yat!** ရပ်။
Get your hands off me!	**Let phae!** လက်ဖယ်။
Let go!	**Hlwut!** လွှတ်။
Stop, thief!	**Yat, tha khohh!** ရပ်၊ သူခိုး။
Could you help me, please?	**Ku nyi payy bar larr?** ကူညီပေးပါလား။
Where's the police station?	**Yell sa khann, bae mhar lell?** ရဲစခန်းဘယ်မှာလဲ။

161

Where's the emergency exit?	**Ayayy baw, htwet pout, bae mhar lell?** အရေးပေါ်ထွက်ပေါက် ဘယ်မှာလဲ။
Where's the fire escape?	**Ayayy baw, hlay garr, bae mhar lell?** အရေးပေါ်လှေကား ဘယ်မှာလဲ။
Call the fire department!	**Mee that, khaw bar!** မီးသတ်ခေါ်ပါ။
Call the police!	**Yell, khaw bar!** ရဲခေါ်ပါ။
Call an ambulance!	**Lunar tin karr, khaw bar!** လူနာတင်ကားခေါ်ပါ။
Where's the nearest phone?	**A nee sone, phone ga, bae mhar lell?** အနီးဆုံးဖုန်းက ဘယ်မှာလဲ။
Could I use your phone?	**Phone, khana ngharr loht, ya ma larr?** ဖုန်းခဏငှားလို့ရမလား။
What's the emergency number?	**Ayayy baw, nan bat, bae lout lell?** အရေးပေါ်နံပါတ်က ဘယ်လောက်လဲ။
What's the number for the police?	**Yell sa khann, phone nan bat ga, bae lout lell?** ရဲစခန်းဖုန်းနံပါတ်က ဘယ်လောက်လဲ။

14.2 Lost items

I've lost my wallet.	**Petsan ate, pyout thwarr dae.** ပိုက်ဆံအိတ်ပျောက်သွားတယ်။
I've lost my laptop.	**Laptop, pyout thwarr dae.** လပ်တော့ပျောက်သွားတယ်။
I've lost my passport.	**Passport, pyout thwarr dae.** ပတ်စ်ပို့ပျောက်သွားတယ်။
I've lost my phone.	**Phone, pyout thwarr dae.** ဖုန်းပျောက်သွားတယ်။
I lost my phone here yesterday.	**Manayt ga, di mhar, phone, pyout thwarr dae.** မနေ့က ဒီမှာဖုန်းပျောက်သွားတယ်။

I left my wallet here.	**Di mhar, petsan ate, kyan gaet dae.** ဒီမှာပိုက်ဆံအိတ်ကျန်ခဲ့တယ်။
Did you find my wallet?	[male speaker] **Kya nawt petsan ate, twayt larr?** ကျွန်တော့်ပိုက်ဆံအိတ်တွေ့လား။
	[female speaker] **Kya ma petsan ate, twayt larr?** ကျွန်မပိုက်ဆံအိတ်တွေ့လား။
It was right here.	**Di mhar bell, sheet nay gaet dar.** ဒီမှာပဲရှိနေခဲ့တာ။
It's very valuable.	**Ae dar ga, a yann, tan bohh sheet dae.** အဲဒါက အရမ်းတန်ဖိုးရှိတယ်။
Where's the lost and found office?	**Pyit see pyout htar na, bae mhar lell?** ပစ္စည်းပျောက်ရှာန ဘယ်မှာလဲ။

14.3 Accidents

There's been an accident.	**Accident phyit htarr dae.** အက်ဆီးဒင့်ဖြစ်ထားတယ်။
Someone's fallen into the water.	**Lu ta yout, yay htell, kya thwarr dae.** လူတစ်ယောက် ရေထဲကျသွားတယ်။
There's a fire.	**Mee laung nay dae.** မီးလောင်နေတယ်။
Is anyone hurt?	**Dan yar ya daet lu, sheet larr?** ဒဏ်ရာရတဲ့လူရှိလား။
Nobody has been injured.	**Dan yar ya daet lu, ma sheet boo.** ဒဏ်ရာရတဲ့လူမရှိဘူး။
Someone has been injured.	**Lu ta yout, dan yar ya htarr dae.** လူတစ်ယောက် ဒဏ်ရာရထားတယ်။
Someone's still trapped inside the car.	**Lu ta yout, karr htell mhar, pate meet nay dae.** လူတစ်ယောက် ကားထဲမှာပိတ်မိနေတယ်။

It's not too bad.	**A yann gyee, a chay a nay, ma sohh boo.** အရမ်းကြီးအခြေအနေမဆိုးဘူး။
Don't worry.	**Ma sohh yain bar naet.** မစိုးရိမ်ပါနဲ့။
Leave everything the way it is, please.	**Arr lone, thoot nay yar naet thu, htarr htarr bar.** အားလုံးသူနေရာနဲ့သူ ထားထားပါ။
I want to talk to the police first.	**A yin zone, yell naet, sagarr pyaww jin dae.** အရင်ဆုံးရဲနဲ့စကားပြောချင်တယ်။
I want to take a photo first.	**A yin zone, dat p'own, yite chin dae.** အရင်ဆုံးဓာတ်ပုံရိုက်ချင်တယ်။
Here's my name, mobile number and address.	[male speaker] **Di mhar, kya nawt nan mae, phone nan bat naet, late sar bar.** ဒီမှာကျွန်တော့်နာမည်၊ ဖုန်းနံပါတ်နဲ့ လိပ်စာပါ။
	[female speaker] **Di mhar, kya ma nan mae, phone nan bat naet, late sar bar.** ဒီမှာကျွန်မနာမည်၊ ဖုန်းနံပါတ်နဲ့ လိပ်စာပါ။
May I have your name, phone number and address?	**Nan mae, phone nan bat naet, late sarr, payy bar?** နာမည်၊ ဖုန်းနံပါတ်နဲ့လိပ်စာပေးပါ။
Could I see your identity card?	**ID card, kyeet loht ya ma larr?** အိုင်ဒီကတ်ကြည့်လို့ရမလား။
Could I see your insurance papers?	**Ar ma gan, sar ywet sar dann dway, kyeet loht ya ma larr?** အာမခံစာရွက်စာတမ်းတွေကြည့်လို့ရမ လား။
Could I see your passport?	**Passport, kyeet loht ya ma larr?** ပတ်စ်ပို့ကြည့်လို့ရမလား။
Will you act as a witness?	**Myet myin thet thay, lote payy ma larr?** မျက်မြင်သက်သေလုပ်ပေးမလား။

I need this information for insurance purposes.	**Ar ma gan lote boht, di achet alet, lo dae.** အာမခံလုပ်ဖို့ ဒီအချက်အလက်လိုတယ်။
Are you insured?	**Ar ma gan, lote htarr larr?** အာမခံလုပ်ထားလား။
Could you sign here, please?	**Di mhar, let mhat, htohh payy bar?** ဒီမှာလက်မှတ်ထိုးပေးပါ။

14.4 Theft

I've been robbed.	**Damya tite khan ya dae.** ဓားပြတိုက်ခံရတယ်။
My phone has been stolen.	**Phone, a khohh khan ya dae.** ဖုန်းအခိုးခံရတယ်။
My car's been broken into.	[male speaker] **Kya nawt karr go, win tite thwarr dae.** ကျွန်တော့်ကားကို ဝင်တိုက်သွားတယ်။
	[female speaker] **Kya ma karr go, win tite thwarr dae.** ကျွန်မကားကို ဝင်တိုက်သွားတယ်။

14.5 Reporting a missing person

I've lost my child.	[male speaker] **Kya nawt kha layy, pyout thwarr dae.** ကျွန်တော့်ကလေးပျောက်သွားတယ်။
	[female speaker] **Kya ma kha layy, pyout thwarr dae.** ကျွန်မကလေးပျောက်သွားတယ်။
Could you help me find him/her?	**Thoot go, waii shar payy bar larr?** သူ့ကိုဝိုင်းရှာပေးပါလား။

He/She's five years old.

Thu ga, athet ngarr nhit, sheet bi.
သူကအသက်ငါးနှစ်ရှိပြီ။

He's got short blond hair.

Thu ga, zabin shway o yaung, atoh layy naet.
သူက ဆံပင်ရွှေအိုရောင်အတိုလေးနဲ့။

She's got long red hair.

Thu ga, zabin ani yaung, ashay layy naet. သူက ဆံပင်အနီရောင် အရှည်လေးနဲ့။

He's got curly brown hair.

Thu ga, zabin anyo yaung, akout naet. သူက ဆံပင်အညိုရောင် အကောက်နဲ့။

She's got straight black hair.

Thu ga, zabin amell yaung, a phyaungt naet.
သူက ဆံပင်အမည်းရောင် အဖြောင့်နဲ့။

He's got frizzy hair.

Thu ga, zabin kout kout naet.
သူက ဆံပင်ကောက်ကောက်နဲ့။

She's wearing a ponytail.

Thu ga, anout mhar, zabin myint myint, see htarr dae.
သူက အနောက်မှာ ဆံပင်မြင့်မြင့်စည်းထားတယ်။

She's wearing braids.

Thu ga, kyit san mee, kyit htarr dae.
သူက ကျစ်ဆံမြီးကျစ်ထားတယ်။

She's wearing her hair in a bun.

Thu ga, za d'own ht'own htarrr dae.
သူက ဆံထုံးထုံးထားတယ်။

He's got blue eyes.

Thu ga, myet lone, apyar yaung naet.
သူက မျက်လုံးအပြာရောင်နဲ့။

She's got brown eyes.

Thu ga, myet lone, anyo yaung naet.
သူက မျက်လုံးအညိုရောင်နဲ့။

He's got green eyes.

Thu ga, myet lone, asein yaung naet.
သူက မျက်လုံးအစိမ်းရောင်နဲ့။

He's wearing a red shirt and jeans.

Thu ga, shat eain gyi ani naet, jinn baungg bi, wit htarr dae.
သူက ရုပ်အင်္ကျီအနီနဲ့ဂျင်းဘောင်းဘီ ဝတ်ထားတယ်။

She's wearing a blue blouse and black pants.	**Thu ga, eain gyi anyo naet, baungg bi amell, wit htarr dae.** သူကအကျီအညိုနဲ့သောင်းဘီအမည်းဝတ်ထားတယ်။
He's wearing glasses.	**Thu ga, myet mhan naet.** သူက မျက်မှန်နဲ့။
She's not wearing glasses.	**Thu ga, myet mhan ma tat boo.** သူက မျက်မှန်မတပ်ဘူး။
She is tall.	**Thu ga, a yat myint dae.** သူက အရပ်မြင့်တယ်။
He is short.	**Thu ga, a yat poot dae.** သူက အရပ်ပုတယ်။
This is his/her photo.	**Dar, thoot dat p'own bar.** ဒါသူ့ဓာတ်ပုံပါ။

14.6 At the police station

An arrest

I don't speak Burmese.	[male speaker] **Kya naw, myanmar zagarr, ma pyaww tat boo.** ကျွန်တော်မြန်မာစကားမပြောတတ်ဘူး။
	[female speaker] **Kya ma, myanmar zagarr, ma pyaww tat boo.** ကျွန်မမြန်မာစကားမပြောတတ်ဘူး။
I didn't see the sign.	**Saii boat ko, ma twayt lite boo.** ဆိုင်းဘုတ်ကို မတွေ့လိုက်ဘူး။
I don't understand. what it says	**Aet mhar, yayy htarr dar go, narr ma lae boo.** အဲ့မှာရေးထားတာကို နားမလည်ဘူး။
I was only doing... kilometers an hour.	**Tanar yi go,...kilometer bell, maungg nay dar bar.** တစ်နာရီကို...ကီလိုမီတာပဲ မောင်းနေတာပါ။

I'll have my car checked.	[male speaker] **Kya nawt karr go, sit kyeet lite mae.** ကျွန်တော့်ကားကို စစ်ကြည့်လိုက်မယ်။
	[female speaker] **Kya ma karr go, sit kyeet lite mae.** ကျွန်မကားကိုစစ်ကြည့်လိုက်မယ်။
I was blinded by oncoming lights.	**Shayt myet nha jinn zai karr ga, mee yaung naet, myet seet pyar thwarr dae.** ရှေ့ မျက်နှာချင်းဆိုင်ကား ကမီးရောင်နဲ့မျက်စိပြာသွားတယ်။

ဂိတက်ပြပါ။	Your (vehicle) documents, please.
အရှိန်နှုန်းများနေတယ်။	You were speeding.
ဒီမှာကားရပ်လို့မရဘူး။	You're not allowed to park here
ရှေ့ မီးတွေမလင်းဘူး။	Your front lights aren't working.
နောက်မီးတွေမလင်းဘူး။	Your rear lights aren't working.
ဒဏ်ငွေ...ဆောင်ရမယ်။	That's a...fine.
အခုဆောင်သွားမလား။	Do you want to pay now?
အခုဆောင်ရမယ်။	You'll have to pay now.

Reporting an incident

I want to report a collision.	**Yin tite mhoot, thadinn payy jin loht bar.** ယာဉ်တိုက်မှုသတင်းပေးချင်လို့ပါ။
I want to file a report for a missing person.	**Lu byout, tai jin loht bar.** လူပျောက်တိုင်ချင်လို့ပါ။
Could you make a statement, please?	**Kyay nyar payy bar larr?** ကြေညာပေးပါလား။
Could I have a copy for the insurance?	**Ar ma gan atwet, mate tu, htote payy bar larr?** အာမခံအတွက် မိတ္တူ၊ထုတ်ပေးပါလား။

I've no money left,
  I'm desperate.

Petsan ma kyan dawt boo. Petsan lo nay dae. ပိုက်ဆံမကျန်တော့ဘူး။
ပိုက်ဆံလိုနေတယ်။

I'd like an interpreter.

Zagabyan khaw jin dae.
စကားပြန်ခေါ်ချင်တယ်။

I'm innocent.

[male speaker] **Kya nawt mhar, apyit ma sheet boo.**
ကျွန်တော့်မှာ အပြစ်မရှိဘူး။

[female speaker] **Kya ma mhar, apyit ma sheet boo.** ကျွန်မမှာ အပြစ်မရှိဘူး။

I want to speak to
  someone from the
  American Embassy.

American than yown ga, ta yout yout naet, zagarr pyaww jin dae.
အမေရိကန်သံရုံးက တစ်ယောက်ယောက်နဲ့
စကားပြောချင်တယ်။

I want a lawyer
  who speaks English.

Ingalate lo pyaww tat taet, shayt nay, ngharr jin dae.
အင်္ဂလိပ်လိုပြောတတ်တဲ့ ရှေ့
နေငှားချင်တယ်။

ဘယ်မှာဖြစ်တာလဲ။	Where did it happen?
ဘယ်အချိန်မှာဖြစ်တာလဲ။	What time did it happen?
ဘာပျောက်နေလဲ။	What's missing?
ဘာယူသွားလဲ။	What's been taken?
မျက်မြင်သက်သေရှိလား။	Are there any witnesses?
စကားပြန်ခေါ်ချင်လား။	Do you want an interpreter?

15. English-Burmese Dictionary

The following dictionary is meant to supplement the chapters in this book. If you cannot find the word you are looking for in this section, you may find it in a relevant chapter of the book.

A

about (approximately) **lout** လောက်

above **apaw** အပေါ်

abroad **nai ngan jarr** နိုင်ငံခြား

accident **ma taw ta sa mhoot** မတော်တဆမှု

adapt **nyheet dae** ညှိတယ်

address **late sar** လိပ်စာ

admission **win gwint** ဝင်ခွင့်

admission price **win jay** ဝင်ကြေး

adult **lu gyee** လူကြီး

advice **akyan** အကြံ

after **pee dawt** ပြီးတော့

afternoon **nayt lae** နေ့လယ်

again **htat** ထပ်

against **sant kyin bet** ဆန့်ကျင်ဘက်

age **athet** အသက်

agree **tha baww tu dae** သဘောတူတယ်

AIDS **A-I-D-S** အေအိုင်ဒီအိတ်စ်

air **lay** လေ

air conditioning **air con** အဲကွန်း

air mattress **mwayt yar** မွေ့ ရာ

air pollution **lay doot nyit nyann jinn** လေထုညစ်ညမ်းခြင်း

airmail **nai ngan jarr ga sar** နိုင်ငံခြားကစာ

airplane **lay yin** လေယာဉ်

airport **lay zate** လေဆိပ်

airport terminal **terminal** တာမင်နယ်

alarm **alann** အလမ်း

alarm clock **nhohh zet nar yi** နိူးစက်နာရီ

alcohol **a yet** အရက်

all day **ta nayt lone** တစ်နေ့လုံး

all the time **tachain lone** တစ်ချိန်လုံး

allergy **ma taet boo** မတည့်ဘူး

alone **ta yout htell** တစ်ယောက်တည်း

also **lell** လည်း

altogether **arr lone atutu** အားလုံးအတူတူ

always **amyell** အမြဲ

ambulance **lu nar tin karr** လူနာတင်ကား

America **american nai ngan** အမေရိကန်နိုင်ငံ

American (people) **american lu myohh** အမေရိကန်လူမျိုး

amount **pamar na** ပမာဏ

amusement park **apann phyay oo yin** အပန်းဖြေဥယျာဉ်

anesthetic (general) **mayt zayy** မေ့ဆေး

anesthetic (local) **ht'own zayy** ထုံဆေး

angry **sate sohh dae** စိတ်ဆိုးတယ်

animal **tarate san** တိရစ္ဆာန်

ankle **chay jinn wit** ခြေကျင်းဝတ်

answer **a phyay** အဖြေ

ant **pa ywet sate** ပုရွက်ဆိတ်

antibiotics **pa teet zi wa sayy** ပဋိဇီဝဆေး

antique **shayy haungg** ရှေးဟောင်း

antiseptic **pohh that sayy** ပိုးသတ်ဆေး

anus **sa oh** စအို

anyone **bae thu ma so** ဘယ်သူမဆို

apartment **tite khann** တိုက်ခန်း

apologies **taungg ban zagarr** တောင်းပန်စကား

apple **pann thee** ပန်းသီး

apple juice **pann thee phyaw yay** ပန်းသီးဖျော်ရည်

appointment (meeting) **a see a wayy** အစည်းအဝေး

April **april la** ဧပြီလ

architecture **beet thoot kar** ဗိသုကာ

area **area** ဧရိယာ

argue **nyinn kh'own dae** ငြင်းခုံတယ်

arm **let maungg** လက်မောင်း

arrange **si zin dae** စီစဉ်တယ်

arrive **yout tae** ရောက်တယ်

art **anoot pyin nyar** အနုပညာ

artery **thwayy hlwut kyaww** သွေးလွတ်ကြော

artificial respiration **a yayy baw, athet kae nee** အရေးပေါ်အသက်ကယ်နည်း

arts and crafts **let mhoot pyin nyar** လက်မှုပညာ

ashtray **salate pyar khwet** ဆေးလိပ်ပြာခွက်

ask **mayy dae** မေးတယ်

ask for **taungg dae** တောင်းတယ်

aspirin **a kite a khell pyout sayy** အကိုက်အခဲပျောက်ဆေး

asthma **pann nar yin kyat** ပန်းနာရင်ကြပ်

at **mhar** မှာ

at home **eain mhar** အိမ်မှာ

at night **nya mhar** ညမှာ

at the back **anout mhar** အနောက်မှာ

at the front **a shayt mhar** အရှေ့မှာ

at the latest **nout sone mhar** နောက်ဆုံးမှာ

August **august la** ဩဂုတ်လ

Australia **australia nai ngan** ဩစတြေးလျနိုင်ငံ

Australian (people) **australia lu myohh** ဩစတြေးလျလူမျိုး

automatic **alo alyout** အလိုအလျောက်

avoid **shaung dae** ရှောင်တယ်

awake **nohh nay dae** နိုးနေတယ်

B

baby **kha layy** ကလေး

baby food **kha layy asarr asar** ကလေးအစားအစာ

babysitter **kha layy htein** ကလေးထိန်း

back (part of body) **kyaww** ကျော

back (rear) **bet mhan** ဘက်မှန်

backpack **kyaww pohh ate** ကျောပိုးအိတ်

backpacker **kyaww pohh ate naet, kha yee thwarr thu** ကျောပိုးအိတ်နဲ့ခရီးသွားသူ

bad (rotting) **pote nay bi** ပုပ်နေပြီ

bad (terrible) **sohh dae** ဆိုးတယ်

bag **ate** အိတ်

baggage **baggage** ဘက်ဂေ့ဂျ်

ball **baw lone** ဘောလုံး

ballpoint pen **baww bin** ဘောပင်

banana **nga pyaww thee** ငှက်ပျောသီး

band aid **plaster** ပလာစတာ

bandage **pat tee** ပတ်တီး

bangs (fringe) **shayt zabin a teet** ရှေ့ဆံပင်အတိ

bank (finance) **ban** ဘဏ်

bank (river) **myit kann** မြစ်ကမ်း

banquet **pann zee** ပန်းစည်း

bar **barr** ဘား

barbecue **barbecue** ဘာဘီကျူး

barber **zabin nyhat sayar** ဆံပင်ညှပ်ဆရာ

bargain **zayy sit tae** ဈေးဆစ်တယ်

baseball **baseball** ဘွေ့စ်ဘော

basketball **basketball** ဘတ်စ်ကတ်ဘော

bath towel **thabet** သဘက်

bathe **yay chohh dae** ရေချိုးတယ်

bathmat **chay thote wit** ခြေသုတ်ဖတ်

bathrobe **yay chohh wit y'own** ရေချိုးဖတ်ရုံ

bathroom (for bathing) **yay chohh gann** ရေချိုးခန်း

bathroom (lavatory) **eain thar** အိမ်သာ

bathtub **yay chohh kan** ရေချိုးကန်

battery **dat khell** ဓာတ်ခဲ

beach **kann jay** ကမ်းခြေ

beautiful **hla dae** လှတယ်

beauty parlor **ahla pyin zai** အလှပြင်ဆိုင်

because **bar phyit loht lell so dawt** ဘာဖြစ်လို့လဲဆိုတော့

bed **ate yar** အိပ်ရာ

bedding **ate yakhinn** အိပ်ရာခင်း

bedroom **ate khann** အိပ်ခန်း

beef **amell tharr** အမဲသား

beer **bee yar** ဘီယာ

before **ma tai gin** မတိုင်ခင်

beggar **patsan taungg daet thu** ပိုက်ဆံတောင်းတဲ့သူ

begin **sa dae** စတယ်

behind **anout** အနောက်

below **out** အောက်

belt **khabat** ခါးပတ်

beside **bayy** ဘေး

best **a kaungg zone** အကောင်းဆုံး

better **po kaungg dae** ပိုကောင်းတယ်

between **gyarr** ကြား

bicycle **set bein** စက်ဘီး

big **kyee dae** ကြီးတယ်

bikini **bikini** ဘီကီနီ

bill **bill** ဘောလ်

billiards **billiard** ဘိလိယက်

bird **nghet** ငှက်

birthday **mwayy nayt** မွေးနေ့

biscuit **biscuit** ဘီစကစ်

bite **kite tae** ကိုက်တယ်

bitter **kharr dae** ခါးတယ်

black **amell yaung** အမည်းရောင်

black eye **myet lone amell** မျက်လုံးအမည်း

bland (taste) **a ya thar, ma sheet boo** အရသာမရှိဘူး

blanket **saung** စောင်

bleach (verb) **phyu aung lote tae** ဖြူအောင်လုပ်တယ်

bleed **thwayy htwet tae** သွေးထွက်တယ်

blind (can't see) **myet ma myin** မျက်မမြင်

blind (on a window) **blind**
ဘလိုင်း

blister **anar** အနာ

blog **blog** ဘလော့

blond **zabin shway yaung**
ဆံပင်ရွှေရောင်

blood **thwayy** သွေး

blood pressure **thwayy paung**
သွေးပေါင်

blood transfusion **thwayy
thwinn dae** သွေးသွင်းတယ်

blouse **blouse cain gyi**
ဘလောက်စ်အကျီ

blue **apyar yaung** အပြာရောင်

boarding gate **boarding gate**
ဘောာဒင်းဂိတ်

boat **hlay** လှေ

body **khan dar ko** ခန္ဓာကိုယ်

boiled water **su pee tharr, yay**
ဆူပြီးသားရေ

bone **a yohh** အရိုး

book **sar oat** စာအုပ်

booked, reserved **booking lote
htarr dae** ဘွတ်ကင်လုပ်ထားတယ်

booking office **booking lote taet,
yone** ဘွတ်ကင်လုပ်တဲ့ရုံး

bookshop **sar oat sai** စာအုပ်ဆိုင်

border **nae zat** နယ်စပ်

bored/boring **pyinn dae/pyinn
zayar kaungg dae** ပျင်းတယ်/
ပျင်းစရာကောင်းတယ်

born **mwayy dae** မွေးတယ်

borrow **ngharr dae** ငှားတယ်

botanic gardens **yote kha bay
da, oo yin** ရုက္ခဗေဒဥယျာဉ်

both **nha khoot lone** နှစ်ခုလုံး

bottle (plastic) **boo** ဘူး

bottle (glass) **palinn** ပုလင်း

bottle opener **palinn phout tan**
ပုလင်းဖောက်တံ

bowl **bagan lone** ပန်းကန်လုံး

box **thayt tar** သေတ္တာ

box office **let mhat y'own**
လက်မှတ်ရုံ

boy **yout kyarr layy**
ယောက်ျားလေး

boyfriend **yee zarr** ရည်းစား

bra **bra si yar** ဘရာစီယာ

bracelet **let kout** လက်ကောက်

brake **brake** ဘရိတ်

brake oil **brake si** ဘရိတ်ဆီ

bread **paung mote** ပေါင်မုန့်

break (verb) **kyohh dae** ကျိုးတယ်

breakfast **manet sar** မနက်စာ

breast **yin tharr** ရင်သား

breathe **athet shu dae**
အသက်ရှုတယ်

bridge **dadarr** တံတား

bring **yu lar dae** ယူလာတယ်

British (general) **byeet teet sha**
ဗြိတိသျှ

British (person) **byeet teet sha
lu myohh** ဗြိတိသျှလူမျိုး

brochure **let kann kyaw nyar**
လက်ကမ်းကြော်ငြာ

broken **kyohh nay dae**
ကျိုးနေတယ်

bronze **kyayy war** ကြေးဝါ

brother (elder) **ako** အစ်ကို

brown **anyo yaung** အညိုရောင်

bruise **yaung kaii dan yar**
ယောင်ကိုင်းဒဏ်ရာ

brush **brush** ဘရပ်ရှ်

Buddhism **bote da bar thar**
ဗုဒ္ဓဘာသာ

building **asout a oo**
အဆောက်အဦး

bulb **mee lone** မီးလုံး

burglary **phout htwinn win yout
tae** ဖောက်ထွင်းဝင်ရောက်တယ်

burn (injury) **apu laung dae**
အပူလောင်တယ်

burn (verb) **mee shoht dae**
မီးရှို့တယ်

bus **bus karr** ဘတ်စ်ကား

bus station **karr mhat tai**
ကားမှတ်တိုင်

bus stop **bus karr mhat tai**
ဘတ်စ်ကားမှတ်တိုင်

bus terminus **karr gate** ကားဂိတ

business **see bwarr yayy, lote
ngann** စီးပွားရေးလုပ်ငန်း

business card **business card**
ဘစ်စနက်စ်ကတ်

business trip **alote kate sa, kha
yee** အလုပ်ကိစ္စခရီး

businessman **see pwarr yayy,
lote ngann shin**
စီးပွားရေးလုပ်ငန်းရှင်

busy (schedule) **alote myarr dae**
အလုပ်များတယ်

busy (traffic) **karr kyat tae**
ကားကြပ်တယ်

but **dar bay maet** ဒါပေမဲ့

butter **htaww bat** ထောပတ်

button (for clothes) **kyae thee**
ကြယ်သီး

button (to press) **khalote** ခလုတ်

buy **wae dae** ဝယ်တယ်

C

cabbage **gaw bi dote** ဂေါ်ဖီထုပ်

cake **kate mote** ကိတ်မုန့်

cake shop **kate mote sai**
ကိတ်မုန့်ဆိုင်

call (verb, name) **nan mae khaw
dae** နာမည်ခေါ်တယ်

call (verb, phone) **phone khaw
dae** ဖုန်းခေါ်တယ်

calligraphy **let yayy hla**
လက်ရေးလှ

camera **camera** ကင်မရာ

can (be able to) **V + nai dae**
V + နိုင်တယ်

can (tin of food) **si thwut boo**
စည်သွတ်ဘူး

can opener **noht zi phout tan**
နို့ဆီဖောက်တံ

cancel **phyet tae** ဖျက်တယ်

candle **pha yaungg dai**
ဖယောင်းတိုင်

candy **tha gyarr lone** သကြားလုံး

car **karr** ကား

card **card** ကတ်

cardigan **thohh mwayy, yin
kwell, eain gyi** သိုးမွေးရင်ကွဲအကျီ

care for **ga yoot site dae**
ဂရုစိုက်တယ်

careful **tha deet htarr** သတိထား

carpet **kaw zaww** ကော်ဇော

carrot **m'own lar oot ni** မုန်လာဥနီ

carry **thae dae** သယ်တယ်

cash (noun) **ngway tharr** ငွေသား

cashier **ngway shinn counter**
ငွေရှင်းကောင်တာ

casino **casino** ကာစီနို

cat **kyaung** ကြောင်

catalog **catalog** ကတ်တလောက်

cauliflower **gaw bi pann** ဂေါ်ဖီပန်း

cause **a kyaungg** အကြောင်း

cave **gu** ဂူ

celebrate **kyinn pa dae**
ကျင်းပတယ်

cemetery **thinn gyaii** သချႋုင်း

center (middle) **alae baho**
အလယ်ဗဟို

center (of city) **myoht lae gaung**
မြို့လယ်ခေါင်

centigrade **centigrade** စင်တီဂရိတ်

centimeter **centimeter**
စင်တီမီတာ

ceramics **kyway** ကြွေ

chair **kh'own** ခုံ

champagne **champagne** ရှန်ပိန်

chance **akhwint a yayy**
အခွင့်အရေး

change (verb, alter, vary)
pyaungg lell dae ပြောင်းလဲတယ်

change (verb, money) **petsan
lell dae** ပိုက်ဆံလဲတယ်

change (verb, swap) **lell dae**
လဲတယ်

change (verb, trains/buses)
pyaungg dae ပြောင်းတယ်

change the baby's diaper **diaper
lell dae** ဒိုင်ဘာလဲတယ်

charge (expense, cost) **k'own
kya zayate** ကုန်ကျစရိတ်

cheap **zayy cho dae** ဈေးချိုတယ်

check (verb) **sit tae** စစ်တယ်

check in **check in lote tae**
ချက်ကင်လုပ်တယ်

check out **check out lote tae**
ချက်ကောက်လုပ်တယ်

Cheers! **Cheers!** ချီးယားစ်

cheese **cheese** ချိစ်

chef **sapho mhoo** စားဖိုမှူး

chess **sit toot yin** စစ်တုရင်

chewing gum **pi kae** ပီကယ်

chicken **kyet tharr** ကြက်သား

child **kha layy** ကလေး

chilled **apann pyay dae**
အပန်းပြေတယ်

chili **nga yote thee** ငရုတ်သီး

chin **mayy zayt** မေးစေ့

China **ta yote nai ngan**
တရုတ်နိုင်ငံ

Chinese (language) **ta yote
zagarr** တရုတ်စကား

Chinese (people) **ta yote lu
myohh** တရုတ်လူမျိုး

chocolate **chocolate** ချောကလက်

choose (verb) **ywayy dae**
ရွေးတယ်

chopsticks **tu** တူ

church **pha yarr kyaungg**
ဘုရားကျောင်း

cigar **salate** ဆေးလိပ်

cigarette **see karet** စီးကရက်

circus **sat kat** ဆပ်ကပ်

citizen **nai ngan tharr** နိုင်ငံသား

city **myoht** မြို့

clean (verb) **thant shinn dae**
သန့်ရှင်းတယ်

clock **nar yi** နာရီ

close (verb) **nee dae** နီးတယ်

closed (shop, etc) **pate tae**
ပိတ်တယ်

closed off (road) **lann pate tae**
လမ်းပိတ်တယ်

clothes, clothing **a wit ahtae**
အဝတ်အထည်

clothes hanger **a wit jate**
အဝတ်ချိတ်

cloud **tain** တိမ်

coach (bus) **express karr**
အိပ်စ်ပရက်စ်ကား

coat (jacket) **jar kin eain gyi**
ဂျာကင်အင်္ကျီ

coat (overcoat) **coat eain gyi,
ashay** ကုတ်အင်္ကျီအရှည်

cockroach **pohh hat** ပိုးဟပ်

coffee **coffee** ကော်ဖီ

cold (not hot) **aye dae** အေးတယ်

cold, flu **a ayy meet dae**
အအေးမိတယ်

collar **kaw lan** ကော်လံ

colleague **lote phaw kai phet**
လုပ်ဖော်ကိုင်ဖက်

collision **yin tite mhoot**
ယာဉ်တိုက်မှု

cologne **a mhwayy yay** အမွှေးရည်

color **a yaung** အရောင်

comb (noun) **bee** ဘီး

come **lar dae** လာတယ်

come back **pyan lar dae**
ပြန်လာတယ်

comedy **har tha** ဟာသ

comfortable **thet taungt thet
thar, sheet dae**
သက်တောင့်သက်သာရှိတယ်

company (business) **company**
ကုမ္ပဏီ

compartment (train) **yah tarr
dwell** ရထားတွဲ

complain (verb) **complain tet
tae** ကွန်ပလိန်းတက်တယ်

complaint **ma kyay nat mhoot**
မကျေနပ်မှု

completely **lone lone** လုံးလုံး

complex **shote tae** ရှုပ်တယ်

computer **computer** ကွန်ပျူတာ

comrade **yell baw** ရဲဘော်

concert **ka bwell** ကပွဲ

concert hall **ka bwell, khann ma**
ကပွဲခန်းမ

condensed milk **noht zi** နို့ဆီ

condom **condom** ကွန်ဒုံး

confectionery **mote tite**
မုန့်တိုက်

Congratulations! **G'own yu bar
dae!** ဂုဏ်ယူပါတယ်

constipation **wann chote tae**
ဝမ်းချုပ်တယ်

consulate **kaung sit win yone**
ကောင်စစ်ဝန်ရုံး

consultation (by doctor) **akyan
payy** အကြံပေး

contact lens **myet kat mhan**
မျက်ကပ်မှန်

contagious **kuu dae** ကူးတယ်

contraceptive **thaday tarr nee**
သန္ဓေတားနည်း

contraceptive pill **thaday tarr
zayy** သန္ဓေတားဆေး

contract **sar jote** စာချုပ်

convenient **asin pyay dae**
အဆင်ပြေတယ်

cook (person) **sapho mhoo**
စားဖိုမှူး

cook (verb) **hinn chet tae**
ဟင်းချက်တယ်

cookie **cookie** ကွတ်ကီး

copper **kyayy ni** ကြေးနီ

copy (noun, replica) **mate tu**
မိတ္တူ

copy (verb) **kuu dae** ကူးတယ်

corner **daungt** ထောင့်

correct **mhan dae** မှန်တယ်

corridor **corridor** ကော်ရစ်ဒါ

corrupt **let sarr dae**
လာဘ်စားတယ်

cosmetics **ahla pyin pyit see**
အလှပြင်ပစ္စည်း

cost (price) **k'own kya za yate**
ကုန်ကျစရိတ်

costly **a k'own a kya, myarr dae**
အကုန်အကျများတယ်

costume **wit s'own** ဝတ်စုံ

cot **pakhet** ပုခက်

cotton **chi** ချည်

cotton wool **gonn** ဂွမ်း

cough (noun) **chaungg sohh**
ချောင်းဆိုး

cough (verb) **chaungg sohh dae**
ချောင်းဆိုးတယ်

cough drops **chaungg sohh
pyout, ng'own zayy**
ချောင်းဆိုးပျောက်ဂုံဆေး

cough syrup **chaungg sohh
pyout, sayy yay**
ချောင်းဆိုးပျောက်ဆေးရည်

count **yay twet tae** ရေတွက်တယ်

counter **counter** ကောင်တာ

country (nation) **nai ngan** နိုင်ငံ

countryside **kyayy let** ကျေးလက်

course of treatment **sayy koot tha, kar la** ဆေးကုသကာလ

cousin **maung nha ma, ta wann kwell** မောင်နှမတစ်ဝမ်းကွဲ

cover (verb) **phone dae** ဖုံးတယ်

cow **nwarr** နွား

crab **ganann** ဂဏန်း

cramp (verb) **kywet tet tae** ကြွက်တက်တယ်

crazy **yoo dae** ရူးတယ်

credit card **credit card** ခရက်ဒစ်ကတ်

crime **yar za wit mhoot** ရာဇဝတ်မှု

cross (the road) **lann koo dae** လမ်းကူးတယ်

crossroads **lann z'own** လမ်းဆုံ

crutch **jaii dout** ချိုင်းထောက်

cry **ngo dae** ငိုတယ်

cubic meter **koot ba meter** ကုဗမီတာ

cucumber **thakhwarr thee** သခွားသီး

cuddly toy **a mwayy pwa yote** အမွေးပွရုပ်

cuff **let aphyarr** လက်အဖျား

cup **khwet** ခွက်

curly **kout tae** ကောက်တယ်

current **hlaii** လှိုင်း

curtains **lite kar** လိုက်ကာ

cushion **cushion** ကူရှင်

custom **dalayt** ဓလေ့

customer **phout thae** ဖောက်သည်

customs **akout khon** အကောက်ခွန်

cut (injury) **sha yar** ရှရာ

cut (verb) **nyhat tae** ညှပ်တယ်

cutlery **darr naet kha yinn** ဓားနဲ့ခက်ရင်း

cycling **set bein see** စက်ဘီးစီး

D

dad **phay phay** ဖေဖေ

daily **nayt tail** နေ့တိုင်း

dairy products **noht htwet pyit see** နို့ထွက်ပစ္စည်း

damage (verb) **pyet see dae** ပျက်စီးတယ်

dance (noun) **aka** အက

dance (verb) **ka dae** ကတယ်

dandruff **bout** ဘောက်

danger **an da yae** အန္တရာယ်

dangerous **an da yae, sheet dae** အန္တရာယ်ရှိတယ်

dark **mhaung dae** မှောင်တယ်

date **yet nayt** ရက်နေ့

date of birth **mwayy nayt** မွေးနေ့

daughter **thamee** သမီး

day **nayt** နေ့

day after tomorrow **thabet khar** သန်ဘက်ခါ

day before yesterday **ho ta nayt ga** ဟိုတစ်နေ့ကေ

dead **thay dae** သေတယ်

deaf **narr ma kyarr** နားမကြား

decaffeinated **caffeine dat, ma par** ကဖင်းဓာတ်မပါ

deceive **hlaet phyarr dae** လှည့်ဖျားတယ်

December **december la** ဒီဇင်ဘာလ

decide **sone phyat tae** ဆုံးဖြတ်တယ်

declare (at customs) **kyay nyar dae** ကြေညာတယ်

deep **net tae** နက်တယ်

deep freeze **yay khell thittar, a ayy khann** ရေခဲသေတ္တာအအေးခန်း

degrees **degree** ဒီဂရီ

delay **nout kya dae** နောက်ကျတယ်

delicious **a ya thar, sheet dae** အရသာရှိတယ်

deliver **payy poht dae** ပေးပို့တယ်

democracy **democracy** ဒီမိုကရေစီ

dentist **thwarr, sayar win** သွားဆရာဝန်

dentures **thwarr aswut** သွားအစွပ်

deny **nyinn dae** ငြင်းတယ်

deodorant **gyaii lein zi** ချိုင်းလိမ်းဆီ

department store **k'own dite** ကုန်တိုက်

departure **htwet khwar** ထွက်ခွာ

departure time **htwet khwar jain** ထွက်ခွာချိန်

deposit (for safekeeping) **sa yan** စရံ

deposit (in bank) **ban at ngway** ဘဏ်အပ်ငွေ

desert **thell gandar ya** သဲကန္တာရ

dessert **acho bwell** အချိုပွဲ

destination **kha yee pann dai** ခရီးပန်းတိုင်

destroy **phyet see dae** ဖျက်ဆီးတယ်

detergent **sat pyar mhont** ဆပ်ပြာမှုန့်

develop **tohh tet tae** တိုးတက်တယ်

diabetic **see jo** ဆီးချို

diamond **sain** စိန်

diaper, nappy **diaper** ဒိုင်ဘာ

diarrhea **wann thwarr dae** ဝမ်းသွားတယ်

dictionary **abeet dan** အဘိဓာန်

diesel oil **diesel si** ဒီဇယ်ဆီ

different **kwell dae** ကွဲတယ်

difficulty **akhet akhell** အခက်အခဲ

dim sum **dim sum** ဒင်းဆမ်း

dining room **hta minn sarr gann** ထမင်းစားခန်း

dinner **nya zar** ညစာ

direct flight **direct flight** တိုက်ရိုက်ဖလိုက်

direction **oo ti bet** ဦးတည်ဘက်

directly **dite yite** တိုက်ရိုက်

dirty **nyit pat tae** ညစ်ပတ်တယ်

disabled **mathan swann** မသန်စွမ်း

disappointment **sate pyet** စိတ်ပျက်

disco **disco** ဒစ်စကို

discount **shawt zayy** လျှော့ဈေး

dish **bagan** ပန်းကန်

dish of the day **yanayt hinn lyar** ယနေ့ဟင်းလျာ

disinfectant **pohh that sayy** ပိုးသတ်ဆေး

dislocate **nay yar pyaungg dae** နေရာပြောင်တယ်

dissatisfied **ma kyay nat boo** မကျေနပ်ဘူး

distance **akwar a wayy** အကွာအဝေး

distilled water **paungg khan yay** ပေါင်းခံရေ

disturb **nhout shet tae** နှောင့်ယှက်တယ်

disturbance **atarr asee** အတားအဆီး

divorced **kwar shinn htarr dae** ကွာရှင်းထားတယ်

dizzy **muu dae** မူးတယ်

do **lote tae** လုပ်တယ်

do not disturb **ma nhout shet ya** မနှောင့်ယှက်ရ

doctor **sayar win** ဆရာဝန်

dog **khwayy** ခွေး

doll **a yote** အရုပ်

domestic **pyi dwinn** ပြည်တွင်း

door **dagarr** တံခါး

double **nhasa** နှစ်ဆ

double bed **nha yout ate, gadin**
နှစ်ယောက်အိပ်ကုတင်

down **out** အောက်

downstairs **out htat** အောက်ထပ်

draught **lay zein tite** လေစိမ်းတိုက်

dream (noun) **eain met** အိပ်မက်

dream (verb) **eain met met tae**
အိပ်မက်မက်တယ်

dress (verb) **a wit wit tae**
အဝတ်ဝတ်တယ်

dress (noun) **wit s'own** ဝတ်စုံ

dress up **kaungg kaungg
mon mon, wit tae**
ကောင်းကောင်းမွန်မွန်ဝတ်တယ်

dressing gown **nya wit ate gar
win** ညဝတ်အိပ်ဝါဂန်

dressing table **mhan tin kh'own**
မှန်တင်ခုံ

drink (noun) **thout sayar**
သောက်စရာ

drink (verb) **thout tae**
သောက်တယ်

drinking water **thout yay**
သောက်ရေ

drive (verb) **maungg dae**
မောင်းတယ်

driver **karr sayar** ကားဆရာ

driver's license **yin maungg, lai
sin** ယာဉ်မောင်းလိုင်စင်

drug **sayy** ဆေး

drugstore **sayy zai** ဆေးဆိုင်

drunk **muu nay dae** မူးနေတယ်

dry (verb) **chout tae**
ခြောက်တယ်

dry cleaning **achout shaw**
အခြောက်လျှော်

dry cleaners **achout shaw set**
အခြောက်လျှော်စက်

duck **bell** ဘဲ

dumpling **phet htote** ဖက်ထုပ်

during **atwinn** အတွင်း

during the day **nayt bet mhar**
နေ့ဘက်မှာ

dust **ph'own** ဖုန်

duty (tax) **akhon** အခွန်

duty-free goods **duty-free pyit
see** ဂျူတီဖရီးပစ္စည်း

duty-free shop **duty-free sai**
ဂျူတီဖရီးဆိုင်

DVD **DVD** ဒီဗီဒီ

dynasty **minn zet** မင်းဆက်

E

each **ta khoot zi** တစ်ခုစီ

each other **ajinn jinn** အချင်းချင်း

ear **narr** နား

earache **narr kite** နားကိုက်

early **saww saww** စောစော

earn **petsan shar dae**
ပိုက်ဆံရှာတယ်

earrings **nagat** နားကပ်

earthquake **ngalyin** ငလျင်

east **ashayt** အရှေ့

easy **lwae dae** လွယ်တယ်

eat **sarr dae** စားတယ်

economy **see bwarr yayy**
စီးပွားရေး

economy class **yohh yohh dann**
ရိုးရိုးတန်း

egg **kyet oot** ကြက်ဥ

eggplant **kha yann thee** ခရမ်းသီး

eight **shit** ရှစ်

eighteen **saet shit** ဆယ့်ရှစ်

eighty **shit sae** ရှစ်ဆယ်

electric fan **pan gar** ပန်ကာ

electricity **hlyat sit** လျှပ်စစ်

electronic **electronic**
အီလက်ထရောနစ်

elephant **sin** ဆင်

elevator **dat hlay garr**
ဓာတ်လှေကား

eleven **saet tit** ဆယ့်တစ်

email **email** အီးမေးလ်

embarrassed **shet tae** ရှက်တယ်

embassy **than yone** သံရုံး

embroidery **pann htohh** ပန်းထိုး

emergency **a yayy baw** အရေးပေါ်

emergency brake **hand brake**
ဟန်းဘရိတ်

emergency exit **a yayy baw
htwet pout** အရေးပေါ်ထွက်ပေါက်

empty **alwut** အလွတ်

end **asone** အဆုံး

England **ingalan nai ngan**
အင်္ဂလန်နိုင်ငံ

English (language) **ingalate
zagarr** အင်္ဂလိပ်စကား

English (people) **ingalate lu
myohh** အင်္ဂလိပ်လူမျိုး

enjoy **pyaww shwin dae** ေ
ပျော်ရွှင်တယ်

enough **lout tae** လောက်တယ်

enter **win dae** ဝင်တယ်

entire **ta khoot lone** တစ်ခုလုံး

entrance **win bout** ဝင်ပေါက်

envelope **sar ate** စာအိတ်

equality **nyi mya mhott** ညီမျှမှု

escalator **set hlay garr**
စက်လှေကား

especially **ahtoo tha phyint**
အထူးသဖြင့်

essential **a yayy kyee dae**
အရေးကြီးတယ်

evening **nya nay** ညနေ

evening wear **nya nay ginn, wit
s'own** ညနေခင်း/ဝတ်စုံ

every **N + daii** N + တိုင်း

everybody **lu daii** လူတိုင်း

everything **a yar daii** အရာတိုင်း

everywhere **nay yar daii**
နေရာတိုင်း

examine **sit sayy dae**
စစ်ဆေးတယ်

example **oot pamar** ဥပမာ

excellent **a yann kaungg dae**
အရမ်းကောင်းတယ်

exchange (money) **ngway lell
dae** ငွေလဲတယ်

exchange rate **ngway lell nhone**
ငွေလဲနှုန်း

excursion **layt lar yayy, kha yee**
လေ့လာရေးခရီး

excuse me **ta chet lout**
တစ်ချက်လောက်

exhausted **pin bann dae**
ပင်ပန်းတယ်

exhibition **pya bwell** ပြပွဲ

exit **htwet pout** ထွက်ပေါက်

export **tin poht dae** တင်ပို့တယ်

expenses **k'own kya za yate**
ကုန်ကျစရိတ်

expensive **zayy kyee dae**
ဈေးကြီးတယ်

explain **shinn pya dae**
ရှင်းပြတယ်

express (letter) **amyan chaww
poht** အမြန်ချောပို့

express (train) **amyan yat htarr**
အမြန်ရထား

external use **apyin bet, loo yan**
အပြင်ဘက်လူးရန်

extension cord **extension kyohh
gway** အိပ်စ်တန်းရှင်းကြိုးခွေ

eye **myet lone** မျက်လုံး

eye drops **myet sinn** မျက်စဉ်း

eye specialist **myet seet ahtoo koot** မျက်စိအထူးကု

F

fabric **pate sa** ပိတ်စ

face **myet nhar** မျက်နှာ

factory **set y'own** စက်ရုံ

Fahrenheit **fahrenheit** ဖာရင်ဟိုက်

faint (verb) **moo lell dae** မူးလဲတယ်

fall (verb) **lell kya dae** လဲကျတယ်

false **mharr dae** မှားတယ်

family **meet tharr zoot** မိသားစု

famous **nan mae kyee dae** နာမည်ကြီးတယ်

fan (cooling device) **yat taung** ယပ်တောင်

fan (person) **parate that** ပရိသတ်

far away **wayy dae** ဝေးတယ်

fare **akha** အခ

farm **taung yar** တောင်ယာ

farmer **lae thamarr** လယ်သမား

fashion show **fashion show** ဖက်ရှင်ရှိုး

fast **myan dae** မြန်တယ်

fat **wa dae** ဝတယ်

father **aphay** အဖေ

father-in-law **yout kahtee** ယောက္ခထီး

fault **amharr** အမှား

fax **fax** ဖက်စ်

February **february la** ဖေဖော်ဝါရီလ

feel **khan zarr ya dae** ခံစားရတယ်

fence **chan zee yohh** ခြံစည်းရိုး

ferry **ferry** ဖယ်ရီ

festival **pwell daw** ပွဲတော်

fever **aphyarr** အဖျား

few **nell nell** နည်းနည်း

fiancé **khin ponn laungg** ခင်ပွန်းလောင်း

fiancée **zanee laungg** ဇနီးလောင်း

fifteen **saet ngarr** ဆယ့်ငါး

fifty **ngarr zae** ငါးဆယ်

fill (verb) **phyayt dae** ဖြည့်တယ်

fill out (form) **form phyayt dae** ဖောင်ဖြည့်တယ်

filling (dental) **thwarr phar** သွားဖာ

filter cigarette **see karat phin** စီးကရက်ဖင်

find **shar dae** ရှာတယ်

fine (money) **dan jayy** ဒဏ်ကြေး

finger **let chaungg** လက်ချောင်း

finish **pee dae** ပြီးတယ်

fire **mee** မီး

fire alarm **mee achet payy** မီးအချက်ပေး

fire department **mee that htar na** မီးသတ်ဌာန

fire escape **a yayy baw hlay garr** အရေးပေါ်လေ့ကား

fire extinguisher **mee that sayy** မီးသတ်ဆေး

first **pa hta ma** ပထမ

first aid **shayy oo thu nar pyoot** ရှေးဦးသူနာပြု

first class **pa hta ma dann** ပထမတန်း

fish (noun) **ngarr** ငါး

fish (verb) **ngarr mhyarr dae** ငါးမျှားတယ်

fishing rod **ngarr mhyarr dan** ငါးမျှားတံ

fitness training **kar ya layt kyint gann, thin dann** ကာယလေ့ကျင့်ခန်းသင်တန်း

fitting room **a wit lell gann** အဝတ်လဲခန်း

five **ngarr** ငါး

fix **pyin dae** ပြင်တယ်

flag **alan** အလံ

flash (camera) **camera mee** ကင်မရာမီး

flashlight **dat mee** ဓာတ်မီး

flavor **a ya thar** အရသာ

flight **flight** ဖလိုက်

flight number **flight nan bat** ဖလိုက်နံပါတ်

flood **yay kyee dae** ရေကြီးတယ်

floor **kyann** ကြမ်း

flour **j'own** ဂျုံ

flu **tote kwayy** တုပ်ကွေး

flush **yay swell cha dae** ရေဆွဲချတယ်

fly (insect) **yin gaung** ယင်ကောင်

fly (verb) **pyan thann dae** ပျံသန်းတယ်

fog **myu** မြူ

foggy **myu saii dae** မြူဆိုင်းတယ်

folklore **yohh yar p'own myin** ရိုးရာပုံပြင်

follow **lite tae** လိုက်တယ်

food **a sarr a sar** အစားအစာ

food poisoning **a sar a sate phyit** အစာအဆိပ်ဖြစ်

foot (anatomy) **chay dout** ခြေထောက်

football (soccer) **baw lone** ဘောလုံး

forbidden **tarr myit htarr dae** တားမြစ်ထားတယ်

foreign **nai ngan jarr** နိုင်ငံခြား

foreign exchange **nai ngan jarr, ngway lell htar na** နိုင်ငံခြားငွေလဲထာန

forget **mayt dae** မေ့တယ်

fork **kha yinn** ခက်ရင်း

form (noun) **form** ဖောင်

formal dress **formal wit s'own** ဖော်မယ်ဝတ်စုံ

forty **layy zae** လေးဆယ်

forward **shayt** ရှေ့

four **layy** လေး

France **pyin thit** ပြင်သစ်

free (no charge) **alagarr** အလကား

free (unoccupied) **arr dae** အားတယ်

free time **arr jain** အားချိန်

freedom **lwut lat mhoot** လွတ်လပ်မှု

freeze **khell dae** ခဲတယ်

French (language) **pyin thit zagarr** ပြင်သစ်စကား

French (people) **pyin thit lu myohh** ပြင်သစ်လူမျိုး

french fries **ar loo gyaungg jaw** အာလူးချောင်းကြော်

fresh **lat sat tae** လတ်ဆတ်တယ်

Friday **thout kyar nayt** သောကြာနေ့

fried **akyaw** အကြော်

friend **tha ngae jinn** သူငယ်ချင်း

friendly **phaw yway dae** ဖော်ရွေတယ်

frightened **kyout tae** ကြောက်တယ်

from **ga nay** ကနေ

front **a shayt** အရှေ့

frozen **khell nay dae** ခဲနေတယ်

fruit **athee** အသီး

fruit juice **athee phyaw yay** အသီးဖျော်ရည်

frying pan **dae ohh** ဒယ်အိုး

full **apyayt** အပြည့်

fun **pyaww zayar** ပျော်စရာ

funeral **athoot ba** အသုဘ

funny **yee ya dae** ရယ်ရတယ်

G

game **game** ဂိမ်း

garage (car repair) **go daung** ဂိုေဒါင်

garbage **amhite** အမှိုက်

garden **oo yin** ဥယျာဉ်

garlic **kyet thwon phyu** ကြက်သွန်ဖြူ

garment **a wit ahtae** အဝတ်အထည်

gas (petrol) **dat si** ဓာတ်ဆီ

gas (petrol) station **si zai** ဆီဆိုင်

gasoline **dat si** ဓာတ်ဆီ

gate (in airport) **gate** ဂိတ်

gem **kyout** ကျောက်

gender **lain** လိင်

genuine **sit mhan dae** စစ်မှန်တယ်

German (language) **German zagarr** ဂျာမန်စကား

German (people) **German lu myohh** ဂျာမန်လူမျိုး

Germany **Germany nai ngan** ဂျာမနီနိုင်ငံ

get off (boat, bus, train) **sinn dae** ဆင်းတယ်

get on (boat, bus, train) **tet tae** တက်တယ်

gift **let saung** လက်ဆောင်

ginger **jinn** ဂျင်း

girl **mein kha layy** မိန်းကလေး

girlfriend **yee zarr** ရည်းစား

give **payy dae** ပေးတယ်

glass (for drinking) **phan khwet** ဖန်ခွက်

glass (material) **phan** ဖန်

glasses **myet mhan** မျက်မှန်

gloves **let ate** လက်အိတ်

glue **kaw** ကော်

go **thwarr dae** သွားတယ်

go back **pyan thwarr dae** ပြန်သွားတယ်

go out **apyin thwarr dae** အပြင်သွားတယ်

gold **shway** ရွှေ

golf **gout** ဂေါက်

golf course **gout yite thin dann** ဂေါက်ရိုက်သင်တန်း

good afternoon **mingalar nayt lae ginn bar** မင်္ဂလာနေ့လယ်ခင်းပါ

good evening **mingalar nya nay ginn bar** မင်္ဂလာညနေခင်းပါ

good morning **mingalar nan net khinn bar** မင်္ဂလာနံနက်ခင်းပါ

good night **mingalar nya jann bar** မင်္ဂလာညချမ်းပါ

goodbye **ta tar** တာ့တာ

gram **gram** ဂရမ်

grandchild **myayy** မြေး

granddaughter **myayy ma** မြေးမ

grandfather **aphohh** အဘိုး

grandmother **aphwarr** အဘွား

grandson **myayy** မြေး

grapes **zabyit thee** စပျစ်သီး

grave **kyinn** ကျင်း

gray **mee khohh yaung** မီးခိုးရောင်

gray-haired **mee khohh yaung zabin** မီးခိုးရောင်ဆံပင်

graze (noun, injury) **ponn paet dan yar** ပွန်းပဲ့ဒဏ်ရာ

greasy (food) **ei dae** အီတယ်

Great Britain **byeet tain nai ngan** ဗြိတိန်နိုင်ငံ

green **asein yaung** အစိမ်းရောင်

green tea **yay nwayy gyann** ရေနွေးကြမ်း

greengrocer **k'own zein sai** ကုန်စိမ်းဆိုင်

greeting **nhote khonn set zagarr** နှုတ်ခွန်းဆက်စကား

grilled **akin** အကင်

groceries **sarr thout k'own** စားသောက်ကုန်

grocery **k'own z'own sai** ကုန်စုံဆိုင်

group **oat soot** အုပ်စု

guide (book) **lann nyon sar oat** လမ်းညွှန်စာအုပ်

guide (person) **aet lann nyon** အညွှန့်လမ်းညွှန်

guided tour **aet lann nyon bar daet, kha yee zin** အညွှန့်လမ်းညွှန်ပါတဲ့ခရီးစဉ်

guilty **apyit sheet dae** အပြစ်ရှိတယ်

gym **gym** ဂျင်

gynecologist **tharr phwarr mee yat, sayar win** သားဖွားမီးယပ်ဆရာဝန်

H

hair **zabin** ဆံပင်

hairbrush **bee** ဘီး

haircut **zabin nyat** ဆံပင်ညှပ်

hairdresser **zabin nyat thu** ဆံပင်ညှပ်သူ

hairdryer **hairdryer** ဟဲဒရိုင်ယာ

hairspray **hairspray** ဟဲစပရေး

hairstyle **zabin kay** ဆံပင်ကေ

half **ta wet** တစ်ဝက်

ham **wet paung jout** ဝက်ပေါင်ခြောက်

hand **let** လက်

hand brake **hand brake** ဟန်းဘရိတ်

hand luggage **let swell ate** လက်ဆွဲအိတ်

hand towel **let thote pawar** လက်သုတ်ပဝါ

handbag **let kai ate** လက်ကိုင်အိတ်

handkerchief **let kai pawar** လက်ကိုင်ပဝါ

handmade **let lote** လက်လုပ်

handsome **chaw dae/khant dae** ချောတယ် / ခန့်တယ်

hanger **jate** ချိတ်

happy **pyaww dae** ပျော်တယ်

harbor **sate kann** ဆိပ်ကမ်း

hard (difficult) **khet tae** ခက်တယ်

hard (firm) **mar dae** မာတယ်

hat **oat htote** ဦးထုပ်

have **sheet dae** ရှိတယ်

have to **V + ya mae** V + ရမယ်

hay fever **nhar mhon** နှာမွှန်

he **thu** သူ

head **gaungg** ခေါင်း

headache **gaungg kite** ခေါင်းကိုက်

headlights **shayt mee gyee** ရှေ့မီးကြီး

healthy **kyann mar dae** ကျန်းမာတယ်

hear **kyarr dae** ကြားတယ်

hearing aid **narr kyarr kareet yar** နားကြားကိရိယာ

heart **nhalone** နှလုံး

heart attack **heart attack** ဟတ်အတက်

heat **apu** အပူ

heavy **layy dae** လေးတယ်

heel (of foot) **phanaungt** ဖနောင့်

heel (of shoe) **dout** ဒေါက်

height **amyint** အမြင့်

height (body) **a yat** အရပ်

hello **mingalarbar** မင်္ဂလာပါ

help (verb) **ku nyi dae** ကူညီတယ်

Help! **Kae gya bar ownn!** ကယ်ကြပါဦး

here **di mhar** ဒီမှာ

high **myint dae** မြင့်တယ်
high chair **kh'own amyint** ခုံအမြင့်
high tide **di yay hlaii amyint** ဒီရေလှိုင်းအမြင့်
highway **amyan lann** အမြန်လမ်း
hiking **taung tet** တောင်တက်
hire **ngarr dae** ငှားတယ်
history **thamaii** သမိုင်း
hitchhike **karr j'own lite see dae** ကားကြုံလိုက်စီးတယ်
hobby **war thanar** ဝါသနာ
holiday (public) **pate yet** ပိတ်ရက်
holiday (vacation) **pate yet kha yee** ပိတ်ရက်ခရီး
homesick **eain lwann** အိမ်လွမ်း
homosexual **lain tu chit thu** လိင်တူချစ်သူ
honest **yohh tharr dae** ရိုးသားတယ်
honey **pyarr yay** ပျားရည်
hope (verb) **myaw lint dae** မျှော်လင့်တယ်
horrible **kyout sayar kaungg dae** ကြောက်စရာကောင်းတယ်
horse **myinn** မြင်း
hospital **sayy y'own** ဆေးရုံ
hospitality **pyu ngar mhoot** ပျူငှာမှု
hot (spicy) **sat tae** စပ်တယ်
hot (warm) **pu dae** ပူတယ်
hot spring **yay pu sann** ရေပူစမ်း
hot water **yay nwayy** ရေနွေး
hot-water bottle **dat boo** ဓာတ်ဘူး
hotel **hotel** ဟိုတယ်
hour **nar yi** နာရီ
house **eain** အိမ်
how **bae lo** ဘယ်လို
How far? **Bae lout wayy lell?** ဘယ်လောက်ဝေးလဲ
How long? **Bae lout kyar lell?** ဘယ်လောက်ကြာလဲ
How many? **Bae nha + counter?** ဘယ်နှစ် + counter
How much? **Bae lout lell?** ဘယ်လောက်လဲ
humid **so htaii dae** စိုထိုင်းတယ်
hundred **yar** ရာ
hungry **bite sar dae** ဗိုက်ဆာတယ်
hurry (quickly) **myan myan** မြန်မြန်
husband **a myohh tharr** အမျိုးသား

I

ice **yay gell** ရေခဲ
ice cream **yay gell m'ownt** ရေခဲမုန့်
idea **idea** အိုင်ဒီယာ
identification (card) **ID card** အိုင်ဒီကတ်
identify **phaw htote tae** ဖော်ထုတ်တယ်
idiot **a yoo** အရူး
if **tagae loht** တကယ်လို့
ill **phyarr dae** ဖျားတယ်
illegal **ta yarr ma win** တရားမဝင်
illness **aphyarr** အဖျား
imagine **sate koo dae** စိတ်ကူးတယ်
immediately **chet jinn** ချက်ချင်း
immigration/arrival **immigration** အင်မီဂရေးရှင်း
important **a yayy kyee dae** အရေးကြီးတယ်
impossible **ma phyit nai boo** မဖြစ်နိုင်ဘူး
improve **tohh tet tae** တိုးတက်တယ်

in **ahtae mhar** အထဲမှာ

in the evening **nya nay mhar** ညနေမှာ

in the morning **ma net mhar** မနက်မှာ

increase **tohh dae** တိုးတယ်

included **bar dae** ပါတယ်

including **apar** အပါ

income **win ngway** ဝင်ငွေ

indicate **nyon dae** ညွှန်တယ်

indicator (car) **achet pya** အချက်ပြမီး

indigestion **a sar ma kyay phyit** အစာမကြေဖြစ်

inexpensive **zayy ma kyee boo** ဈေးမကြီးဘူး

infected **pohh sheet dae** ပိုးရှိတယ်

infectious **koo dat tae** ကူးတတ်တယ်

inflammation **yaung dae** ယောင်တယ်

inflation **ngway phaungg pwa mhoot** ငွေဖောင်းပွမှု

information **thadinn a chet a let** သတင်းအချက်အလက်

information desk **information counter** အင်ဖော်မေးရှင်းကောင်တာ

injection **sayy htohh dae** ဆေးထိုးတယ်

injured **dan yar ya htarr dae** ဒဏ်ရာရထားတယ်

innocent **apyit kinn sin dae** အပြစ်ကင်းစင်တယ်

inquire **s'own zann dae** စုံစမ်းတယ်

insect **insect** အင်းဆက်

insect bite **insect kite yar** အင်းဆက်ကိုက်ရာ

insect repellent **insect sayy** အင်းဆက်ဆေး

inside **ahtell mhar** အထဲမှာ

instead of **asarr** အစား

instructions **nyon kyarr chet** ညွှန်ကြားချက်

insurance **ar ma gan** အာမခံ

intelligent **nyan kaungg dae** ဉာဏ်ကောင်းတယ်

interested **sate win zarr dae** စိတ်ဝင်စားတယ်

interesting **sate win zarr zayar kaungg dae** စိတ်ဝင်စားစရာကောင်းတယ်

internal use (medicine) **atwinn bet lein yan** အတွင်းဘက်လိမ်းရန်

international **nai ngan dagar** နိုင်ငံတကာ

Internet **internet** အင်တာနက်

Internet cafe, cybercafe **internet sai** အင်တာနက်ဆိုင်

interpreter **zagabyan** စကားပြန်

intersection **lann z'own** လမ်းဆုံ

introduce **mate set tae** မိတ်ဆက်တယ်

introduce oneself **koht ko ko, mate set tae** ကိုယ့်ကိုကိုယ်မိတ်ဆက်တယ်

invite **phate tae** ဖိတ်တယ်

invoice **k'own kya za yate sa yinn** ကုန်ကျစရိတ်စာရင်း

Ireland **Ireland** အိုင်းယာလန်

iron (for clothes) **mee bu** မီးပူ

iron (metal) **than** သံ

iron (verb) **mee bu tite tae** မီးပူတိုက်တယ်

island **kyonn** ကျွန်း

Italian (language) **Italy zagarr** အီတလီစကား

Italian (people) **Italy lu myohh** အီတလီလူမျိုး

Italy **Italy nai ngan** အီတလီနိုင်ငံ

itchy **yarr dae** ယားတယ်

itinerary **kha yee zin** ခရီးစဉ်

J

jack (for a car) **jite** ဂျ္ဂက်

jack (verb) **jite htout tae**
ဂျ္ဂက်ထောက်တယ်

jacket **jarkin** ဂျာကင်

jade **kyout sein** ကျောက်စိမ်း

jam **yo** ယို

January **january la** ဇန်နဝါရီလ

Japan **japan nai ngan**
ဂျပန်နိုင်ငံ

Japanese (language) **japan
zagarr** ဂျပန်စကား

Japanese (people) **japan lu
myohh** ဂျပန်လူမျိုး

jazz **jazz** ဂျက်စ်

jeans **jinn** ဂျင်း

jellyfish **jelly ngarr** ဂျယ်လီငါး

jewelry **yadanar** ရတနာ

jewelry shop **yadanar sai**
ရတနာဆိုင်

job **alote** အလုပ်

joke **har tha** ဟာသ

journalist **thadinn dout**
သတင်းထောက်

journey **kha yee** ခရီး

juice **phyaw yay** ဖျော်ရည်

July **july la** ဇူလိုင်လ

jumper **sweater eain gyi**
ဆွယ်တာအင်္ကျီ

June **june la** ဇွန်လ

just (only) **bell** ပဲ

just (very recently) **saww saww
ga bell** စောစောကပဲ

K

keep **thein htarr dae**
သိမ်းထားတယ်

kerosene **yay nan** ရေနံ

key **thawt** သော့

kilogram **kilogram** ကီလိုဂရမ်

kilometer **kilometer** ကီလိုမီတာ

king **ba yin** ဘုရင်

kitchen **mee pho jaung**
မီးဖိုချောင်

knee **doo** ဒူး

knife **darr** ဓား

know **theet dae** သိတယ်

L

laces (for shoes) **phanat kyohh**
ဖိနပ်ကြိုး

lake **yay kan** ရေကန်

lamp **mee eain** မီးအိမ်

land (ground) **myay gyee** မြေကြီး

land (verb) **sinn dae** ဆင်းတယ်

landscape **shoot ginn** ရှုခင်း

lane (of traffic) **lann thwae**
လမ်းသွယ်

language **zagarr** စကား

large **kyee dae** ကြီးတယ်

last (endure) **khan dae** ခံတယ်

last (final) **nout sone** နောက်ဆုံး

last night **ma nayt nya ga**
မနေ့ညက

late **nout kya dae** နောက်ကျတယ်

later **nout mha** နောက်မှ

laugh (verb) **yee dae** ရယ်တယ်

laundry soap **a wit shaw sat
pyar** အဝတ်လျှော်ဆပ်ပြာ

law **oot baday** ဥပဒေ

lawyer **shayt nay** ရှေ့ နေ

laxative **wann nhote sayy**
ဝမ်းနှုတ်ဆေး

lazy **apyinn kyee dae**
အပျင်းကြီးတယ်

leak (verb) **yo saint dae**
ယိုစိမ့်တယ်

learn **layt lar dae** လေ့လာတယ်

least (at least) **anell sone**
အနည်းဆုံး

leather **tha yay** သားရေ

leave **htwet tae** ထွက်တယ်

left (direction) **bae bet** ဘယ်ဘက်

left behind **kyan gaet dae** ကျန်ခဲ့တယ်

leg **chay dout** ခြေထောက်

legal **ta ya win** တရားဝင်

leisure **arr lat chain** အားလပ်ချိန်

lemon **shout thee** ရှောက်သီး

lend **chayy ngarr dae** ချေးငှားတယ်

lens (camera) **mhan baloo** မှန်ဘီလူး

less **po nell dae** ပိုနည်းတယ်

letter **sar** စာ

lettuce **salat ywet** ဆလပ်ရွက်

library **sar kyeet tite** စာကြည့်တိုက်

license **lai sin** လိုင်စင်

lie (verb, not tell the truth) **lain dae** လိမ်တယ်

lie down **hlell dae** လှဲတယ်

lift (elevator) **dat hlay garr** ဓာတ်လှေကား

light (lamp) **mee** မီး

light (not dark) **linn dae** လင်းတယ်

light (not heavy) **pawt dae** ပေါ့တယ်

light bulb **mee lone** မီးလုံး

lighter (for cigarettes) **mee jit** မီးခြစ်

lightning **shat see let** လျှပ်စီးလက်

like (verb) **kyite tae** ကြိုက်တယ်

linen **li nin** လီနင်

lip **nhakhann** နှုတ်ခမ်း

lipstick **nhakhann ni** နှုတ်ခမ်းနီ

listen **narr htaung dae** နားထောင်တယ်

liter **liter** လီတာ

little (amount) **nell nell** နည်းနည်း

little (small) **thayy dae** သေးတယ်

live (verb) **nay dae** နေတယ်

liver **athell** အသည်း

lobster **pazon dote** ပုစွန်ထုပ်

local **day tha khan** ဒေသခံ

lock **lock cha dae** လော့ချတယ်

long **shay dae** ရှည်တယ်

long-distance call **nae wayy khaw** နယ်ဝေးခေါ်

look at **kyeet dae** ကြည့်တယ်

look for **shar dae** ရှာတယ်

look up **mawt kyeet dae** မော့ကြည့်တယ်

lose (to not win) **shone dae** ရှုံးတယ်

loss **sone shone mhoot** ဆုံးရှုံးမှု

lost (can't find the way) **lann pyout tae** လမ်းပျောက်တယ်

lost (missing) **pyout thwarr dae** ပျောက်သွားတယ်

lost and found office **pyit see pyout, shar phway yayy yone** ပစ္စည်းပျောက်ရှာဖွေရေးရုံး

loud **athan kyae dae** အသံကျယ်တယ်

love **achit** အချစ်

love (verb) **chit tae** ချစ်တယ်

low **naint dae** နိမ့်တယ်

low tide **di yay anaint** ဒီရေအနိမ့်

luck **kan kaungg mhoot** ကံကောင်းမှု

luggage **luggage** လက်ဝွေ့ဂျ်

luggage locker **luggage locker** လက်ဝွေ့ဂျ်လော့ကာ

lunch **nayt lae zar** နေ့လယ်စာ

lungs **asote** အဆုတ်

lychees **lychee thee** လိုင်ချီးသီး

M

magazine **magazine** မဂ္ဂဇင်း

mail (letters) **sar** စာ

mail (verb) **sar poht dae**
စာပို့တယ်

mailbox **sar dite bone** စာတိုက်ပုံး

main **adeet ka** အဓိက

main road **lann ma gyee**
လမ်းမကြီး

make, create **lote tae** လုပ်တယ်

make an appointment **appointment lote tae** အပွိုင့်မန့်လုပ်တယ်

make love **chit tinn nhaww dae**
ချစ်တင်းနှောတယ်

makeshift **yar yi** ယာယီ

makeup **makeup** မိတ်ကပ်

man **yout kyarr / a myohh tharr**
ယောက်ျား / အမျိုးသား

manager **manager** မန်နေဂျာ

manicure **let thell ahla pyin**
လက်သည်းအလှပြင်

many **a myarr gyee** အများကြီး

map **myay b'own** မြေပုံ

March **march la** မတ်လ

marital status **eain daung sheet,
ma sheet** အိမ်ထောင်ရှိ၊ မရှိ

market **zayy** ဈေး

married **eain daung sheet dae**
အိမ်ထောင်ရှိတယ်

massage **mar sat** မာဆတ်

match (competition) **pwell** ပွဲ

matchstick **mee jit san** မီးခြစ်ဆံ

mattress **mwayt yar** မွေ့ရာ

May **may la** မေလ

maybe **V + yin + V + mae** V +
ရင် + V + မယ်

meal **a sarr a sar** အစားအစာ

meaning **a date bae** အဓိပ္ပါယ်

measure (verb) **taii tar dae**
တိုင်းတာတယ်

meat **atharr** အသား

medicine **sayy** ဆေး

meet **twayt dae** တွေ့တယ်

meeting **a see a wayy**
အစည်းအဝေး

mend **pyin dae** ပြင်တယ်

menu **menu** မီနူး

merchant **k'own thae** ကုန်သည်

message **message** မက်ဆေ့ဂျ်

metal **that htoot** သတ္တု

metal detector **that htoot, sit
sayy set** သတ္တုစစ်ဆေးစက်

meter **meter** မီတာ

method **nee lann** နည်းလမ်း

midday **nay monn taet**
နေ့မွန်းတည့်

middle **alae** အလယ်

midnight **tha gaung yan**
သန်းခေါင်ယံ

migraine **gaungg htohh kite** ေ
ခါင်းထိုးကိုက်

milk **nwarr noht** နွားနို့

millimeter **millimeter** မီလီမီတာ

million **thann** သန်း

mine (male speaker) **kya nawt
har** ကျွန်တော့ဟာ

mine (female speaker) **kya ma
har** ကျွန်မဟာ

minute **minit** မိနစ်

mirror **mhan** မှန်

miss (flight, train) **lwut thwarr
dae** လွတ်သွားတယ်

Miss (term of address) **Ma +
name** မ + နာမည်

miss (long for) **lwann dae**
လွမ်းတယ်

missing **pyout nay dae**
ပျောက်နေတယ်

missing person **pyout nay daet
lu** ပျောက်နေတဲ့လူ

mist **myu** မြူ
mistake (noun) **amharr** အမှား
mistaken **mharr thwarr dae** မှားသွားတယ်
misunderstanding **narr lae mhoot lwell dae** နားလည်မှုလွဲတယ်
misty **myu htu nay dae** မြူထူနေတယ်
modern **khit mi** ခေတ်မီ
Monday **ta ninn lar nayt** တနင်္လာနေ့
money **petsan** ပိုက်ဆံ
monkey **myout** မျောက်
month **la** လ
moon **la** လ
morning **manet** မနက်
more **po** ပို
mosquito **chin** ခြင်
mosquito net **chin daung** ခြင်ထောင်
mother **amay** အမေ
mother-in-law **yout khama** ယောက္ခမ
motorbike **sai kae** ဆိုင်ကယ်
mountain **taung** တောင်
mouse **kywet** ကြွက်
mouth **bazat** ပါးစပ်
move **shwayt dae** ရွှေ့တယ်
movie **yote shin** ရုပ်ရှင်
Mr. **U (pronounced "oo") + name** ဦး + နာမည်
Mrs **Daw + name** ဒေါ် + နာမည်
MSG **a cho mh'ownt** အချိုမှုန့်
much **thate** သိပ်
mud **shont** ရွှံ့
muscle **kywet tharr** ကြွက်သား
museum **pya dite** ပြတိုက်
mushrooms **mho** မှို
music **gi ta** ဂီတ
musical instrument **gi ta tu reet yar** ဂီတတူရိယာ
Muslim **muslim** မူစလင်
must **V + ya mae** V + ရမယ်
mutton (goat's meat) **sate tharr** ဆိတ်သား
my [male] **kya nawt** ကျွန်တော့်
[female] **kya ma** ကျွန်မ

N

nail (finger) **let thell** လက်သည်း
nail (metal) **than** သံ
nail clippers **let thell nyat** လက်သည်းညှပ်
nail file **let thell pwut tan** လက်သည်းပွတ်တံ
nail scissors **let thell nyat, kat kyayy** လက်သည်းညှပ်ကတ်ကြေး
napkin **let thote pawar** လက်သုတ်ပဝါ
nappy, diaper **diaper** ဒိုင်ဘာ
nationality **lu myohh** လူမျိုး
natural **thabar wa kya dae** သဘာဝကျတယ်
nature **thabar wa** သဘာဝ
nauseous **an jin dae** အန်ချင်တယ်
near **anee anarr** အနီးအနား
nearby **di narr mhar** ဒီနားမှာ
necessary **lo dae** လိုတယ်
neck **lae binn** လည်ပင်း
necklace **swell kyohh** ဆွဲကြိုး
necktie **necktie** နက်ကတိုင်
needle **at** အပ်
neighbor **eain nee jinn** အိမ်နီးချင်း
nephew **tu** တူ
never **bae dawt mha** ဘယ်တော့မှ
new **athit** အသစ်
news **thadinn** သတင်း

newsstand **thadinn zar sin** သတင်းစာစင်

newspaper **thadinn zar** သတင်းစာ

next **nout** နောက်

next to **bayy** ဘေး

nice **kaungg dae** ကောင်းတယ်

niece **tu ma** တူမ

night **nya** ည

night view **nya shoot ginn** ညရှုခင်း

nightclub **nightclub** နိုက်ကလပ်

nine **kohh** ကိုး

nineteen **saet kohh** ဆယ့်ကိုး

ninety **kohh zae** ကိုးဆယ်

nipple (on baby's bottle) **noht thee gaungg** နို့သီးခေါင်း

no **ma hote boo** မဟုတ်ဘူး

no entry **ma win ya** မဝင်ရ

no one **bae thu mha** ဘယ်သူမှ

noise **su nyan than** ဆူညံသံ

noisy **su nyan dae** ဆူညံတယ်

noodles **khout swell** ခေါက်ဆွဲ

noon **nay monn taet** နေ့မွန်းတည့်

normal **p'own mhan** ပုံမှန်

north **myout bet** မြောက်ဘက်

nose **nhakhaungg** နှာခေါင်း

nosebleed **nhakhaungg thwayy shan dae** နှာခေါင်းသွေးလျှံတယ်

notebook **mhat soot sar oat** မှတ်စုစာအုပ်

notepad **mhat soot sar oat** မှတ်စုစာအုပ်

nothing **bar mha ma hote boo** ဘာမှမဟုတ်ဘူး

novel **wit htoot** ဝတ္ထု

November **november la** နိုဝင်ဘာလ

now **akhoot** အခု

number **nan bat** နံပါတ်

number plate **nan bat pyarr** နံပါတ်ပြား

nurse **thu nar pyoot** သူနာပြု

O

obvious **theet thar dae** သိသာတယ်

occupation **alote akai** အလုပ်အကိုင်

October **october la** အောက်တိုဘာလ

of course **hote tar bawt** ဟုတ်တာပေါ့

off (turned off) **pate htarr dae** ပိတ်ထားတယ်

office **yone** ရုံး

oil **si** ဆီ

ointment **lein zayy** လိမ်းဆေး

okay **ok** အိုကေ

old (used for people) **athet kyee dae** အသက်ကြီးတယ်

old (used for things) **haungg dae** ဟောင်းတယ်

Olympics **Olympic** အိုလံပစ်

on **apaw** အပေါ်

on (turned on) **phwint htarr dae** ဖွင့်ထားတယ်

on the left **bae bet mhar** ဘယ်ဘက်မှာ

on the right **nyar bet mhar** ညာဘက်မှာ

on the way **lann mhar** လမ်းမှာ

once **da jain** တစ်ကြိမ်

one **tit** တစ်

one-way traffic **talann thwarr** တစ်လမ်းသွား

onion **kyet thon ni** ကြက်သွန်နီ

online chat **online chat** အွန်လိုင်းချက်

only **bell** ပဲ

open (adj.) **phwint htarr dae**
ဖွင့်ထားတယ်

open (verb) **phwint dae** ဖွင့်တယ်

opera **opera pya zat**
အော်ပရာပြဇာတ်

operate (surgeon) **khwell sate
tae** ခွဲစိတ်တယ်

operator (telephone) **telephone
operator** တယ်လီဖုန်းအော်ပရေတာ

opportunity **akhwint a yayy**
အခွင့်အရေး

opposite **sant kyin bet**
ဆန့်ကျင်ဘက်

optician **myet mhan lote thu**
မျက်မှန်လုပ်သူ

orange (color) **lain maw yaung**
လိမ္မော်ရောင်

orange (fruit) **lain maw thee**
လိမ္မော်သီး

order (verb, in a restaurant)
mhar dae မှာတယ်

ordinary **thar man** သာမန်

other **tacharr** တခြား

our [male] **kya naw doht yaet**
ကျွန်တော်တို့ရဲ့

[female] **kya ma doht yaet**
ကျွန်မတို့ရဲ့

outside **apyin** အပြင်

over there **ho mhar** ဟိုမှာ

overseas **nai ngan jarr** နိုင်ငံခြား

overtake (vehicle) **kyaw thwarr
dae** ကျော်သွားတယ်

owe **akywayy tin dae**
အကြွေးတင်တယ်

P

packed lunch **hta minn boo**
ထမင်းဘူး

packet **ahtote** အထုပ်

page **sar myet nhar** စာမျက်နှာ

pagoda **pha yarr** ဘုရား

pain **a kite a khell** အကိုက်အခဲ

painkiller **a kite a khell pyout
sayy** အကိုက်အခဲပျောက်ဆေး

painting **baji** ပန်းချီ

pair **a s'own** အစုံ

pajamas **nya wit eain gyi**
ညဝတ်အင်္ကျီ

palace **nann daw** နန်းတော်

pan **dae ohh** ဒယ်အိုး

panties **atwinn khan baungg bi**
အတွင်းခံဘောင်းဘီ

pants **baungg bi** ဘောင်းဘီ

pantyhose **atharr gat baungg bi**
အသားကပ်ဘောင်းဘီ

paper **sar ywet** စာရွက်

parcel **parcel** ပါဆယ်

parents **meet ba** မိဘ

park, gardens **pann jan** ပန်းခြံ

parking space **karr parkin**
ကားပါကင်

partner **partner** ပါတနာ

party (event) **party** ပါတီ

passenger **kha yee thae** ခရီးသည်

passport **passport** ပတ်စ်ပို့

passport number **passport nan
bat** ပတ်စ်ပို့နံပါတ်

pay (verb) **payy dae** ပေးတယ်

peach **met mon thee** မက်မွန်သီး

peanut **myay bell** မြေပဲ

pear **thit taw thee** သစ်တော်သီး

pearl **palell** ပုလဲ

peas **pell** ပဲ

pedestrian crossing **lu koo myinn
gyarr** လူကူးမျဉ်းကြား

pen **baww bin** ဘောပင်

pencil **khell dan** ခဲတံ

penis **lain dan** လိင်တံ

penknife **khell dan chon daet
darr** ခဲတံချွန်တဲ့ဓား

people **lu** လူ

pepper (black) **nga yote kaungg**
ငရုတ်ကောင်း

pepper (chilli) **nga yote pwa**
ငရုတ်ပွ

performance **phyaw phyay yayy**
ဖျော်ဖြေရေး

perfume **yay mwayy** ရေမွှေး

perhaps **phyit nai dae**
ဖြစ်နိုင်တယ်

period (menstruation) **yar thi**
ရာသီ

permit (noun) **khwint pyoot
maint** ခွင့်ပြုမိန့်

permit (verb) **khwint pyoot dae**
ခွင့်ပြုတယ်

person **lu** လူ

personal **ko yayy ko dar**
ကိုယ်ရေးကိုယ်တာ

perspire **chwayy htwet tae**
ချွေးထွက်တယ်

pharmacy **sayy zai** ဆေးဆိုင်

phone (noun) **phone** ဖုန်း

phone (verb) **phone set tae**
ဖုန်းဆက်တယ်

phone number **phone nan bat**
ဖုန်းနံပါတ်

photo **dat p'own** ဓာတ်ပုံ

photocopier **mate tu set**
မိတ္တူစက်

photocopy (verb) **mate tu koo
dae** မိတ္တူကူးတယ်

phrasebook **zagabyaww sar oat**
စကားပြောစာအုပ်

pick up (collect meet someone)
kyo dae ကြိုတယ်

picnic **pyaww bwell zarr**
ပျော်ပွဲစား

pill (contraceptive) **tarr zayy**
တားဆေး

pillow **gaungg ownn** ခေါင်းအုံး

pillowcase **gaungg ownn swut**
ခေါင်းအုံးစွပ်

pills, tablets **sayy** ဆေး

pin **pin at** ပင်အပ်

pineapple **narnat thee** နာနတ်သီး

pink **pann yaung** ပန်းရောင်

pity **thanarr dae** သနားတယ်

place **nay yar** နေရာ

place of interest **sate win zarr
zayar nay yar** စိတ်ဝင်စားစရာနေရာ

plain (simple) **yohh yohh** ရိုးရိုး

plan (noun, intention) **a si a zin**
အစီအစဉ်

plane **lay yin** လေယာဉ်

plant **apin** အပင်

plastic **plastic** ပလတ်စတစ်

plastic bag **plastic ate**
ပလတ်စတစ်အိတ်

plate **bagan** ပန်းကန်

platform **platform** ပလက်ဖောင်း

play (drama) **pya zat** ပြဇာတ်

play (verb) **gazarr dae**
ကစားတယ်

play golf **gout yite tae**
ဂေါက်ရိုက်တယ်

play tennis **tennis gazarr dae**
တင်းနစ်ကစားတယ်

playground **gazarr gwinn**
ကစားကွင်း

playing cards **phell yite tae**
ဖဲရိုက်တယ်

please **kyayy zoo pyoot pee**
ကျေးဇူးပြုပြီး

plug (electric) **plug** ပလတ်

plum **zee thee** ဇီးသီး

pocket **ate kat** အိတ်ကပ်

pocketknife **ate saung darr**
အိတ်ဆောင်ဓား

point out **nyon pya dae**
ညွှန်ပြတယ်

poisonous **asate sheet dae**
အဆိပ်ရှိတယ်

police **yell** ရဲ

police station **yell sakhann** ရဲခန်း

pond **yay kan** ရေကန်

poor (not rich) **sinn yell dae**
ဆင်းရဲတယ်

poor (pitiful) **thanarr
zayar kaungg dae**
သနားစရာကောင်းတယ်

population **lu oo yay** လူဦးရေ

pork **wet tharr** ဝက်သား

portable power **power bank**
ပါဝါဘဏ်

portable Wi-Fi router **Wi-Fi set**
ဝိုင်ဖိုင်စက်

porter (for bags) **ku li** ကူလီ

possible **phyit nai dae** ဖြစ်နိုင်တယ်

post (verb) **sar poht dae** စာပို့တယ်

post office **sar dite** စာတိုက်

postage **sar poht kha** စာပို့ခ

postcard **postcard** ပို့စ်ကတ်

postcode **sar poht thin gay ta**
စာပို့သင်္ကေတ

postpone **saii htarr dae**
ဆိုင်းထားတယ်

potato **ar loo** အာလူး

potato chips **ar loo gyaw**
အာလူးကြော်

poultry **kyet bell** ကြက်ဘဲ

powdered milk **noht mh'ownt**
နို့မှုန့်

practice (verb) **layt kyint dae** ေ
လ့ကျင့်တယ်

prawn **bazon** ပုစွန်

precious stone **kyout myet**
ကျောက်မျက်

prefer **po kyite dae** ပိုကြိုက်တယ်

preference **po kyite dar**
ပိုကြိုက်တာ

pregnant **ko win sheet dae**
ကိုယ်ဝန်ရှိတယ်

prepaid phone card **phone
ngway phyayt card**
ဖုန်းငွေဖြည့်ကတ်

prepare **pyin sin dae** ပြင်ဆင်တယ်

prescription **sayy zar** ဆေးစာ

present (gift) **let saung**
လက်ဆောင်

present (in attendance) **sheet
dae** ရှိတယ်

pressure **pheet arr** ဖိအား

pretty **hla dae** လှတယ်

price **zayy nhone** ဈေးနှုန်း

price list **zayy nhone sayinn**
ဈေးနှုန်းစာရင်း

print (noun, picture) **yite tae**
ရိုက်တယ်

print (from computer) **print
htote tae** ပရင့်ထုတ်တယ်

private **pote galeet ka** ပုဂ္ဂလိက

probably **phyit nai dae**
ဖြစ်နိုင်တယ်

problem **pyet thanar** ပြဿနာ

product **pyit see** ပစ္စည်း

profession **alote akai**
အလုပ်အကိုင်

profit (noun) **amyat** အမြတ်

program **program** ပရိုဂရမ်

promise **gadeet** ကတိ

pronounce **athan htwet tae**
အသံထွက်တယ်

prostitute **pyayt dazar**
ပြည့်တန်ဆာ

protect **kar gwae dae**
ကာကွယ်တယ်

public **amyarr pyi thu**
အများပြည်သူ

pull **swell dae** ဆွဲတယ်

pull a muscle **a ywut pyell dae**
အရွတ်ပြဲတယ်

purchase **wae dae** ဝယ်တယ်
pure **thant sin dae** သန့်စင်တယ်
purple **kha yann yaung** ခရမ်းရောင်
purse **petsan ate** ပိုက်ဆံအိတ်
push (verb) **tonn dae** တွန်းတယ်
put (in) **htaet dae** ထည့်တယ်
put (on) **tin dae** တင်တယ်
pyjamas **nya wit eain gyi** ညဝတ်အင်္ကျီ

Q

quality **a yay athwayy** အရည်အသွေး
quantity **a yay atwet** အရေအတွက်
quarrel **nyinnn kh'own dae** ငြင်းခုံတယ်
quarter **dazate** တစ်စိတ်
quarter of an hour **saet ngarr minit** ဆယ့်ငါးမိနစ်
queen **ba yin ma** ဘုရင်မ
question **mayy zayar** မေးစရာ
queue (verb) **tann si dae** တန်းစီတယ်
quick **myan dae** မြန်တယ်
quiet **tate sate tae** တိတ်ဆိတ်တယ်
quilt **gonn gat** ဂွမ်းကပ်

R

rabbit **y'own** ယုန်
radio **radio** ရေဒီယို
railway **yat htarr than lann** ရထားသံလမ်း
railway station **bu tar** ဘူတာ
rain (noun) **mohh** မိုး
rain (verb) **mohh ywar dae** မိုးရွာတယ်
raincoat **mohh gar eain gyi** မိုးကာအင်္ကျီ
rape **madein kyint dae** မုဒိမ်းကျင့်တယ်
rapids **yay see than daet nay yar** ရေစီးသန်တဲ့နေရာ
rare **sharr dae** ရှားတယ်
rash **ma sinn zarr bell, lote tae** မစဉ်းစားဘဲလုပ်တယ်
rat **kywet** ကြွက်
raw **asein** အစိမ်း
razor blade **blade darr** ဘလိတ်ဓား
read **phat tae** ဖတ်တယ်
ready **asin thint** အဆင်သင့်
really **dagae** တကယ်
reason **akyaungg pya jet** အကြောင်းပြချက်
receipt **pyay zar** ပြေစာ
receive **let khan ya sheet dae** လက်ခံရရှိတယ်
reception desk **reception** ရီဆက်ရှင်
recommend **htout khan payy dae** ထောက်ခံပေးတယ်
rectangle **daungt mhan satoot gan** ထောင့်မှန်စတုဂံ
red **ani** အနီ
red wine **wine ani** ဝိုင်အနီ
reduction **shawt cha** လျှော့ချ
refrigerator **yay gell thittar** ရေခဲသေတ္တာ
refund **pyan ann ngway** ပြန်အမ်းငွေ
refuse **nyinn dae** ငြင်းတယ်
region **day tha** ဒေသ
registered **mhat p'own tin htarr dae** မှတ်ပုံတင်ထားတယ်
registered mail **register sar** ရက်ဂျစ်စတာစာ
regret **naung ta ya dae** နောင်တရတယ်
relatives **sway myohh** ဆွေမျိုး

reliable **arr kohh ya dae**
အားကိုးရတယ်

religion **bar thar yayy** ဘာသာရေး

remember **mhat meet dae**
မှတ်မိတယ်

rent/hire **ngarr dae** ငှားတယ်

repair **pyin dae** ပြင်တယ်

repeat (say) **htat pyaww dae**
ထပ်ပြောတယ်

repeat (do) **htat lote tae**
ထပ်လုပ်တယ်

represent **ko zarr pyoot dae**
ကိုယ်စားပြုတယ်

reserve **reserve lote htarr dae**
ရီဇတ်လုပ်ထားတယ်

responsible **tar win sheet dae**
တာဝန်ရှိတယ်

rest **narr dae** နားတယ်

restaurant **sarr thout sai**
စားသောက်ဆိုင်

restroom **eain thar** အိမ်သာ

result **ya let** ရလဒ်

retired **anyein zarr** အငြိမ်းစား

return (come back) **pyan lar dae**
ပြန်လာတယ်

return (give back) **pyan payy
dae** ပြန်ပေးတယ်

return (go back) **pyan thwarr
dae** ပြန်သွားတယ်

return ticket **athwarr apyan let
mhat** အသွားအပြန်လက်မှတ်

rheumatism **asit yaung**
အဆစ်ယောင်

ribbon **phell byarr** ဖဲပြား

rice (cooked) **htaminn** ထမင်း

rice (grain) **san** ဆန်

rice (paddy) **zabarr** စပါး

ridiculous **yoo dae** ရူးတယ်

riding (horseback) **see dae**
စီးတယ်

right (correct) **mhan dae**
မှန်တယ်

right (side) **nyar** ညာ

right of way **lann athone pyoot
khwint** လမ်းအသုံးပြုခွင့်

ring (noun) **let swut** လက်စွပ်

rinse **sayy dae** ဆေးတယ်

ripe **mhaet dae** မှည့်တယ်

risk **sont zarr mhoot** စွန့်စားမှု

river **myit** မြစ်

road **lann ma** လမ်းမ

roadway **lann** လမ်း

roasted **akin** အကင်

rock (stone) **kyout tone**
ကျောက်တုံး

roof **khaung mohh** ခေါင်မိုး

room **akhann** အခန်း

room number **akhann nan bat**
အခန်းနံပါတ်

room service **akhann win saung
mhoot** အခန်းဝန်ဆောင်မှု

rope **kyohh** ကြိုး

round **a waii** အဝိုင်း

route **lann gyaungg** လမ်းကြောင်း

rowing boat **laungg hlay**
လှောင်လှေ

rubber (eraser) **khell byet** ခဲဖျက်

rubber (material) **rabar** ရာဘာ

rude **yaii dae** ရိုင်းတယ်

ruin (noun) **phyet see dae**
ဖျက်ဆီးတယ်

run (verb) **pyayy dae** ပြေးတယ်

running shoes **pyayy daet
phanat** ပြေးတဲ့ဖိနပ်

S

sad **wann nell dae** ဝမ်းနည်းတယ်

safe (adj.) **l'own j'own dae**
လုံခြုံတယ်

safe (for cash) **mee gan thittar**
မီးခံသေတ္တာ

safety pin **hloht wet nan bat**
လျှို့ပွက်နံပါတ်

salad **athote** အသုပ်

sale **yaungg arr** ရောင်းအား

sales clerk **a yaungg sa yayy**
အရောင်းစာရေး

salt **sarr** ဆား

same **tu dae** တူတယ်

sandals **gwinn dohh phanat**
ကွင်းထိုးဖိနပ်

sanitary napkin/towel **a myohh
tha mee, la zin thone pyit see**
အမျိုးသမီးလစဉ်သုံးပစ္စည်း

satisfied **kyay nat tae**
ကျေနပ်တယ်

Saturday **sa nay nayt** စနေနေ့

sauce **sauce** ဆော့စ်

saucepan **dae ohh** ဒယ်အိုး

sauna **chwayy htote khann**
ချွေးထုတ်ခန်း

say **pyaww dae** ပြောတယ်

scald (injury) **apu laung dan yar**
အပူလောင်ဒဏ်ရာ

scarf **mar phalar** မာဖလာ

scarf (headscarf) **gaungg zee**
ခေါင်းစည်း

scenery **shoot ginn** ရှုခင်း

schedule **achain za yarr**
အချိန်ဇယား

school **kyaungg** ကျောင်း

scissors **kat kyayy** ကတ်ကြေး

screwdriver **wet ou hlaet**
ဝက်အူလှည့်

sculpture **baboot** ပန်းပု

sea **pinlae** ပင်လယ်

seafood **pinlae zar** ပင်လယ်စာ

season **yar thi** ရာသီ

seat **htai kh'own** ထိုင်ခုံ

second (in line) **doot ta ya**
ဒုတိယ

second (measurement of time)
second စက္ကန့်

sedative **sate nyain dae**
စိတ်ငြိမ်တယ်

see **myin dae** မြင်တယ်

seem **htin ya dae** ထင်ရတယ်

send **poht dae** ပို့တယ်

sentence **sar gyaungg** စာကြောင်း

separate **thee jarr** သီးခြား

September **september la**
စက်တင်ဘာလ

serious **layy net tae** ေ
လးနက်တယ်

serious (injury) **pyinn htan dae**
ပြင်းထန်တယ်

service **win saung mhoot**
ဝန်ဆောင်မှု

seven **khunit** ခုနစ်

seventeen **saet khunit** ဆယ့်ခုနစ်

seventy **khunasae** ခုနစ်ဆယ်

sew **chote tae** ချုပ်တယ်

shade **a yate** အရိပ်

shallow **tain dae** တိမ်တယ်

shampoo **shampoo** ရှန်ပူ

shark **ngamann** ငါးမန်း

shave (verb) **yate tae** ရိတ်တယ်

shaver **yate set** ရိတ်စက်

shaving cream **amwayy yate
cream** အမွေးရိတ်ကရင်မ်

she **thu** သူ

sheet **akhinn** အခင်း

shirt **shat eain gyi** ရှပ်အင်္ကျီ

shoe **shoe phanat** ရှူးဖိနပ်

shoe polish **phanat a yaung tin
si** ဖိနပ်အရောင်တင်ဆီ

shop, store **sai** ဆိုင်

shop (verb) **zayy wae dae**
ဈေးဝယ်တယ်

shop assistant **sai aku** ဆိုင်အကူ
shop window **sai byadinn bout** ဆိုင်ပြတင်းပေါက်
shopping center **zayy wae center** ဈေးဝယ်စင်တာ
short (height) **poot dae** ပုတယ်
short (length) **toh dae** တိုတယ်
shorts (short trousers) **baungg bi toh** ဘောင်းဘီတို
shoulder **pakhone** ပခုံး
show to **pya dae** ပြတယ်
shower (for washing) **yay bann** ရေပန်း
shrimp **bazon** ပုစွန်
shuttle bus **bus karr** ဘတ်စ်ကား
shy **shet tae** ရှက်တယ်
sightseeing **shoot ginn kyeet** ရှုခင်းကြည့်
sign (road) **thin gay ta** သင်္ကေတ
sign (verb) **let mhat htohh dae** လက်မှတ်ထိုးတယ်
signature **let mhat** လက်မှတ်
silk **pohh** ပိုး
silver **ngway** ငွေ
simple **yohh yohh** ရိုးရိုး
since (until now) **V + gadell ga** V + ကတည်းက
sing **thajinn so dae** သီချင်းဆိုတယ်
single (only one) **ta khoot dell** တစ်ခုတည်း
single (unmarried) [male] **lu byo** လူပျို [female] **apyo** အပျို
single ticket **da gyangg zar, let mhat** တစ်ကြောင်းစာလက်မှတ်
sir **sayar** ဆရာ
sister (older) **ama** အစ်မ
sister (younger) **nyi ma** ညီမ
sit **htai dae** ထိုင်တယ်
six **chout** ခြောက်
sixteen **saet chout** ဆယ့်ခြောက်
sixty **chout sae** ခြောက်ဆယ်
size **a ywae asarr** အရွယ်အစား
size (clothes) **size** ဆိုဒ်
skin **a yay byarr** အရေပြား
skirt **skirt** စကတ်
sky **kaungg gin** ကောင်းကင်
sleep (verb) **ate tae** အိပ်တယ်
sleeping pills **ate sayy** အိပ်ဆေး
sleepy **ate chin dae** အိပ်ချင်တယ်
sleeve **eain gyi let** အင်္ကျီလက်
slippers **chay nhyat phanat** ခြေညှပ်ဖိနပ်
slow **nhayy dae** နှေးတယ်
small **thayy dae** သေးတယ်
small change **akyway** အကြွေ
smelly **nan dae** နံတယ်
smile **apyone** အပြုံး
smoke (verb) **salate thout tae** ဆေးလိပ်သောက်တယ်
smoke detector **salate ngwayt, achet payy set** ဆေးလိပ်ငွေ့ အချက်ပေးစက်
snack **m'ownt** မုန့်
snake **mway** မြွေ
snow (noun) **nhinn** နှင်း
snow (verb) **nhinn kya dae** နှင်းကျတယ်
soap **sat pyar** ဆပ်ပြာ
soap powder **sat pyar mh'ownt** ဆပ်ပြာမှုန့်
soccer **baw lone** ဘောလုံး
soccer match **baw lone bwell** ဘောလုံးပွဲ
social media **lu mhoot kon yet** လူမှုကွန်ရက်
socket (electric) **palat pout** ပလတ်ပေါက်
socks **chay ate** ခြေအိတ်
soft **pyawt dae** ပျော့တယ်

soft drink **a aye** အအေး

software **software** ဆော့ဖ်ဝဲ

soil **myay gyee** မြေကြီး

sole (of shoe) **phanat out chay** ဖိနပ်အောက်ခြေ

some **achoht** အချို့

someone **ta yout yout** တစ်ယောက်ယောက်

something **ta khoot khoot** တစ်ခုခု

sometimes **takhar talay** တစ်ခါတစ်လေ

somewhere **tanay yar yar** တစ်နေရာရာ

son **tharr** သား

song **thajinn** သီချင်း

soon **ma kyar gin** မကြာခင်

sore (painful) **nar dae** နာတယ်

sore (ulcer) **anar** အနာ

sore throat **lae gyaungg nar dae** လည်ချောင်းနာတယ်

sorry **taungg ban bar dae** တောင်းပန်ပါတယ်

soup **hinn yay** ဟင်းရည်

sour **chin dae** ချဉ်တယ်

south **taung bet** တောင်ဘက်

souvenir **amhat taya, let saung pyit see** အမှတ်တရလက်ဆောင်ပစ္စည်း

soy sauce (salty) **pell ngan pyar yay (angan)** ပဲငံပြာရည် (အငံ)

soy sauce (sweet) **pell ngan pyar yay (acho)** ပဲငံပြာရည် (အချို)

space **nay yar lwut** နေရာလွတ်

speak **pyaww dae** ပြောတယ်

special **ahtoo** အထူး

specialist (doctor) **ahtoo koot** အထူးကု

specialty (cooking) **ahtoo pyoot** အထူးပြု

speed limit **amyan nhone, kant that chet** အမြန်နှုန်းကန့်သတ်ချက်

spell **salone paungg dae** စာလုံးပေါင်းတယ်

spend money **petsan thone dae** ပိုက်ဆံသုံးတယ်

spices **hinn khat amwayy akyai** ဟင်းခတ်အမွေးအကြိုင်

spicy **sat tae** စပ်တယ်

spider **pint gu** ပင့်ကူ

spoon **zonn** ဇွန်း

sport **arr gazarr** အားကစား

sports center **arr gazarr y'own** အားကစားရုံ

spouse **khin ponn** (husband) ခင်ပွန်း **zanee** (wife) ဇနီး

sprain (verb) **asit lwell dae** အဆစ်လွဲတယ်

square (shape) **layy daungt** လေးထောင့်

square meter **satoot yann meter** စတုရန်းမီတာ

stadium **arr gazarr y'own** အားကစားရုံ

stain **asonn** အစွန်း

stain remover **asonn chut sayy** အစွန်းချွတ်ဆေး

stairs **hlay garr** လှေကား

stale **out thohh thouh nant htwet** အောက်သိုးသိုးနံ့နဲ့ထွက်

stamp **dazate gaungg** တံဆိပ်ခေါင်း

stand up **mat tat yat tae** မတ်တတ်ရပ်တယ်

star **kyae** ကြယ်

start **sa dae** စတယ်

station (train) **bu tar** ဘူတာ

statue **yote toot** ရုပ်တု

stay overnight **nya ate nay dae** ညအိပ်နေတယ်

steal **khohh dae** ခိုးတယ်

steamed **paungg htarr dae**
ပေါင်းထားတယ်

stepfather **pahtwayy** ပထွေး

stepmother **meet dwayy** မိထွေး

steps **chay hlann** ခြေလှမ်း

sterilize (clean) **pohh that tae**
ပိုးသတ်တယ်

sterilize (stop having children)
tharr gyaww phyat tae
သားကြောဖြတ်တယ်

sticky tape **tate** တိပ်

stockings **atharr kat baungg bi**
အသားကပ်ဘောင်းဘီ

stomach (abdomen) **bite** ဗိုက်

stomach (organ) **asar eain**
အစာအိမ်

stomachache **bite aungt dae**
ဗိုက်အောင့်တယ်

stool (seat) **khwayy chay kh'own**
ခွေးခြေခုံ

stop **yat tae** ရပ်တယ်

stopover **khana yat** ခဏရပ်

store, shop **sai** ဆိုင်

storm **m'own daii** မုန်တိုင်း

story (building) **ahtat** အထပ်

straight **phyaungt dae**
ဖြောင့်တယ်

straight ahead **taet taet**
တည့်တည့်

strange **htoo zann dae**
ထူးဆန်းတယ်

straw (drinking) **pite** ဗိုက်

street **lann** လမ်း

street vendor **lann bayy zayy
thae** လမ်းဘေးဈေးသည်

strike (verb, refuse to work)
sanda pya dae ဆန္ဒပြတယ်

string **kyohh** ကြိုး

strong **than mar dae** သန်မာတယ်

study (verb) **sar lote tae**
စာလုပ်တယ်

stupid **mite mell dae** မိုက်မဲတယ်

sturdy **khai khant dae**
ခိုင်ခံ့တယ်

subtitles **sar dann htohh**
စာတန်းထိုး

suburb **sin jay phone** ဆင်ခြေဖုံး

succeed **aung myin dae**
အောင်မြင်တယ်

sugar **thagyarr** သကြား

suit **wit s'own** ဝတ်စုံ

suitcase **thitttar** သေတ္တာ

summer **nway yar thi** နွေရာသီ

sun **nay** နေ

Sunday **ta ninn ga nway nayt**
တနင်္ဂနွေနေ့

sunglasses **nay gar myet mhan**
နေကာမျက်မှန်

sunrise **nay htwet chain**
နေထွက်ချိန်

sunscreen **nay laung khan lotion**
နေလောင်ခံလိုးရှင်း

sunset **nay win chain** နေဝင်ချိန်

sunshade **nay gar** နေကာ

supermarket **supermarket**
စူပါမားကတ်

sure **thay char dae** သေချာတယ်

surname **meet tharr zoot nan
mae** မိသားစုနာမည်

surprise **ant aww mhoot** အံ့သြမှု

swallow (verb) **myo cha dae**
မျိုချတယ်

swamp **shont bwet** ရွှံ့ဗွက်

sweat (verb) **chwayy htwet tae**
ချွေးထွက်တယ်

sweater **sweater eain gyi**
ဆွယ်တာအင်္ကျီ

sweet **cho dae** ချိုတယ်

swim (verb) **yay koo dae**
ရေကူးတယ်

swimming costume **yay koo wit
s'own** ရေကူးဝတ်စုံ

swimming pool **yay koo kan**
ရေကူးကန်

switch (light) **mee khalote**
မီးခလုတ်

swollen **yaung dae** ယောင်တယ်

syrup **thagyarr yay** သကြားရည်

T

table **zabwell** စားပွဲ

table tennis **zabwell tin tennis**
စားပွဲတင်တင်းနစ်

tablecloth **zabwell khinn** စားပွဲခင်း

tablemat **apu khan out khan
byarr** အပူခံအောက်ခံပြား

tablespoon **zabwell tin zonn**
စားပွဲတင်ဇွန်း

tablets **sayy byarr** ဆေးပြား

tableware **zonn dway bagan
dway** ဇွန်းတွေပန်းကန်တွေ

tailor's **at chote sai** အပ်ချုပ်ဆိုင်

take (medicine) **sayy thout tae**
ဆေးသောက်တယ်

take (photograph) **dat p'own
yite tae** ဓာတ်ပုံရိုက်တယ်

take (time) **kyar dae** ကြာတယ်

takeaway **par sae** ပါဆယ်

talk **zagarr pyaww dae**
စကားပြောတယ်

tall **a yat myint dae**
အရပ်မြင့်တယ်

tampon **tampon** တမ်ပွန်

tap **pite gaungg** ပိုက်ခေါင်း

tap water **pite yay** ပိုက်ရေ

tape measure **pay kyohh**
ပေကြိုး

taste (flavor) **a ya thar** အရသာ

taste (style) **a kyite** အကြိုက်

taste (verb) **myee dae**
မြည်းတယ်

tasty **a ya thar sheet dae**
အရသာရှိတယ်

tax **akhon** အခွန်

tax-free shop **akhon lwut sai**
အခွန်လွတ်ဆိုင်

taxi **taxi** တက္ကစီ

tea (green) **yay nwayy gyann**
ရေနွေးကြမ်း

tea (with condensed milk)
laphet yay လက်ဖက်ရည်

tea house **laphet yay sai**
လက်ဖက်ရည်ဆိုင်

teacup **laphet yay khwet**
လက်ဖက်ရည်ခွက်

teapot **yay nwayy kayarr**
ရေနွေးကရား

teaspoon **laphet yay zonn**
လက်ဖက်ရည်ဇွန်း

teat (on baby's bottle) **noht thee
gaungg** နို့သီးခေါင်း

television **TV** တီဗီ

tell **pyaww pya dae** ပြောပြတယ်

temperature **apu jain** အပူချိန်

temple **phayarr kyaungg**
ဘုရားကျောင်း

temporary **yar yi** ယာယီ

ten **ta sae** တစ်ဆယ်

ten thousand **ta thaungg**
တစ်သောင်း

tender, sore **aungt dae** ေ
အာင့်တယ်

tennis **tennis** တင်းနစ်

tennis court **tennis kwinn**
တင်းနစ်ကွင်း

tent **ywet phyin tell** ရွက်ဖျင်တဲ

terminal (airport) **terminal**
တာမင်နယ်

terminus (bus) **karr gate**
ကားဂိတ်

thank **kyayy zoo tin dae**
ကျေးဇူးတင်တယ်

thanks **kyayy zoo bar** ကျေးဇူးပါ

thank you **kyayy zoo tin bar dae**
ကျေးဇူးတင်ပါတယ်

that **ho har** ဟိုဟာ

thaw (verb) **a yay pyaww dae**
အရည်ပျော်တယ်

theater **pya zat y'own** ပြဇာတ်ရုံ

theft **khohh mhoot** ခိုးမှု

their **thu doht yaet** သူတို့ရဲ့

there **ho mhar** ဟိုမှာ

there is (are) **...sheet dae**
...ရှိတယ်

thermometer **thermometer**
သာမိုမီတာ

they **thu doht** သူတို့

thick **htu dae** ထူတယ်

thief **thakhohh** သူခိုး

thigh **paung** ပေါင်

thin (not fat) **pain dae** ပိန်တယ်

thin (not thick) **parr dae** ပါးတယ်

thing **pyitsee** ပစ္စည်း

think (believe) **htin dae** ထင်တယ်

think (ponder) **sinn zarr dae**
စဉ်းစားတယ်

third (in a series) **tat ta ya**
တတိယ

third (⅓) **thone b'own dab'own**
သုံးပုံတစ်ပုံ

thirsty **yay sar dae** ရေဆာတယ်

this **dar** ဒါ

this afternoon **di nayt ginn**
ဒီနေ့ခင်း

this evening **di nya nay** ဒီညနေ

this morning **di ma net** ဒီမနက်

thousand **htaung** ထောင်

thread **at chi** အပ်ချည်

three **thone** သုံး

throat **lae gyaungg** လည်ချောင်း

throat lozenges **ng'own zayy
byarr** ဂုံဆေးပြား

through (passage) **phyat pee**
ဖြတ်ပြီး

thunder (verb) **mohh gyohh pyit
tae** မိုးကြီးပစ်တယ်

thunderstorm **mohh gyohh
m'own daii** မိုးကြီးမုန်တိုင်း

Thursday **kyar thar badayy nayt**
ကြာသပတေးနေ့

ticket **let mhat** လက်မှတ်

ticket office **let mhat y'own**
လက်မှတ်ရုံ

tide **di yay** ဒီရေ

tidy **that yat tae** သပ်ရပ်တယ်

tie (necktie) **necktie** နက်ကတိုင်

tie (verb) **chi dae** ချည်တယ်

tights **baungg bi akyat**
ဘောင်းဘီအကြပ်

time **achain** အချိန်

times (multiplied by) **asa** အဆ

timetable **achain zayarr**
အချိန်ဇယား

tin (can) **than boo** သံဘူး

tin opener **noh zi phout tan**
နို့ဆီဖောက်တံ

tip (gratuity) **tip** တစ်ပ်

tire (tyre) **tar yar** တာယာ

tired **maww dae** မောတယ်

tissues (facial) **tissue** တစ်ရှူး

toast (noun, bread) **paung
m'ownt mee kin** ပေါင်မုန့်မီးကင်

tobacco **sayy ywet kyee**
ဆေးရွက်ကြီး

today **di nayt** ဒီနေ့

toe **chay gyaungg** ခြေချောင်း

together **atutu** အတူတူ

toilet **eain thar** အိမ်သာ

toilet (seated) **bo htai eain thar**
ဘိုထိုင်အိမ်သာ

toilet (squat) **yohh yohh eain thar** ရိုးရိုးအိမ်သာ

toilet paper **tissue** တစ်ရှူး

toiletries **yay chohh gann thone, pyit see** ရေချိုးခန်းသုံးပစ္စည်း

tomato **kha yann jin thee** ခရမ်းချဉ်သီး

tomb **oat gu** အုတ်ဂူ

tomorrow **ma net phyan** မနက်ဖြန်

tongue **shar** လျှာ

tonight **di nya** ဒီည

too **lell** လည်း

tool **kareet yar** ကိရိယာ

tooth **thwarr** သွား

toothache **thwarr kite tae** သွားကိုက်တယ်

toothbrush **thabwut tan** သွားပွတ်တံ

toothpaste **thwarr tite sayy** သွားတိုက်ဆေး

toothpick **thwarr gyarr htohh dan** သွားကြားထိုးတံ

top **htate** ထိပ်

top up **ngway phyayt dae** ငွေဖြည့်တယ်

torch, flashlight **let nhate dat mee** လက်နှိပ်ဓာတ်မီး

total **soot soot paungg** စုစုပေါင်း

touch **hteet dae** ထိတယ်

tour **kha yee zin** ခရီးစဉ်

tour group **kha yee thwarr aph-waet** ခရီးသွားအဖွဲ့.

tour guide **aet lann nhyon** ဧည့်လမ်းညွှန်

toward **shayt go** ရှေ့.ကို

towel **thabet** သဘက်

tower **mhyaw zin** မျှော်စင်

town **myoht** မြို့.

toy **a yote** အရုပ်

trade **k'own thwae yayy** ကုန်သွယ်ရေး

traffic **yin gyaww** ယာဉ်ကြော

traffic light **mee point** မီးပွိုင့်

train **yat htarr** ရထား

train station **bu tar** ဘူတာ

train ticket **yat htarr let mhat** ရထားလက်မှတ်

train timetable **yat htarr achain za yarr** ရထားအချိန်ဇယား

transfer (bank) **ngway hlwell dae** ငွေလွှဲတယ်

translate **bar thar pyan dae** ဘာသာပြန်တယ်

translator **bar thar pyan** ဘာသာပြန်

travel **kha yee thwarr dae** ခရီးသွားတယ်

travel agent **kha yee thwarr kozalae** ခရီးသွားကိုယ်စားလှယ်

traveler **kha yee thwarr** ခရီးသွား

traveling bag **a wit ate** အဝတ်အိတ်

treatment **sayy koot tha mhoot** ဆေးကုသမှု

tree **thit pin** သစ်ပင်

triangle **tareet gan** တြိဂံ

trim (haircut) **teet dae** တိတယ်

trip (travel) **kha yee** ခရီး

trouble **dote kha** ဒုက္ခ

trousers **baungg bi** ဘောင်းဘီ

truck **k'own tin karr** ကုန်တင်ကား

true **mhan dae** မှန်တယ်

trustworthy **y'own kyi ya dae** ယုံကြည်ရတယ်

try **kyohh zarr dae** ကြိုးစားတယ်

try on **wit kyeet dae** ဝတ်ကြည့်တယ်

Tuesday **ingar nayt** အင်္ဂါနေ့

tunnel **hlai gaungg** လိုဏ်ခေါင်း

turn (verb, change direction) **kwayt dae** ကွေ့တယ်
turn off **pate tae** ပိတ်တယ်
turn on **phwint dae** ဖွင့်တယ်
TV **TV** တီဗီ
TV guide **TV lann nhyon** တီဗီလမ်းညွှန်
tweezers **zar ganar** ဇာဂနာ
twelve **saet nhit** ဆယ့်နှစ်
twice **nhasa** နှစ်ဆ
Twitter **Twitter** တွစ်တာ
two **nhit** နှစ်
typhoon **typhoon m'own daii** တိုင်ဖွန်းမုန်တိုင်း
tyre (tire) **tar yar** တာယာ

U

ugly **yote sohh dae** ရုပ်ဆိုးတယ်
ulcer **pyi** ပြည်
umbrella **htee** ထီး
under **out** အောက်
underpants **atwinn khan baungg bi** အတွင်းခံဘောင်းဘီ
understand **narr lae dae** နားလည်တယ်
underwear **atwinn khan** အတွင်းခံ
undress **a wit chwut tae** အဝတ်ချွတ်တယ်
unemployed **alote ma sheet boo** အလုပ်မရှိဘူး
uneven **ma nyi nyar boo** မညီညာဘူး
university **takkatho** တက္ကသိုလ်
until **ahteet** အထိ
up **apaw** အပေါ်
upset (unhappy) **sate nyit tae** စိတ်ညစ်တယ်
upset stomach **bite ma kaungg boo** ဗိုက်မကောင်းဘူး
upstairs **apaw htat** အပေါ်ထပ်
urgent **alyin lo** အလျင်လို
urine **see** ဆီး
urinate **see thwarr dae** ဆီးသွားတယ်
us [male speaker] **kya naw doht go** ကျွန်တော်တို့ကို
us [female speaker] **kya ma doht go** ကျွန်မတို့ကို
use **thone dae** သုံးတယ်
used up **k'own thwarr bi** ကုန်သွားပြီ
useful **athone win dae** အသုံးဝင်တယ်
useless **athone ma win boo** အသုံးမဝင်ဘူး
usually **amyarr arr phyint** အများအားဖြင့်

V

vacancy **nay yar lwut** နေရာလွတ်
vacant **nay yar lwut tae** နေရာလွတ်တယ်
vacation **arr lat yet** အားလပ်ရက်
vacuum flask **dat boo** ဓာတ်ဘူး
vagina **mein ma ko** မိန်းမကိုယ်
valid **ta yarr win dae** တရားဝင်တယ်
valley **jite whann** ချိုင့်ဝှမ်း
valuable **tan bohh sheet dae** တန်ဖိုးရှိတယ်
valuables **aphohh tan pyitsee** အဖိုးတန်ပစ္စည်း
value **tan bohh** တန်ဖိုး
van **van karr** ဗန်ကား
vase **pann ohh** ပန်းအိုး
vegetable **hinn thee hinn ywet** ဟင်းသီးဟင်းရွက်
vegetarian **thet that lwut** သက်သတ်လွတ်
vein **thwayy byan gyaww** သွေးပြန်ကြော

velvet **gadibar** ကတ္တီပါ

venereal disease **kar la tharr yaww gar** ကာလသားရောဂါ

venomous **asate sheet dae** အဆိပ်ရှိတယ်

vertical **daung lite** ဒေါင်လိုက်

very **a yann** အရမ်း

via **naet** နဲ့

vicinity **anee ta wite** အနီးတစ်ဝိုက်

video camera **video camera** ဗီဒီယိုကင်မရာ

view **shoot ginn** ရှုခင်း

village **ywar** ရွာ

vinegar **shar lakar yay** ရှာလကာရည်

visa **visa** ဗီဇာ

visit **alae apat** အလည်အပတ်

visiting time **lae pat chain** လည်ပတ်ချိန်

volleyball **volleyball** ဘော်လီဘော

vomit **an dae** အန်တယ်

W

wage **lote arr kha** လုပ်အားခ

waist **kharr** ခါး

wait **saungt dae** စောင့်တယ်

waiter/waitress **zabwell htohh** စားပွဲထိုး

waiting **saungt nay dae** စောင့်နေတယ်

room **akhann** အခန်း

wake **nohh dae** နိုးတယ်

wake up **nohh dae** နိုးတယ်

walk **lann shout tae** လမ်းလျှောက်တယ်

walking stick **dote kout** တုတ်ကောက်

wall **nan yan** နံရံ

wallet **petsan ate** ပိုက်ဆံအိတ်

want **N + lo jin dae** N + လိုချင်တယ် **V + jin dae** V + ချင်တယ်

war **sit pwell** စစ်ပွဲ

warm **nwayy dae** နွေးတယ်

warn, warning **thadeet payy dae** သတိပေးတယ်

wash (hands) **sayy dae** ဆေးတယ်

wash (clothes, hair) **shaw dae** လျှော်တယ်

wash (face) **myet nhar thit tae** မျက်နှာသစ်တယ်

washing machine **a wit shaw zet** အဝတ်လျှော်စက်

washing powder **sat pyar mh'ownt** ဆပ်ပြာမှုန့်

watch (look after) **saungt kyeet dae** စောင့်ကြည့်တယ်

watch (wristwatch) **let pat nar yi** လက်ပတ်နာရီ

watch out **tha deet htarr** သတိထား

water **yay** ရေ

waterfall **yay dagon** ရေတံခွန်

watermelon **phayell thee** ဖရဲသီး

waterproof **yay so khan** ရေစိုခံ

way (direction) **lann** လမ်း

way (method) **nee lann** နည်းလမ်း

we [male] **kya naw doht** ကျွန်တော်တို့ [female] **kya ma doht** ကျွန်မတို့

weak **arr nell dae** အားနည်းတယ်

wealthy **chann thar dae** ချမ်းသာတယ်

wear (clothing) **wit tae** ဝတ်တယ်

wear (glasses, contact lenses) **tat tae** တပ်တယ်

weather **yar thi oot doot** ရာသီဥတု

weather forecast **mohh lay watha** မိုးလေဝသ

wedding **mingalar zaung** မင်္ဂလာဆောင်

Wednesday **bote da hoo nayt** ဗုဒ္ဓဟူးနေ့

week **apat** အပတ်

weekday **gyarr yet** ကြားရက်

weekend **sa nay, ta ninn ga nway** စနေ၊ တနင်္ဂနွေ

weigh (verb) **layy dae** လေးတယ်

weight **alayy jain** အလေးချိန်

welcome **kyo zo dae** ကြိုဆိုတယ်

well (good) **kaungg dae** ကောင်းတယ်

well (of water) **yay dwinn** ရေတွင်း

west **anout bet** အနောက်ဘက်

West (Occident) **anout taii** အနောက်တိုင်း

Western style **anout taii p'own zan** အနောက်တိုင်းပုံစံ

Westernized **anout taii san san** အနောက်တိုင်းဆန်ဆန်

wet **so dae** စိုတယ်

what **bar lell** ဘာလဲ

wheelchair **wheelchair** ဝှီးချဲလ်

when (past tense) **bae d'ownn ga lell** ဘယ်တုန်းကလဲ

when (future tense) **bae dawt lell** ဘယ်တော့လဲ

where (at) **bae mhar lell** ဘယ်မှာလဲ

where (to) **bae go lell** ဘယ်ကိုလဲ

which **bae har lell** ဘယ်ဟာလဲ

wide **kyae dae** ကျယ်တယ်

white **aphyu yaung** အဖြူရောင်

white wine **wine aphyu** ဝိုင်အဖြူ

who **bae thu lell** ဘယ်သူလဲ

whose **bae thoot har lell** ဘယ်သူ့ဟာလဲ

whole **ta khoot lone** တစ်ခုလုံး

why **bar phyit loht lell** ဘာဖြစ်လို့လဲ

widow **mote sohh ma** မုဆိုးမ

widower **mote sohh bo** မုဆိုးဖို

wife **a myohh thamee** အမျိုးသမီး

wildlife (animals) **taww yaii tarate san** တောရိုင်းတိရစ္ဆာန်

win (verb) **nai dae** နိုင်တယ်

wind **lay** လေ

window (in room) **byadinn bout** ပြတင်းပေါက်

windscreen, windshield **lay gar mhan** လေကာမှန်

windshield wiper **wiper** ဝိုက်ဘာ

wine **wine** ဝိုင်

winter **saungg yar thi** ဆောင်းရာသီ

wire **wire kyohh** ဝါယာကြိုး

wish **soot taungg dae** ဆုတောင်းတယ်

withdraw (money) **htote tae** ထုတ်တယ်

without **ma par bell** မပါဘဲ

witness **myet myin thet thay** မျက်မြင်သက်သေ

woman **amyohh thamee** အမျိုးသမီး

wonderful **nhit thet sayar kaungg dae** နှစ်သက်စရာကောင်းတယ်

wood **thit tharr** သစ်သား

wool (material) **thohh mwayy** သိုးမွေး

word **salone** စာလုံး

work **alote** အလုပ်

working day **alote lote yet** အလုပ်လုပ်ရက်

world **gabar** ကမ္ဘာ

worried **sate pu dae** စိတ်ပူတယ်

worse **po sohh dae** ပိုဆိုးတယ်

worst **asohh zone** အဆိုးဆုံး

wound **dan yar** ဒဏ်ရာ

wrap **pat tae** ပတ်တယ်

wrapping (paper) **parkin set ku** ပါကင်စက္ကူ

wrench, spanner **gwa** ဂွ

wrist **let kout wit** လက်ကောက်ဝတ်

wristwatch **let pat nar yi** လက်ပတ်နာရီ

write **yayy dae** ရေးတယ်

write down **cha yayy dae** ချရေးတယ်

writer [male] **sar yayy sayar** စာရေးဆရာ [female] **sar yayy sayarma** စာရေးဆရာမ

writing pad **sarr yayy out khan amar byarr** စာရေးအောက်ခံအမာပြား

wrong **mharr dae** မှားတယ်

X

X-ray **dat mhan** ဓာတ်မှန်

Y

year **nhit** နှစ်

yellow **a war yaung** အဝါရောင်

yes **hote kaet** ဟုတ်ကဲ့

yes (true; approval) **hote tae** ဟုတ်တယ်

yesterday **ma nayt ga** မနေ့က

you [male] **kha myarr** ခင်ဗျား [female] **shin** ရှင်

you (plural) [male] **kha myarr doht** ခင်ဗျားတို့ [female] **shin doht** ရှင်တို့

you're welcome **ya bar dae** ရပါတယ်

young **ngae dae** ငယ်တယ်

youth hostel **lu ngae asaung** လူငယ်အဆောင်

Z

zero **th'own nya** သုည

zip **zip** ဇစ်

zip (verb) **zip swell dae** ဇစ်ဆွဲတယ်

zoo **tarate san y'own** တိရစ္ဆာန်ရုံ

The Tuttle Story
"Books to Span the East and West"

Our core mission at Tuttle Publishing is to create books which bring people together one page at a time. Tuttle was founded in 1832 in the small New England town of Rutland, Vermont (USA). Our fundamental values remain as strong today as they were then—to publish best-in-class books informing the English-speaking world about the countries and peoples of Asia. The world has become a smaller place today and Asia's economic, cultural and political influence has expanded, yet the need for meaningful dialogue and information about this diverse region has never been greater. Since 1948, Tuttle has been a leader in publishing books on the cultures, arts, cuisines, languages and literatures of Asia. Our authors and photographers have won numerous awards and Tuttle has published thousands of books on subjects ranging from martial arts to paper crafts. We welcome you to explore the wealth of information available on Asia at **www.tuttlepublishing.com**.

Published by Tuttle Publishing, an imprint of Periplus Editions (HK) Ltd.

www.tuttlepublishing.com

Copyright © 2020 Periplus Editions (HK) Ltd

ISBN 978-0-8048-4683-7

First edition
23 22 21 20   8 7 6 5 4 3 2 1
2001TP

Printed in Singapore

TUTTLE PUBLISHING® is a registered trademark of Tuttle Publishing, a division of Periplus Editions (HK) Ltd.

Distributed by

North America, Latin America & Europe
Tuttle Publishing
364 Innovation Drive
North Clarendon, VT 05759-9436 U.S.A.
Tel: 1 (802) 773-8930
Fax: 1 (802) 773-6993
info@tuttlepublishing.com
www.tuttlepublishing.com

Japan
Tuttle Publishing
Yaekari Building, 3rd Floor, 5-4-12 Osaki
Shinagawa-ku, Tokyo 141 0032
Tel: (81) 3 5437-0171
Fax: (81) 3 5437-0755
sales@tuttle.co.jp
www.tuttle.co.jp

Asia Pacific
Berkeley Books Pte Ltd
3 Kallang Sector #04-01
Singapore 349278
Tel: (65) 6741 2178
Fax: (65) 6741 2179
inquiries@periplus.com.sg
www.periplus.com